REVELATION EXPLAINED

REVELATION EXPLAINED

Copyright © 2011 by Charles R. Thompson

Tisip Company
Wesley Chapel Fl. 33543

Printed in the United States of America
ISBN 978-0-615-23334-5

REVELATION
EXPLAINED

Charles R. Thompson

TISIP COMPANY

Wesley Chapel, Florida

Contents

PREFACE

THERE are several different perceptions of the book of Revelation. Some people choose not to read it because, to them, it is too hard to understand. Others are fearful when they read about a beast with seven heads and ten horns in Revelation 13:1, "And saw a beast rise up out of the sea, having seven heads and ten horns." There are those who think Revelation is a book of condemnation. Still others find the book of Revelation to be a book of peace and comfort. The people who experience peace and comfort believe Revelation is God's word revealed to his followers. Whether fear or peace, either viewpoint is valid because the book of Revelation promises both, a blessing and a curse. The blessing is promised in Revelation 1:3, "Blessed is he that readeth, and they that hear the words of this prophecy." And the curse is promised in Revelation 22:18–19, "God shall add unto him the plagues that are written in this book."

This book will answer most, if not all, of the questions ever raised about the book of Revelation. It is not an attempt to prove or disprove theories about the timing of the rapture; however, it will address the horsemen, seals, trumpets, vials, tribulation, and the beasts, among other things. This book will analyze the mysteries that most readers of Revelation have looked upon with obscurity while illuminating some of Revelation's enigmas.

The meaning of the word *revelation* is "the act of making known." It also means God's disclosure of himself and his will to his creation. The word *revelation* comes from the word *reveal*, which means "to make known, to divulge, to display, and to make known something that is hidden or secret." Another word we must consider when discussing the book of Revelation is *prophecy*, the act of telling what will happen, foretelling future events, a divinely inspired utterance, or to predict. The difference between the words *prophecy* and *revelation* is that prophecy refers to future events and revelation is any combination of past, present, and future events. Revelation is a book of prophecy, causing some people to believe it has already been fulfilled. Still others believe it is all future. Revelation speaks briefly of the past and the present, but also speaks about the future in vivid detail. Reading this book will definitely give more insight concerning these different beliefs: past, present, or future.

This journey through the book of Revelation will not be complicated at all. It will be easy to read, but, more importantly, easy to understand. After all, Jesus is our example. He did not make life complicated. He kept it simple. Jesus usually associated his message with sowing and reaping, fishermen and nets, or shepherds and flocks when he taught the gospel to his followers. He used examples relative to common occupations in order to bring about a more personal and meaningful understanding of his doctrine. His examples are better known as parables. An example of a parable is when Jesus taught his disciples about a sower sowing seed in Matthew 13:3–9, "A sower went forth to sow." Jesus explained he was the sower in Matthew 13:37, "He that soweth the good seed is the Son of man."

The book of Revelation is no different. Things stated in Revelation will be interpreted somewhere else within the confines of the Bible.

The only foolproof way to interpret Revelation is with the scriptures. As 2 Timothy 3:16 tells us, "All scripture is given by inspiration of God." Revelation will be interpreted from within the Bible, not current events. Where current events are mentioned, it is only as an example, not to prove or disprove anything.

Unless otherwise noted, all scripture used in this book is from the King James Version. We chose this version so we would not be interpreting an interpretation. Our goal was to stick as close as possible to the original text.

In general, most people like to study the book of Revelation with a telescope, that is, far away. Revelation actually reveals more of itself when viewed under a microscope. It will become evident that Revelation actually interprets itself most of the time. An example of this can be found in Revelation 1:20, "The seven stars are the angels of the seven churches: and the seven candlesticks which thou sawest are the seven churches." There can be no mistake because this scripture tells us exactly what the stars represent and what the candlesticks represent.

As the study of Revelation progresses, it will become apparent that Revelation is not written in chronological order. Time is measured in minute-by-minute episodes or events. Take, for example, the actions of two different people in the same time frame. Both are doing entirely two different things at the exact same time. The best way to explain or understand exactly what is happening is to isolate all of the events.

- Set apart all the events pertaining to the first individual.
- Set apart all the events pertaining to the second individual.
- Go back and establish what really happened, based on a timeline of all the events from both individuals in a chronological order.

This method of separating different events produces a much clearer picture of what really took place. For example, many television shows give a timeline to show what each individual was doing at a particular time. This method cuts down on a lot of confusion. The book of Revelation is written very much the same way, that is, in segments. For example, the verses in Revelation 1 should be read in this order: 1–3, 8, 11, 9–10, 12–20, and 4–7. This order depicts a better view of the chapter. Because Revelation is not written in chronological order, this book will skip around to gather all related verses to establish a broader basis of understanding of the topic at hand. Upon conclusion of this book, the entire book of Revelation will be addressed.

Some important factors in understanding Revelation is to first ask a series of questions: who, what, when, where and how.

- Ask, "Who are the parties involved?"
- Seek exactly what roles each party plays.
- Establish when in time these events did take place.
- Ask, "Where is the location that these events are taking place?"
- Determine how these parties and their actions influenced the immediate situation and history.

Another important concept about the book of Revelation is that it is divided into three separate parts. Revelation 1:19 reveals the breakdown:

- The things which thou hast seen (chapter 1)
- The things which are (chapters 2 and 3)
- The things which shall be hereafter (chapter 4–22)

Here is another way of looking at this scenario. The things that were seen represent the past, the things that are represent the present, and the things that shall be hereafter represent the future. Because chapters 1 through 3 covers the past and present, with regards to the time it was written, one can see that almost the entire book of Revelation is dedicated to the future.

The book of Revelation is also a book that is often spiritualized. Many do not take this book to be literal. Revelation is no more spiritual than the book of Acts. For instance, some supernatural events took place in the book of Acts. For example, Acts 2:4 states, "All filled with the Holy Ghost, and began to speak with other tongues, as the Spirit gave them utterance." Being filled with the Holy Ghost is a spiritual event originating in heaven, but the manifestation of it was literally revealed on earth when they spoke in other tongues. Revelation is written precisely the same way. Upon completion of this book, identifying which events are spiritual and which events are literal can be accomplished with greater ease.

Revelation is also a book of many symbolisms. Each and every symbol will be analyzed and cross-referenced with scripture. Defining the symbolism is equivalent to being handed the keys to a locked vault. With the keys, the vault can be unlocked. Then one has access to its contents. The same is true with regard to Revelation. With the keys, Revelation can be unlocked, providing access to its understanding. Revelation 1:3 states, "Blessed is he that readeth, and they that hear the words of this prophecy." But how can one hear this prophecy if he does not understand the words of this prophecy?

I pray your relationship with Christ will be greatly enhanced after reading this book. This preface will close with the last verse of the Bible, Revelation 22:21; "The grace of our Lord Jesus Christ be with you all. Amen."

CHAPTER 1

THE VISION

Rev. 1:1   The Revelation of Jesus Christ, which God gave unto him, to shew unto his servants things which must shortly come to pass; and he sent and signified it by his angel unto his servant John:

Rev. 1:2   Who bare record of the word of God, and of the testimony of Jesus Christ, and of all things that he saw.

Rev. 1:3   Blessed is he that readeth, and they that hear the words of this prophecy, and keep those things which are written therein: for the time is at hand.

FROM the three verses above, one can identify the parties in this chapter as God, Jesus, an angel, John, and the readers and hearers of this prophesy. Let's examine each one to see the role each party plays in this chapter.

God, who knows all things, gives a revelation to Jesus in Revelation 1:1–2. Jesus then gives the revelation to an angel. Likewise, the angel then gives the revelation to John. John then witnesses and records the revelation that he receives from the angel. The revelation that John received is the word of God, the testimony of Jesus Christ, and all things that John witnessed (Rev. 1:2). This record, or revelation, is the book of Revelation, the last book of the Bible and the last time God spoke to his people through scripture. The readers and hearers are the people who read the book of Revelation and heard the words recorded in the book of Revelation.

Now, let's take a closer look at why God gave this revelation to his son, Jesus. God gave the revelation to show events that must shortly come to pass to the servants of Jesus (Rev. 1:1). The phrase (things that must shortly come to pass) indicates God is referencing things of the future from the time the book of Revelation was written. The book of Revelation was written around 95 or 96 AD, so, at the time it was written, most of the events described in the book of Revelation had not happened. So, it is concluded that God gave this revelation to Jesus so he could reveal things of the future to his followers.

Once Jesus received the revelation from God, he was charged with the task of revealing it to his servants. Jesus did not go to John himself. He sent an angel in his place to give the revelation to John. Jesus could not go to John himself because some things had to happen (shortly come to pass) before his return. Revelation 1:7 states, "Behold, he cometh with clouds; and every eye shall see him, and they also which pierced him."

God does things in order. Jesus is expected to return in the clouds, so he could not go to John himself because, the next time he comes, it will be to receive his followers unto himself. John 14:2–3 states, "I go to prepare a place for you. And if I go and prepare a place for you, I will come again, and receive you unto myself; that where I am, there ye may be also." Jesus wants to reveal the future to his servants, but, when he returns, it is to receive the saints, so he sent an angel in his stead to reveal the revelation to John.

The Bible does not specify the name of the angel sent to John, but two candidates come to mind. It can possibly be Gabriel because he was used in similar incidents in times past. For example, in Luke 1:19, he was sent to make known the birth of John the Baptist to Zacharias. Another possibility can be Michael, the archangel, according to Jude 1:9. Michael is a chief angel, so he definitely has access to Jesus. The name of the angel really doesn't matter. The important thing is that the will of God is established and fulfilled. The will of God, in this case, is to get his revelation into the hearts and minds of his servants.

John, one of the twelve disciples, received the revelation from the angel. There's no indication as to why John was chosen over the other disciples to receive this revelation. Perhaps he was a special disciple. John 21:20–24 states, "The disciple that Jesus loved." Or, better still, he was a good steward of the gospel of Jesus Christ. Revelation 1:9–10 states, "Was in the isle that is called Patmos, for the word of God, and for the testimony of Jesus Christ. I was in the Spirit on the Lord's day." Some believe John was chosen to reveal this revelation because he was Jesus' favorite disciple, at least in John's mind

(Joh. 21:20–24). Regardless as to why John was chosen, the fact remains that he wrote the book of Revelation.

The readers and the hearers can be categorized into two groups, the blessed and the cursed. There is a stipulation in Revelation 1:3 that only those who keep the things written in the book of Revelation will be blessed. In order to be blessed, one must first read, hear, and do the things in Revelation:

- The one who reads Revelation and understands it, but does not do the things in Revelation, is classified as a reader and hearer, but he is not a doer. So he is not blessed.
- The one who reads Revelation, understands it, and lives accordingly is a reader, a hearer, and a doer, so he is therefore blessed.

One cannot keep or do the things written in Revelation unless one first understands its principles. It's like flying an airplane. One has to read the manual, understand it, and do the things in the manual before expecting to lift the plane off the ground. Revelation is exactly the same. Once it is read and understood, one can expect and know that certain events will take place in a specific manner.

The Angel Finds John

Rev. 1:9   I John, who also am your brother, and companion in tribulation, and in the kingdom and patience of Jesus Christ, was in the isle that is called Patmos, for the word of God, and for the testimony of Jesus Christ.

Rev. 1:10   I was in the Spirit on the Lord's day, and heard behind me a great voice, as of a trumpet,

The angel sought John and found him on the Lord's Day, which is another way of saying Sabbath day. Exodus 20:11 says, "For in six days the LORD made heaven and earth, the sea, and all that in them is, and rested the seventh day: wherefore the LORD blessed the sabbath day, and hallowed it." John was in the spirit (in the presence of God), giving reverence to God.

Being a good steward of the word of God, John was rejoicing in the Lord, praying continually and giving thanks for all things.

The angel found John on an island named Patmos, an island off the southwest coast of Asia Minor. Asia Minor is better known as present-day Turkey. John was probably a prisoner on this island because he was a Christian. There wasn't much tolerance for Christians in John's day. If he was not a prisoner, then he was there for the word of God and the testimony of Jesus Christ. As John was praying and seeking God, he heard a voice behind him as the sound of a trumpet. Musicians often refer to their instrument as talking while they are playing and under the influence of their musical notes. From behind him, John heard someone talking to him in rhythmic or poetic tone.

The Vision

> Rev. 1:8   I am Alpha and Omega, the beginning and the ending, saith the Lord, which is, and which was, and which is to come, the Almighty.

While John was praying, the angel introduced whom he represented, not himself. Revelation 1:8 states, "I am Alpha and Omega, the beginning and the ending." He stated he was the beginning and the end. He was the beginning in John 1:1, "In the beginning was the Word, and the Word was with God, and the Word was God." He was the end in John 14:6, "I am the way, and the truth, and the life: no one cometh unto the Father, but by me."

In conclusion, the angel represented Jesus or God Almighty. In case there is some confusion as to who the angel represents, consult John 10:30, "I and my Father are one." John14:9 states, "He that hath seen me hath seen the Father." The angel represented either God or Jesus. For the rest of this study, we will refer to the angel in John's vision as the Angel of Jesus because many angels are in Revelation. Identifying the angel in John's vision as such will help eliminate confusion.

> Rev. 1:10   I was in the Spirit on the Lord's day, and heard behind me a great voice, as of a trumpet,

Rev. 1:12   And I turned to see the voice that spake with me. And being turned, I saw seven golden candlesticks;

Rev. 1:13   And in the midst of the seven candlesticks one like unto the Son of man, clothed with a garment down to the foot, and girt about the paps with a golden girdle.

Rev. 1:14   His head and his hairs were white like wool, as white as snow; and his eyes were as a flame of fire;

Rev. 1:15   And his feet like unto fine brass, as if they burned in a furnace; and his voice as the sound of many waters.

Rev. 1:16   And he had in his right hand seven stars: and out of his mouth went a sharp twoedged sword: and his countenance was as the sun shineth in his strength.

While John was praying, he heard this great voice behind him. He turned to see who was behind him. John saw a figure standing in the middle of seven candlesticks. He did not see Jesus. He saw the angel. Revelation 1:13 states, "And in the midst of the candlesticks one like unto the Son of man." John saw the angel standing in the middle of the candlesticks, not Jesus. The angel represented Jesus in verbal and physical form.

Rev. 1:17   And when I saw him, I fell at his feet as dead. And he laid his right hand upon me, saying unto me, Fear not; I am the first and the last:

When John saw the angel, he fell at the feet of the angel as a dead man. Remember, John was in the spirit and praying to God. John might have thought the angel was Jesus returning for his saints because he immediately fainted. As John lay before the angel, passed out, the angel touched John and told him to "fear not." Usually in scripture, whenever an angel appears to man, he always reassures him first by saying, "Fear not." This theory is also demonstrated in Revelation 1:17, "He laid his right hand upon me, saying unto me, Fear not."

Once the angel revived John, the angel began his salutation all over again.

Rev. 1:8   I am the Alpha and the Omega, saith the Lord God, who is and who was and who is to come, the Almighty.

Rev. 1:11   Saying, I am Alpha and Omega, the first and the last: and, What thou seest, write in a book, and send it unto the seven churches which are in Asia; unto Ephesus, and unto Smyrna, and unto Pergamos, and unto Thyatira, and unto Sardis, and unto Philadelphia, and unto Laodicea.

Remember, the angel started speaking to John in Revelation 1:8. Revelation 1:11 is just a continuation. John did not hear the contents of what the angel said because, as soon as he heard the voice behind him, he turned to see who was talking to him. John did not hear the part of the conversation where the angel told him to write a book and send it to the seven churches. John did not hear the contents of the conversation because, when he turned and saw the angel, he passed out as a dead man (Rev. 1:17). The angel was still talking, but John did not comprehend what the Angel of Jesus said the first time because he was temporarily unconscious. That was why the Angel of Jesus repeated himself in Revelation 1:17–19.

The Angel Revives John

Rev. 1:17   And when I saw him, I fell at his feet as dead. And he laid his right hand upon me, saying unto me, Fear not; I am the first and the last:

Rev. 1:18   I am he that liveth, and was dead; and, behold, I am alive for evermore, Amen; and have the keys of hell and of death.

Rev. 1:19   Write the things which thou hast seen, and the things which are, and the things which shall be hereafter;

As soon as the angel revived John, he identified himself to John again. The angel then gave John a threefold command to write "the things which thou hast seen, and the things which are, and the things which shall be hereafter" (Rev. 1:19). The angel had already given John the instructions in Revelation 1:11, but John did not hear them. At this point, the angel repeated what he told John in Revelation 1:11.

Now let's go back and put it in perspective. In Revelation 1:8–10, the angel started speaking to John while John was praying. John was startled when he heard a great voice behind him. John immediately turned to see who was talking to him. Revelation 1:12–16 tells us what John saw when he turned to see who was talking to him. Revelation 1:17–19 tells us that John passed out when he saw the angel. The angel revived John and started speaking again in Revelation 1:17–19, where he introduced himself again. The following all occurred in a split second:

- The time John first heard the angel speaking in Revelation 1:8 *until*
- The time he turned to see who was speaking in Revelation 1:12 *until*
- The time he saw the angel in Revelation 1:13 *until*
- The time he passed out and was revived by the angel in Revelation 1:17

Rev. 1:11   Saying, I am Alpha and Omega, the first and the last: and, What thou seest, write in a book, and send it unto the seven churches which are in Asia; unto Ephesus, and unto Smyrna, and unto Pergamos, and unto Thyatira, and unto Sardis, and unto Philadelphia, and unto Laodicea.

The angel also gave John some instructions. He told John to write what he saw in a book and send them to the seven churches. The angel named these seven churches and gave their geographical location. The seven churches are in Asia.

Rev. 1:20   The mystery of the seven stars which thou sawest in my right hand, and the seven golden candlesticks. The seven stars are the angels of the seven churches: and the seven candlesticks which thou sawest are the seven churches.

The angel explains in Revelation 1:20, "The mystery of the seven stars which was in the right hand of the angel, and the seven golden candlesticks. The seven stars are the angels of the seven churches, and the seven candlesticks are the seven churches."

Here, the book of Revelation interprets itself, a common practice throughout Revelation. Often, Revelation explains itself undoubtedly to minimize confusion and misinterpretation.

The Salutation

Rev. 1:4   John to the seven churches which are in Asia: Grace be unto you, and peace, from him which is, and which was, and which is to come; and from the seven Spirits which are before his throne;

Rev. 1:5   And from Jesus Christ, who is the faithful witness, and the first begotten of the dead, and the prince of the kings of the earth. Unto him that loved us, and washed us from our sins in his own blood,

Rev. 1:6   And hath made us kings and priests unto God and his Father; to him be glory and dominion for ever and ever. Amen.

Rev. 1:7   Behold, he cometh with clouds; and every eye shall see him, and they also which pierced him: and all kindreds of the earth shall wail because of him. Even so, Amen.

John began to write what he saw. He began his salutation of the book to whom the book was written to the seven churches in Asia. The church was actually started in Asia. As the world's population increased, other continents became inhabited. The migration of man from Asia to other continents brought forth the growth of the church to other parts of Asia, Europe, North Africa, and so forth. Although John was writing to the seven churches in Asia, indirectly, he was writing to churches all over the world. John wished grace and peace to the seven churches.

John told the name of the author of the book to the seven churches. The book comes from Revelation 1:4–5, "Him which is, and which was, and which is to come; and from the seven Spirits which are before his throne; and from Jesus Christ." The phrase (which is, which was, and which is to come) is the Almighty God, according to Revelation 1:8, "Which is, and which was, and which is to come, the Almighty." The author of the book to the seven churches is God, Jesus, and the seven spirits before the throne. The seven spirits will be discussed in more detail later in this study.

John explained exactly who Jesus was. Jesus was introduced with admiration. Revelation 1:5–6 states:

> The faithful witness, and the first begotten of the dead, and the prince of the kings of the earth. Unto him that loved us, and washed us from our sins in his own blood, and hath made us kings and priests unto God and his Father; to him be glory and dominion for ever and ever.

Jesus Christ made all of those who are born again kings and priests unto God and his father. John also told the seven churches exactly how Jesus would return. Revelation 1:7 says, "He cometh with clouds; and every eye shall see him." This is again confirmed in Acts 1:9–11, "While they beheld, he was taken up; and a cloud received him … this same Jesus, which is taken up from you into heaven, shall so come in like manner as ye have seen him go into heaven." John had not yet gotten to the contents of the letter. That would come later, beginning in Chapter 2. This was only his salutation to the seven churches.

Topics of the Letters

Rev. 1:19 Write the things which thou hast seen, and the things which are, and the things which shall be hereafter;

In Revelation 1:11, we know to whom the book is written, the seven churches in Asia. In Revelation 1:19, we learn the basic contents of the things John is supposed to write about: the things which thou hast seen, the things which are, and the things which shall be hereafter.

The things that John saw, refers to the angel standing in the midst of the candlesticks (vision). The things that are, refers to things in existence at the exact point in time when John received the revelation from the Angel of Jesus. For example, you are reading this book right now. Another example is that you are in a physical body right now. These examples show present conditions or things that are in existence right now. The things that shall be hereafter, refers to things that had not occurred at that exact time.

John received the revelation from the Angel of Jesus. Some examples of hereafter would be tomorrow, next week, or after receiving a glorified body. These things will occur some time in the future or after John received the revelation. Category 1 was completed in chapter 1. The other two categories will be examined as this study progresses.

The Proper Order of Things

The revelation is handed down from God to Jesus, from Jesus to an angel, from an angel to John, and then from John to the servants. Why was the revelation not given directly to the servants? First, the book of Revelation is scripture, just like the rest of the Bible. As 2 Timothy 3:16 states, "All scripture is given by inspiration of God, and is profitable for doctrine, for reproof, for correction, for instruction in righteousness." God did not write the Bible himself. He inspired men to write the Bible. As 2 Peter 1:21 states, "For the prophecy came not in old time by the will of man: but holy men of God spake as they were moved by the Holy Ghost." God used a man to write the book of Revelation. In this case, it was John, one of the twelve disciples. Revelation was written in God's natural order of doing things, for man and by man, but inspired by God.

You might ask, "Why didn't God give the revelation directly to John?" There is no definitive answer given in Revelation 1:1–3, but my opinion on this matter is a simple one. God has a natural order of things. In the Old Testament, God talked directly to man, for example, in Genesis 17:9, it states, "And God said unto Abraham, thou shalt keep my covenant therefore, thou, and thy seed after thee in their generations." Between the book of Malachi and the book of Matthew is a period of about four hundred years when God did not talk to man. This is called the silent years. In the New Testament, God spoke to man through Jesus. After Jesus died, God spoke to man through the Holy Ghost. God follows his own laws: God the father,

God the son, and God the Holy Ghost. Once a human being dies, he cannot talk to man again except in the supernatural, such as visions, dreams, and ghosts. It is true that Jesus did come back to earth after his resurrection, but that was a supernatural act to prove to mankind that Jesus Christ was raised from the dead with a new body. Jesus had to show himself shortly after being raised from the dead to prove that his dead body was not stolen and hidden. Without mankind actually seeing his glorified body, his death would have been no different than the death of all others who died before him. He walked on earth approximately forty days, exposing his glorified body to mankind before ascending into heaven. It is not recorded anywhere in the scriptures that mankind saw Jesus on earth after he went to prepare a place for his followers. Jesus sent the Holy Ghost or Comforter after his ascension into heaven because he himself could not return to earth until it was the proper time, that is, when he returned to earth for his saints. John 14:3 states, "If I go and prepare a place for you, I will come again, and receive you unto myself; that where I am, there ye may be also." His ghost or the Holy Ghost is with us, but Jesus the man cannot reappear until he returns on a white horse to judge and make war (Rev. 19:11). According to God's natural order of life and death, Jesus himself cannot appear before man anymore because he died as a man. He would have to appear in the form of a vision, dream, or ghost. This is why I believe Jesus did not give the revelation directly to John.

CHAPTER 2

THE CHURCHES

Rev. 2:1   Unto the angel of the church of Ephesus write; These things saith he that holdeth the seven stars in his right hand, who walketh in the midst of the seven golden candlesticks;

WE will start by first understanding all the people or beings involved. The different beings involved in Revelation 2–3 are the seven angels of the seven churches, John, and the Angel of Jesus who showed the revelation to John.

The Angel of Jesus, in Revelation 1:11 and 1:19, instructed John to write three different things in a book and send it to the seven churches in Asia. John was to write the things that he saw, the things that are, and the things that shall be hereafter. We have already discussed the first thing in chapter 1, that is, what John saw, the Angel of Jesus, the vision.

Now we will explore the second thing of which John was to write. The second thing (the things that are) describes the present state of the seven churches. It is like a state of the union address. John only wrote to the seven churches what the Angel of Jesus revealed to him. Notice that John wrote to the angel of these churches, not to the churches themselves. These are not John's words, but they are the words that the Angel of Jesus revealed to him.

It's important to establish the fact that John was to write a book concerning the future events (things that must be hereafter) to the seven churches in Asia. Along with the book, he wrote individual letters to each of the seven churches (the things that are) because each church had different issues, at that particular time. The contents of the letters to the seven churches are all different, but the content of the book that he sent to the seven churches is exactly the same.

Ephesus

Rev. 2:1   Unto the angel of the church of Ephesus write; These things saith he that holdeth the seven stars in his right hand, who walketh in the midst of the seven golden candlesticks;

Rev. 2:2   I know thy works, and thy labour, and thy patience, and how thou canst not bear them which are evil: and thou hast tried them which say they are apostles, and are not, and hast found them liars:

Rev. 2:3   And hast borne, and hast patience, and for my name's sake hast laboured, and hast not fainted.

Rev. 2:4   Nevertheless I have somewhat against thee, because thou hast left thy first love.

Rev. 2:5   Remember therefore from whence thou art fallen, and repent, and do the first works; or else I will come unto thee quickly, and will remove thy candlestick out of his place, except thou repent.

Rev. 2:6   But this thou hast, that thou hatest the deeds of the Nicolaitans, which I also hate.

Rev. 2:7   He that hath an ear, let him hear what the Spirit saith unto the churches; To him that overcometh will I give to eat of the tree of life, which is in the midst of the paradise of God.

John wrote of the good deeds of the church of Ephesus that the angel revealed to him. When talking about the church of Ephesus, the angel told John that he knew of their works, labor, and patience and how they abhorred evil. He knew how the church had tried those who said they were apostles and found them to be liars, not apostles. He knew how the church of Ephesus had not fainted concerning the name of Jesus, and he knew they hated the deeds of the Nicolaitans, just like Jesus did. The Nicolaitans could be described as part-time Christians.

John now turned to the evil deeds of the church of Ephesus. Even though the church had done many good deeds, they still had done wrong by leaving their first love. The meaning of "first love," as it is used here, is explained best in Matthew 22:37–40, "Love the Lord thy God with all thy heart, and with all thy soul, and with all thy mind … Thou shalt love thy neighbour as thyself." John told the church they had to make some changes. They had to remember from where they had fallen, repent, and do their first works. Their first works were to love. Love God first. Then love thy neighbor.

Now John made them some promises. He promised them that, if they did not repent and return their first works, then he would come to them quickly and remove their candlestick out of its place. Remember that, in Revelation 1:20, the candlestick represented the churches. John was now saying he would remove this church. He also promised that, if they did repent and overcome, he would give them to eat from the tree of life, which is in the midst of the paradise of God, which is referred to as heaven or the garden of Eden. Adam lived in the garden of Eden (paradise), and he had access to the tree of life before his disobedience.

While Jesus was hanging on the cross, being crucified, he told the thief who repented, "To day shalt thou be with me in paradise" (Luke 23:43). We know the tree of life was in the garden of Eden and the tree of life was in paradise, thus signifying that paradise and garden of Eden are synonymous.

Smyrna

Rev. 2:8   And unto the angel of the church in Smyrna write; These things saith the first and the last, which was dead, and is alive;

Rev. 2:9   I know thy works, and tribulation, and poverty, (but thou art rich) and I know the blasphemy of them which say they are Jews, and are not, but are the synagogue of Satan.

Rev. 2:10 Fear none of those things which thou shalt suffer: behold, the devil shall cast some of you into prison, that ye may be tried; and ye shall have tribulation ten days: be thou faithful unto death, and I will give thee a crown of life.

Rev. 2:11   He that hath an ear, let him hear what the Spirit saith
             unto the churches; He that overcometh shall not be hurt
             of the second death.

John now wrote of the good deeds of the church of Smyrna. The angel
revealed to him that he knew of their works, tribulations, and poverty. He
told them that, although they were in poverty, they were still rich because
faithfulness in God amounted to more than material things.

Then John turned to the evil deeds of the church of Smyrna. He knew
some had been blaspheming. They claimed to be Jews, but, in reality,
were not. They were straight from the school of Satan because they were
constantly learning and teaching new ways to take advantage of one another.
They would say or do anything in an effort to deceive anyone, including
family, friends, and associates.

Next, John warned the church of Smyrna that they would suffer some
things. They would experience several different trials and tribulation, but
do not faint from well doing and do not fear anything that the devil would
force upon them. He encouraged them to be faithful and endure their entire
life. At the end, they would receive a crown of life. Those individuals that
overcame should not be hurt of the second death or second resurrection.
This parallels with the teaching of Jesus that we must endure to the end
(Mat. 10:22).

Pergamos

Rev. 2:12   And to the angel of the church in Pergamos write; These
             things saith he which hath the sharp sword with two
             edges;

Rev. 2:13   I know thy works, and where thou dwellest, even where
             Satan's seat is: and thou holdest fast my name, and hast
             not denied my faith, even in those days wherein Antipas
             was my faithful martyr, who was slain among you, where
             Satan dwelleth.

Rev. 2:14   But I have a few things against thee, because thou hast
             there them that hold the doctrine of Balaam, who taught
             Balac to cast a stumblingblock before the children of

Israel, to eat things sacrificed unto idols, and to commit fornication.

Rev. 2:15   So hast thou also them that hold the doctrine of the Nicolaitans, which thing I hate.

Rev. 2:16   Repent; or else I will come unto thee quickly, and will fight against them with the sword of my mouth.

Rev. 2:17   He that hath an ear, let him hear what the Spirit saith unto the churches; To him that overcometh will I give to eat of the hidden manna, and will give him a white stone, and in the stone a new name written, which no man knoweth saving he that receiveth it.

John now began to write the letter to the church of Pergamos. As usual, he first talked about the good deeds of the church. He told the church of Pergamos that he knew their lifestyle. He knew they were experiencing some struggles just because of where they resided. Their home was located in the town where Satan's headquarters was located. Their hometown was Satan's stronghold, and this was shown by his martyrdom of Antipas, for no reason other than he worshipped me. Although difficult, he knew they continued to adhere to the name of Jesus, and they had not denied their faith, even in trying times.

Even though the church of Pergamos was strong in the faith, they still had faults. John exposed some of their faults. They had, among them, some people who held the doctrines of Balaam, which was in opposition to the teachings of Jesus and responsible for teaching the children of Israel to eat things sacrificed to idols. By eating things sacrificed to idols, they were putting other gods before the Almighty God (Exo. 20:3). Another group of traitors among them adopted the doctrines of the Nicolaitanes, who taught abominable things. They were engaged in sexual immorality, such as adultery, incest, homosexuality, and so forth.

The Angel of Jesus promised the church of Pergamos that, if they did not repent, he would come and fight against them with the sword of his mouth, the word of God. Not only would he return, but he would return quickly, shortening their lives. The other part of the promise was that, if they did repent and overcome, he would give them the hidden manna, the food that God fed the children of Israel while they were in the wilderness.

While eating the manna for forty years, their clothes did not wear out, and they were immune to sickness and disease (Deu. 8:3–4). He also promised to give them a white stone with a new name written in it. The only person who knew this new name was the person who received it. Having a secret name made them equivalent to the angels (Jud. 13:18).

Thyatira

Rev. 2:18   And unto the angel of the church in Thyatira write; These things saith the Son of God, who hath his eyes like unto a flame of fire, and his feet are like fine brass;

Rev. 2:19   I know thy works, and charity, and service, and faith, and thy patience, and thy works; and the last to be more than the first.

Rev. 2:20   Notwithstanding I have a few things against thee, because thou sufferest that woman Jezebel, which calleth herself a prophetess, to teach and to seduce my servants to commit fornication, and to eat things sacrificed unto idols.

Rev. 2:21   And I gave her space to repent of her fornication; and she repented not.

Rev. 2:22   Behold, I will cast her into a bed, and them that commit adultery with her into great tribulation, except they repent of their deeds.

Rev. 2:23   And I will kill her children with death; and all the churches shall know that I am he which searcheth the reins and hearts: and I will give unto every one of you according to your works.

Rev. 2:24   But unto you I say, and unto the rest in Thyatira, as many as have not this doctrine, and which have not known the depths of Satan, as they speak; I will put upon you none other burden.

Rev. 2:25   But that which ye have already hold fast till I come.

Rev. 2:26   And he that overcometh, and keepeth my works unto the end, to him will I give power over the nations:

Rev. 2:27   And he shall rule them with a rod of iron; as the vessels of a potter shall they be broken to shivers: even as I received of my Father.

Rev. 2:28   And I will give him the morning star.

Rev. 2:29   He that hath an ear, let him hear what the Spirit saith unto the churches.

John first told the church of Thyatira that he knew their works. He listed their good deeds as charity, service, faith, and patience. He told them that their last works were better than their first works. It appeared that the church of Thyatira really had it together until he listed their bad deeds.

He only listed one thing that the church of Thyatira was doing that was against God. In their midst, they welcomed a woman named Jezebel. She wasn't literally in their presence because she lived centuries earlier. The Angel of Jesus referred to her false doctrine that was alive and well within the church. Not all of the church took part in Jezebel's doctrine. Only a small group did. They allowed Jezebel's doctrine to be taught openly, which led to the seduction of members, fornication, and eating things sacrificed to idols. They were given several opportunities to repent, but they never did.

As usual, the church of Thyatira was given some promises based on their choices. The ones who did not follow Jezebel's doctrine weren't given anything else to do. They were only to continue in their good works until Jesus returned. The followers of Jezebel's doctrine were to be cast into great tribulation, and their children would die. The great tribulation mentioned here is not the great tribulation. It is only a period of time in which they, as individuals, would have to endure some annoying and frustrating situations because of their own actions. If they repented of Jezebel's doctrine and continued in their good deeds until Jesus returned, then he would give them power over the nations. They would rule the nations with a rod of iron, signifying they would be kings and priests and they would reign with Christ (Rev. 1:6) and (Rev. 20:4), respectively. He would also give them the morning star, Jesus. Revelation 22:16 states, "I am the root and the offspring of David, and the bright and morning star." Anyone who receives the morning star (Jesus) has endured this world to the very end and will rule and reign with Jesus when he returns.

Sardis

Rev. 3:1   And unto the angel of the church in Sardis write; These things saith he that hath the seven Spirits of God, and the seven stars; I know thy works, that thou hast a name that thou livest, and art dead.

Rev. 3:2   Be watchful, and strengthen the things which remain, that are ready to die: for I have not found thy works perfect before God.

Rev. 3:3   Remember therefore how thou hast received and heard, and hold fast, and repent. If therefore thou shalt not watch, I will come on thee as a thief, and thou shalt not know what hour I will come upon thee.

Rev. 3:4   Thou hast a few names even in Sardis which have not defiled their garments; and they shall walk with me in white: for they are worthy.

Rev. 3:5   He that overcometh, the same shall be clothed in white raiment; and I will not blot out his name out of the book of life, but I will confess his name before my Father, and before his angels.

Rev. 3:6   He that hath an ear, let him hear what the Spirit saith unto the churches.

John first told the church of Sardis that the Angel of Jesus knew their works, which were not perfect before God. The angel knew they were professing to be on fire for God, but, in reality, they were just keeping the pews warm. He also told them to be watchful and develop the few good things they had left because even the little fire they had remaining was almost ready to be extinguished. They should remember how excited they were when they first received the word of God. This church also had a division in it because some members there had not been influenced by the world while others could not be distinguished from the non-Christians.

He promised the backsliders of the church of Sardis that, if they were not watchful and did not repent, he would come to them unexpectedly when they least expected it. It was very clear that, if they did not repent then, their names would be blotted out of the Book of Life. It was also implied that their continual disobedience could and would cause Jesus to return sooner than later to execute their judgment. On the other hand, if they were watchful and repented, then Jesus would confess their names before the Father and the angels, along with the names of those who had not been unfaithful. All who were found worthy would be given the privilege of walking with Jesus when he returned. Anyone who did not receive Jesus' approval on judgment day would not be permitted to dwell with Christ in his kingdom. In his kingdom, all residents live without debt, pain, and hunger and lack for nothing.

Philadelphia

Rev. 3:7   And to the angel of the church in Philadelphia write; These things saith he that is holy, he that is true, he that hath the key of David, he that openeth, and no man shutteth; and shutteth, and no man openeth;

Rev. 3:8   I know thy works: behold, I have set before thee an open door, and no man can shut it: for thou hast a little strength, and hast kept my word, and hast not denied my name.

Rev. 3:9   Behold, I will make them of the synagogue of Satan, which say they are Jews, and are not, but do lie; behold, I will make them to come and worship before thy feet, and to know that I have loved thee.

Rev. 3:10   Because thou hast kept the word of my patience, I also will keep thee from the hour of temptation, which shall come upon all the world, to try them that dwell upon the earth.

Rev. 3:11   Behold, I come quickly: hold that fast which thou hast, that no man take thy crown.

Rev. 3:12   Him that overcometh will I make a pillar in the temple of my God, and he shall go no more out: and I will write upon him the name of my God, and the name of the city of my God, which is new Jerusalem, which cometh down out of heaven from my God: and I will write upon him my new name.

Rev. 3:13   He that hath an ear, let him hear what the Spirit saith
            unto the churches.

John started the letter to the church of Philadelphia by stating the Angel of Jesus knew their works. He also gave a brief description of Jesus. The church of Philadelphia had kept the words of Jesus, had not denied his name, and had been patient. Notice that he did not list bad deeds. He promised that, because the church of Philadelphia had kept the word of his patience, the unbelievers would worship before their feet. He would also keep them from the hour of temptation.

Everybody in the whole world will be tempted, but it is ultimately up to each and every individual to continue to keep the word of God. If you keep the word of God, no one can take your crown or cause you to lose your salvation. For all of those who overcome the world, he will make a pillar in the temple of God. Upon them, he will write the name of God, the name of the city of God, and his new name, which Jesus gives. The name of the city of God is New Jerusalem. Mankind will see this city descending down from heaven at the second coming of Christ (Rev. 21:1–2). This city will also be the residence of all the saints at the return of Jesus.

Laodicea

Rev. 3:14   And unto the angel of the church of the Laodiceans
            write; These things saith the Amen, the faithful and true
            witness, the beginning of the creation of God;
Rev. 3:15   I know thy works, that thou art neither cold nor hot: I
            would thou wert cold or hot.
Rev. 3:16   So then because thou art lukewarm, and neither cold
            nor hot, I will spue thee out of my mouth.
Rev. 3:17   Because thou sayest, I am rich, and increased with
            goods, and have need of nothing; and knowest not that
            thou art wretched, and miserable, and poor, and blind,
            and naked:
Rev. 3:18   I counsel thee to buy of me gold tried in the fire, that
            thou mayest be rich; and white raiment, that thou
            mayest be clothed, and that the shame of thy nakedness

	do not appear; and anoint thine eyes with eyesalve, that thou mayest see.
Rev. 3:19	As many as I love, I rebuke and chasten: be zealous therefore, and repent.
Rev. 3:20	Behold, I stand at the door, and knock: if any man hear my voice, and open the door, I will come in to him, and will sup with him, and he with me.
Rev. 3:21	To him that overcometh will I grant to sit with me in my throne, even as I also overcame, and am set down with my Father in his throne.
Rev. 3:22	He that hath an ear, let him hear what the Spirit saith unto the churches.

John started his letter to the church of Laodicea by telling them that Jesus knew their works. He told them that they were neither cold nor hot. Notice he did not say that they were doing anything positive. He described them as being lukewarm, straddling the fence, and in the middle of the road. He told them that they were trusting in their riches and they thought they had need of nothing. John wrote that they were not aware that they were wretched, miserable, poor, blind, and naked. Because the church of Laodicea was lukewarm, Jesus would spew them out of his mouth, that is, he would reject them. He told them that they should trust in Jesus because the gold that came with his name had been tried in the fire. His gold would not burn up like the gold in which they were trusting. His gold was spiritual or righteousness while their gold was physical or monetary. If they trusted in Jesus, they would be rich, and their sin would be forgiven because the righteousness of Jesus covered a multitude of sins. He told the Laodiceans that Jesus was waiting for all of them to come and seek him.

John also told the church of Laodicea that Jesus had made them some promises. He promised that, if they overcame the world and repented, Jesus would have dinner with them. The dinner mentioned here references his future kingdom when he returns. He will also grant those who overcome this world system to sit with him when he sits on his throne. Just as Jesus overcame the world, the Laodiceans can overcome it also.

Summary of the Letters to the Churches

All the letters to the churches begins with "I know thy works" and ends with "He that hath an ear let him hear what the Spirit saith unto the churches." Five of the churches have pros and cons: Ephesus, Smyrna, Pergamos, Thyatira, and Sardis. The only church with no cons listed is Philadelphia. Laodicea is the only church with no pros listed.

Promises were made to all the churches. These promises come in the form of blessings and curses. Each and every one of these promises is the same promises that are made to all believers. They are not isolated to just one church. Because people make up churches, all the promises, whether it is a blessing or a curse, applies to each and every individual who has ever lived. See Appendix in the back of the book for more information.

Interesting Facts

We should consider some interesting facts. Patmos, the island where John had been frequenting when he first saw the Angel of Jesus, is off the coast of Asia Minor, a region in Asia now known as present-day Turkey. All seven of these churches listed in Revelation 1:11 are located in the region known today as the nation of Turkey. Turkey is a Gentile nation, not a Jewish nation. Although the book of Revelation is for everybody, it was written to Gentile churches.

CHAPTER 3

THE THRONE ROOM

Rev. 4:1   After this I looked, and, behold, a door was opened in heaven: and the first voice which I heard was as it were of a trumpet talking with me; which said, Come up hither, and I will shew thee things which must be hereafter.

Rev. 4:2   And immediately I was in the spirit: and, behold, a throne was set in heaven, and one sat on the throne.

Rev. 4:3   And he that sat was to look upon like a jasper and a sardine stone: and there was a rainbow round about the throne, in sight like unto an emerald.

Rev. 4:4   And round about the throne were four and twenty seats: and upon the seats I saw four and twenty elders sitting, clothed in white raiment; and they had on their heads crowns of gold.

Rev. 4:5   And out of the throne proceeded lightnings and thunderings and voices: and there were seven lamps of fire burning before the throne, which are the seven Spirits of God.

The Open Door

REVELATION 4–5 takes place in heaven. This is a scene in the throne room itself. Those involved are John, the writer, the one who sits on the throne, twenty-four elders, four beasts, and the Lamb. Other objects found in the throne room are the seven lamps of fire, twenty-four seats for the crowned twenty-four elders, white raiment, stones, rainbow, lightning, thundering, and voices.

Let's get a picture in our minds as to what exactly is taking place. John saw a door open in heaven. When he looked through the opened door, John saw someone sitting on a throne with twenty-four elders sitting around the throne. Seven lamps of fire were burning before the throne. Four beasts were in the midst of the throne. In front of the throne, there was a sea of glass, and lightning, thundering, and voices were coming from the throne.

Next, we'll examine and explain all of the events that are taking place. A door opened in heaven. John heard a voice, the Angel of Jesus, asking him to come up into heaven. This same angel was chosen to reveal the revelation to John. The angel invited John to come up to heaven so he could reveal future things to John. Remember, John was to write of three different things: the things that he saw (the vision of the angel), the things that are (the state of the seven churches of Asia), and the things that must be hereafter (future events). The first part or the vision was discussed in chapter 1. The second part, or the state of the churches, was discussed in chapters 2 and 3. The third and final part of John's revelation is all future and begins in chapter 4 and ends in chapter 22. Chapter 4 is the beginning of the actual prophecy.

Some people reference "Come up hither" (Rev. 4:1) as God calling his saints home. This is only the Angel of Jesus, requesting John's presence in the throne room. The angel extended this invitation to John in order to show John the future so he could record the revelation accurately. Another indication that the angel was only requesting John to come into heaven to the throne room and not the saints is because John is the only one who was in the spirit and witnessed the throne room. Other than the twenty-four elders, the text does not mention any other saints in the throne room.

After the angel invited John to come up in heaven to the throne room, John was immediately in the spirit, that is, in the presence or anointing of God. He saw a throne in heaven, and someone was sitting on it. The one on the throne looked like a jasper and a sardine stone, and the throne had a rainbow, like an emerald, around it.

Stones

The Old Testament gives a lot of information concerning the stones. To better understand the meaning of the stones, one has to look at the Levitical priesthood. The tribe of Levi was the priestly tribe, and their duties were to perform all of the ceremonial rituals under the law.

Aaron, Moses' brother, was from the tribe of Levi. The priest had to wear special garments during the performance of their duties, for example, the breastplate of judgment. In Exodus 28:15–21, the breastplate of judgment was to have four rows of three stones for a total of twelve stones, each representing one of the tribes of Israel. Each stone on the breastplate of judgment had a meaning:

- The jasper stone represented the tribe of Benjamin.
- The sardine stone represented the tribe of Reuben.
- The emerald stone represented the tribe of Judah.

The name of each tribe also had its own unique meaning. The meaning of *Reuben* is "see, a son."[1] The meaning of *Benjamin* is "son of the right hand."[2] The meaning of *Judah*, taken from Genesis 29:35, is "praise the Lord." The list of tribes in the back of the book contains the names of all the tribes, the meaning of their names, and the stone symbolizing each tribe.

This is the picture. The one sitting on the throne is God and the glory round about him. It looks like a sardine stone and a jasper stone. The two stones represent this glow. The sardine stone signifies that God has a son, and this is confirmed in Matthew 3:17, "A voice from heaven, saying, this is my beloved Son." The jasper stone signifies that God's son sits on the right hand of the Father, and this is confirmed in Hebrews 10:12, "After he had offered one sacrifice for sins for ever, sat down on the right hand of God." A rainbow arches round about the throne. The color of the rainbow is emerald and the emerald stone signifies praise around the throne. The significance of the three stones is that:

- God has a son.
- God's son sits on his right side.
- The throne is surrounded by praise.

The emerald rainbow round about the throne testifies that the throne

---

[1] The New Strong's Complete Dictionary (Thomas Nelson Publishers, 1996), 216.

[2] The New Strong's Complete Dictionary (Thomas Nelson Publishers, 1996), 26.

room is a place of praise and worship. There is something else of importance about the rainbow. The bow in Genesis represents a promise that God made, that is, he will never again destroy mankind by water. Genesis 9:15 states, "I will remember my covenant, which is between me and you and every living creature of all flesh; and the waters shall no more become a flood to destroy all flesh." This promise or covenant was an everlasting promise. Genesis 9:16 states, "And I will look upon it, that I may remember the everlasting covenant between God and every living creature." A twofold message is here. The rainbow round about the throne represents an everlasting covenant. The color of the rainbow (emerald) represents praise. The rainbow is round about the throne, so praise fills the throne room. The rainbow is a reminder that God does not violate his covenants.

Twenty-four Seats and Twenty-four Elders

John also saw twenty-four seats around the throne, with twenty-four elders sitting in those seats. Elders are usually thought of as older people or people who are older than you are. The twenty-four elders sitting in the seats around the throne is where the Old Testament and New Testament come together. Twelve of these elders are the twelve sons of Jacob, which make up the twelve tribes of Israel in the Old Testament. The remaining twelve elders are the twelve apostles of Jesus from the New Testament. In Revelation 21:10–14, when John describes the wall around New Jerusalem, it mentions the twelve gates, named for the twelve tribes. The twelve foundations are named for the twelve apostles of Jesus. So, to enter the New Jerusalem, one enters the gates built on Old Testament promises, whose foundation is based on New Testament assurances.

The twenty-four elders are Jacob's twelve sons and Jesus' twelve disciples. Bear with me now while I explain how these twenty-four men, who have all died in the flesh, are in heaven sitting around the throne. Jesus told the disciples that they would sit on twelve thrones or twelve seats. Matthew 19:28 states, "Ye which have followed me, in the regeneration when the Son of man shall sit in the throne of his glory, ye also shall sit upon twelve thrones, judging the twelve tribes of Israel." Do not be confused. The twelve disciples will not be judging the men for whom the twelve tribes are named. The twelve disciples, along with the twelve tribes (sons of Jacob), will be judging mankind. Romans 2:12 states, "For as many as have sinned without law shall also perish without law: and as many as have sinned in the law shall be judged by the law." Judgment will come by the twelve tribes that lived by the law and the twelve disciples that lived under grace or the New Testament, not under the law.

All twenty-four of these men are dead in the flesh, but their souls are still alive. To explain further, Genesis 2:7 tells us that man has a body, "And the LORD God formed man of the dust of the ground"; a spirit, "And breathed into his nostrils the breath of life"; and a soul, "And man became a living soul." The meaning of spirit is "wind" or "breath."[3] Man's spirit is literally the breath of life, so we can conclude that man is a tripartite being, consisting of a body, a soul, and a spirit.

When a person dies, a series of things take place. Death occurs when a body no longer has a spirit or breath of God. James 2:26 states, "For as the body without the spirit is dead." When a person dies, his body is then buried. Ecclesiates12:7 states, "Then shall the dust return to the earth as it was." When a person dies, his spirit goes back to God. Ecclesiastes 12:7 further states, "And the spirit shall return unto God who gave it." At death, the spirit (or breath) leaves the body. The body is buried, and the part of man left is the soul. The soul is the part of man that is made in God's own image. Genesis 1:26–27 states, "God said, Let us make man in our image, after our likeness … God created man in his own image, in the image of God created he him." The soul is abstract. It is the mind, heart, or conscience of man. Man looked like God before he was given a body. Man was created in Genesis 1:27. At that point, man looked like God. Man was given a body in Genesis 2:7. At that point, man took a form and looked like man does today. Once a person dies, his spirit returns to God, the body returns to the earth, and the soul goes either to heaven or hell, depending upon that person's state of righteousness at the time of his death.

In order to establish that souls are still alive and active after physical death, we turn to Luke 9:28–31, "Behold, there talked with him two men, which were Moses and Elias … who appeared in glory, and spake of his decease." This setting is in the New Testament, and Jesus is talking to Old

---

[3] The New Strong's Complete Dictionary of Bible Words (Thomas Nelson Publishers, 1996), 517.

Testament saints, Moses and Elias. Jesus is speaking with their souls, not their physical bodies.

In the book of Luke, Lazarus and the rich man are both dead, but they are aware of their surrounding. Luke 16:22–24 states:

> And it came to pass, that the beggar died, and was carried by the angels into Abraham's bosom: the rich man also died, and was buried. And in hell he lift up his eyes, being in torments, and seeth Abraham afar off, and Lazarus in his bosom. And he cried and said, Father Abraham, have mercy on me, and send Lazarus that he may dip the tip of his finger in water, and cool my tongue; for I am tormented in this flame.

These men had died in the flesh, but their souls continued to live. Lazarus' soul experienced pleasure; the rich man's soul experienced suffering.

In the book of Revelation, we see that the souls (not the body) under the altar are aware of what is happening on earth. Revelation 6:9–10 states:

> I saw under the altar the souls of them that were slain for the word of God, and for the testimony which they held: and they cried with a loud voice, saying, how long, O Lord, holy and true, dost thou not judge and avenge our blood on them that dwell on the earth?

So there is consciousness after death. These are the souls of men who previously died in righteousness. Their souls are in heaven, and they witness the events happening on earth. These souls continue to live, and they can talk directly to God. Souls do not die. They move on to life eternal or everlasting damnation.

White Raiment

Now that it has been established that the elders are souls from both the Old and New Testaments, something else should be noted. The elders are clothed with white raiment. Revelation conveys the meaning of the fine linen. Revelation 19:8 states, "Arrayed in fine linen, clean and white; for the fine linen is the righteousness of saints." The twenty-four elders are clothed in righteousness. You have to be righteous in order to be in heaven, as 2 Peter 3:13 states: "Nevertheless we, according to his promise, look for new heavens and a new earth, wherein dwelleth righteousness."

Crowns

The elders are also wearing crowns of gold. Crowns are a covering for the head, worn to represent a specific title. Kings, queens, and priests often wear them, but they are not only limited to royalty. Miss America, for example, wears a crown. A headdress usually signifies a state of accomplishment, victory, or royalty. The twenty-four elders are worthy to wear crowns because they are royalty. Revelation 1:6 states, "And hath made us kings and priests unto God and his Father." Saints are kings and priests in the sight of God in the throne room, a place for worship and praise. The twenty-four elders throw their crowns before the throne as they worship. Revelation 4:10 states, "Cast their crowns before the throne."

Seven Lamps of Fire

Seven lamps of fire burn before the throne. The seven lamps of fire are interpreted in Revelation 4:5, "Which are the seven Spirits of God." We know then that the seven lamps of fire are the seven spirits of God. The purpose of the seven spirits of God is to be sent forth into the world. Revelation 5:6 states, "Sent forth into all the earth." Think back to John's vision in chapter 1 when the angel was standing in the midst of seven candlesticks. The Greek word for candlestick is *luchnia*, which means the same thing as lamp stand.

The presence of a lamp stand alone does not generate any light. The lamp stand has to be lit before there is any illumination. In the time of Jesus, the torch or lamp stand gave light when it was lit with a fire. Stars are sources of illumination from a distance, and the star, in this case, is the fire. Therefore, the lamps of fire or candlesticks and the fire represent the stars that are the churches with their respective angels. Revelation 1:20 states, "The seven stars are the angels of the seven churches: and the seven candlesticks which thou sawest are the seven churches."

To summarize, in Revelation 4:5, the seven lamps of fire are the seven spirits of God. In Revelation 5:6, the seven spirits of God are sent forth into all the earth. The seven lamps of fire are the seven spirits of God. The seven spirits of God are the seven lamp stands. The seven lamp stands are the seven candlesticks. The seven candlesticks are the seven churches in Revelation 1:20. The fire on those lamps or candlesticks is the same as the stars shown in Revelation 1:20. In Ephesians 5:23, Christ is the head of the church.

In Revelation 1:12–13, Christ is in the midst of the seven candlesticks (churches). In Revelation 5:6, the Lamb is standing with the seven spirits of God (churches). Revelation 1:13 and 5:6 both reference Jesus as being the head of the churches.

Rev. 4:6   And before the throne there was a sea of glass like unto crystal: and in the midst of the throne, and round about the throne, were four beasts full of eyes before and behind.

Rev. 4:7   And the first beast was like a lion, and the second beast like a calf, and the third beast had a face as a man, and the fourth beast was like a flying eagle.

Rev. 4:8   And the four beasts had each of them six wings about him; and they were full of eyes within: and they rest not day and night, saying, Holy, holy, holy, Lord God Almighty, which was, and is, and is to come.

Rev. 4:9   And when those beasts give glory and honour and thanks to him that sat on the throne, who liveth for ever and ever,

Rev. 4:10   The four and twenty elders fall down before him that sat on the throne, and worship him that liveth for ever and ever, and cast their crowns before the throne, saying,

Rev. 4:11   Thou art worthy, O Lord, to receive glory and honour and power: for thou hast created all things, and for thy pleasure they are and were created.

Sea of Glass

A sea of glass is before the throne. The phrase "sea of glass" indicates it is a large, open space and it is smooth and transparent, like glass. Picture a dance floor or a ballroom where all the ceremonial activities take place.

Four Beasts

In the midst of the throne are four beasts full of eyes. They have eyes in front and behind them, literally all over their bodies. The first beast looks like a lion. The second beast looks like a calf. The third beast looks like a man. The fourth beast looks like a flying eagle. All four of these beasts have six wings. They do not rest at all. Do you remember the emerald rainbow of praise round about the throne? They praise and worship God day and night continually.

These beasts are some type of angelic being. They are not physical because they are worshipping God in heaven at the throne. Actually, other than the angels (messengers of God), there are at least two other kinds of being in heaven. To understand more about these beings, we have to go to Ezekiel 1:1–28 and 10:9–22.

In Ezekiel 1:1–28, we have the description of a beast unlike any beast we have ever seen. Each beast has four faces: the face of a lion, the face of a man, the face of an ox, and the face of an eagle. Each has four wings. They have straight legs. The sole of their feet is like the soles of a calf's foot. Each has hands under their wings, and they do not turn when they move. They have eyes all over their bodies, and they have wheels.

In Ezekiel 10:9–22, the description of the beast is the same as the description in Ezekiel 1. The name of the creature is given, and they are called cherubim. Ezekiel 10:15 states, "And the cherubim were lifted up. This is the living creature that I saw by the river of Chebar." This verse also verifies that the creature in Ezekiel 10:15 is the same creature that was seen in Ezekiel 1:1–28.

There is a discrepancy between the beast described in Ezekiel and the beast described in Revelation 4:6–8. The creature or beast described in Ezekiel has only four wings, but the beast or creature in Revelation 4:6–8 has six wings. The beasts in Revelation 4:6–8 cannot be cherubim because of the difference in the number of wings and lack of wheels. It is some other kind of angelic being.

There is another beast very similar to the cherubim, named a seraph or seraphim in Isaiah 6:2–6. They are very similar, but one of the differences is that the cherubim have four wings. The seraphim have six wings. Isaiah 6:2 states, "Above it stood the seraphim: each one had six wings." The description of the seraphim is exactly the same as the being described in Revelation 4:6–8. Cherubim means "a keeper, a warder, or a guard of the deity."[4] Seraphim means "burning ones" or "angels of fire."[5] The four beasts that John witnessed in heaven (Rev. 4:6–8) are seraphim. These are not beasts in the sense that we know beast. The beasts, or creatures, described in Revelation 4:6–8 are heavenly beings, and there is no reason to be afraid of them because their duty is to praise God continually.

> Rev. 5:1   And I saw in the right hand of him that sat on the throne a book written within and on the backside, sealed with seven seals.
>
> Rev. 5:2   And I saw a strong angel proclaiming with a loud voice, Who is worthy to open the book, and to loose the seals thereof?
>
> Rev. 5:3   And no man in heaven, nor in earth, neither under the earth, was able to open the book, neither to look thereon.
>
> Rev. 5:4   And I wept much, because no man was found worthy to open and to read the book, neither to look thereon.

Book with Seven Seals

Revelation 5 is a continuation of Revelation 4. The setting is still in the throne room of heaven. John saw a scroll or book in the right hand of the one sitting on the throne. This book was written on both sides, and it was sealed with seven seals. An angel wanted to know who was worthy to break the seals on the book so it could be opened and have its contents read. It was determined that no man in heaven, no man on earth, no man under the earth, and no man in the sea was worthy to open this book. John began to weep because no one was found worthy to break the seals on the book. Without the seals being broken, it is impossible to open the book and

---

4 Smith's Bible Dictionary revised edition (Nashville: Holman Bible Publishers), 54.

5 Smith's Bible Dictionary revised edition (Nashville: Holman Bible Publishers), 273.

view the contents of the book. An elder told John that he should not worry because one is worthy to break the seven seals. Revelation 5:5 states, "The Lion of the tribe of Juda, the Root of David." In other words, Jesus Christ is the only one worthy to open this book. He is the only one without sin, and he has already conquered death. Revelation 1:18 states, "I am he that liveth, and was dead; and, behold, I am alive for evermore, Amen; and have the keys of hell and of death."

In order to understand more about the book with the seven seals, we have to go to the Old Testament to the book of Daniel. The archangel, Gabriel, told Daniel about End-time events. He finally told Daniel to seal up the book. Daniel 12:4 states, "Seal the book, even to the time of the end." While man waits until the End-time, he will learn more and more about prophecy. Daniel 12:4 states, "Many shall run to and fro, and knowledge shall be increased." Gabriel again told Daniel that the words were closed and sealed. Daniel 12:9 states, "Go thy way, Daniel: for the words are closed up and sealed till the time of the end." This could very well be the book that has the seven seals in the throne room.

The setting of Revelation 4 and 5 is the setting in heaven at the End-time. It is time for the seals to be broken to reveal the contents of the book with seven seals. When the seals are broken, the things that are recorded in the book will begin to come to pass on earth.

The book described in Revelation 5 had seals on it. The only way it could be read was for the seals to be broken. Seals are bands or stamps to make sure unauthorized persons do not tamper with a document. Obviously, this book contained classified information. Not just anyone could break the seals on a document. Only authorized personnel, depending on one's clearance, are permitted to break seals. In this case, only a person with the highest possible clearance, a person without sin, was authorized to break the seals. That person is Jesus Christ.

Rev. 5:5   And one of the elders saith unto me, Weep not: behold, the Lion of the tribe of Juda, the Root of David, hath prevailed to open the book, and to loose the seven seals thereof.

Rev. 5:6   And I beheld, and, lo, in the midst of the throne and of the four beasts, and in the midst of the elders, stood a

Lamb as it had been slain, having seven horns and seven
eyes, which are the seven Spirits of God sent forth into
all the earth.

Lion of the Tribe of Judah

The phrases "lion of the tribe of Judah" and the "root of David" are
synonymous. This fact is referenced in Revelation 5:5, "Weep not: behold,
the Lion of the tribe of Juda, the Root of David." It is known that Jesus is
from the tribe of Judah. Hebrews 7:14 states, "For it is evident that our Lord
sprang out of Juda; of which tribe." Once again, Revelation makes it posi-
tively clear who is the lion of the tribe of Judah. Revelation 22:16 states, "I
Jesus have sent mine angel to testify unto you these things in the churches. I
am the root and the offspring of David." Jesus clearly identified himself and
then continued to explain his genealogy. The lion of the tribe of Judah is
none other than Jesus Christ. Jesus is also called the Lamb. John 1:29 states,
"John seeth Jesus coming unto him, and saith, Behold the Lamb of God,
which taketh away the sin of the world."

John looked around about the throne, and he saw a lamb as it had been
slain, standing in the midst of the seraphim and the twenty-four elders. This
lamb had seven horns and seven eyes, the seven spirits of God. The seven
spirits of God was determined earlier to be the seven candlesticks with their
seven stars, the seven churches and their seven angels in Revelation 1:20:

> The mystery of the seven stars which thou sawest in my right hand,
> and the seven golden candlesticks. The seven stars are the angels of
> the seven churches: and the seven candlesticks which thou sawest are
> the seven churches.

The description in Revelation 5:6 of the lamb having seven spirits is
synonymous with the description of the vision in Revelation 1:12–13, where
the son of man has seven candlesticks. The lamb approached the throne and
took the book from the one sitting on the throne. The lamb appearing to be
slain is a symbol of Jesus because Jesus died on the cross (slain). Nevertheless,
he rose from the dead and was now alive and well. In Revelation 1:18, the

angel states that Jesus Christ is the one who lives. He was dead, but now he was alive forevermore, and he had the keys of hell and of death.

Rev. 5:7   And he came and took the book out of the right hand of him that sat upon the throne.

Rev. 5:8   And when he had taken the book, the four beasts and four and twenty elders fell down before the Lamb, having every one of them harps, and golden vials full of odours, which are the prayers of saints.

Rev. 5:9   And they sung a new song, saying, Thou art worthy to take the book, and to open the seals thereof: for thou wast slain, and hast redeemed us to God by thy blood out of every kindred, and tongue, and people, and nation;

Rev. 5:10 And hast made us unto our God kings and priests: and we shall reign on the earth.

Rev. 5:11 And I beheld, and I heard the voice of many angels round about the throne and the beasts and the elders: and the number of them was ten thousand times ten thousand, and thousands of thousands;

Rev. 5:12 Saying with a loud voice, Worthy is the Lamb that was slain to receive power, and riches, and wisdom, and strength, and honour, and glory, and blessing.

Rev. 5:13 And every creature which is in heaven, and on the earth, and under the earth, and such as are in the sea, and all that are in them, heard I saying, Blessing, and honour, and glory, and power, be unto him that sitteth upon the throne, and unto the Lamb for ever and ever.

Rev. 5:14 And the four beasts said, Amen. And the four and twenty elders fell down and worshipped him that liveth for ever and ever.

When the lamb took the book from the right hand of the one sitting on the throne, all the elders and beasts fell down before the throne to worship. They all had harps and golden vials, full of odors. The harps are musical instruments. The vials are small containers or bowls. The odors are some type of incense or aroma. The vials full of odors are the prayers of the saints. Revelation 5:8 states, "And golden vials full of odours, which are the prayers of saints." In the Old Testament, the odors were sweet savours to the Lord. Leviticus 4:31 states, "Shall burn it upon the altar for a sweet savour unto the LORD." In the New Testament, the odors were of a sweet smell. Philippians 4:18 states, "An odour of a sweet smell, a sacrifice acceptable, well pleasing to God."

All of the beings in the throne room were spiritual beings, including John the writer, his soul only, not his physical body. Revelation 4:2 states, "Immediately I was in the spirit: and, behold, a throne was set in heaven." Nothing physical is in the throne room, including the book with seven seals. Books are words. The words in the book with seven seals came from God, so the book with seven seals is a spiritual book. John 6:63 states, "The words that I speak unto you, they are spirit."

CHAPTER 4

THE HORSEMEN

Rev. 6:1   And I saw when the Lamb opened one of the seals, and I heard, as it were the noise of thunder, one of the four beasts saying, Come and see.

Rev. 6:2   And I saw, and behold a white horse: and he that sat on him had a bow; and a crown was given unto him: and he went forth conquering, and to conquer.

Rev. 6:3   And when he had opened the second seal, I heard the second beast say, Come and see.

Rev. 6:4   And there went out another horse that was red: and power was given to him that sat thereon to take peace from the earth, and that they should kill one another: and there was given unto him a great sword.

Rev. 6:5   And when he had opened the third seal, I heard the third beast say, Come and see. And I beheld, and lo a black horse; and he that sat on him had a pair of balances in his hand.

Rev. 6:6   And I heard a voice in the midst of the four beasts say, A measure of wheat for a penny, and three measures of barley for a penny; and see thou hurt not the oil and the wine.

Rev. 6:7   And when he had opened the fourth seal, I heard the voice of the fourth beast say, Come and see.

Rev. 6:8   And I looked, and behold a pale horse: and his name that sat on him was Death, and Hell followed with him. And power was given unto them over the fourth part of the earth, to kill with sword, and with hunger, and with death, and with the beasts of the earth.

The Four Horses

FOUR horses are mentioned in Revelation 6:1–8. Each horse has a different color; each horse performs a different function. There is a lot of speculation as to who or what these horses represent. Some say the white horse represents Jesus Christ, but it's best to let the scriptures discern their meaning.

Let's take a closer look at these four horses: a white horse, red horse, black horse, and a pale horse. Because there are four different colored horses, there must be something significant about each of them. To better understand the symbolization of these horses, let's go to the Old Testament to the book of Zechariah.[6]

Zec. 6:1   And I turned, and lifted up mine eyes, and looked, and, behold, there came four chariots out from between two mountains; and the mountains were mountains of brass.

Zec. 6:2   In the first chariot were red horses; and in the second chariot black horses;

Zec. 6:3   And in the third chariot white horses; and in the fourth chariot grisled and bay horses.

Zec. 6:4   Then I answered and said unto the angel that talked with me, What are these, my lord?

Zec. 6:5   And the angel answered and said unto me, These are the four spirits of the heavens, which go forth from standing before the Lord of all the earth.

Zec. 6:6   The black horses which are therein go forth into the north country; and the white go forth after them; and the grisled go forth toward the south country.

Zec. 6:7   And the bay went forth, and sought to go that they might walk to and fro through the earth: and he said, Get you hence, walk to and fro through the earth. So they walked to and fro through the earth.

---

[6] Torah Light Ministries, Stanley Chester, taped message.

Zec. 1:8	I saw by night, and behold a man riding upon a red horse, and he stood among the myrtle trees that were in the bottom; and behind him were there red horses, speckled, and white.
Zec. 1:9	Then said I, O my lord, what are these? And the angel that talked with me said unto me, I will shew thee what these be.
Zec. 1:10	And the man that stood among the myrtle trees answered and said, These are they whom the LORD hath sent to walk to and fro through the earth.
Zec. 1:11	And they answered the angel of the LORD that stood among the myrtle trees, and said, We have walked to and fro through the earth, and, behold, all the earth sitteth still, and is at rest.

Zechariah 6:5 points out that the horses are the spirits of heaven, which goes forth from standing before the Lord of the whole earth. Zechariah 1:10 discloses that the horses are those who walk to and fro throughout all the earth. Both of these scriptures parallel Revelation 5:6, "Which are the seven Spirits of God sent forth into all the earth." So the four horses represent spirits or influences. The horses are not literal. They represent spiritual influences on the earth. The horses themselves should not be the focus of one's attention, but their colors should be.

The Colors

Throughout the Bible, different colors stand for different things, so it is imperative that the colors of the horses be studied a little more carefully. These four different colors have to be understood in order to establish the relevance of each horse.

- The color white is associated with righteousness in Revelation 19:8, "Clean and white: for the fine linen is the righteousness of saints." The color white is also associated with being pure. Revelation 15:6 states, "Clothed in pure and white linen."

- The color red is always associated with struggle or stumbling blocks. Do you remember Esau in Genesis 25:21–34? When he was born, he was red and hairy, and he struggled with his brother Jacob while still in the womb. The red pottage that Esau traded for his birthright was red. Another example is the exodus of the Israelites from Egypt. The Egyptian army was pursuing them from behind, and the Red Sea obstructed their forward progression. The Red Sea was their stumbling block. They had nowhere to go.
- The color black is associated with grief or mourning. Revelation 6:12 indicates the color is associated with sackcloth of hair. Sackcloth is exactly what the name implies. It is the rough cloth of which sacks are made. It is a garment that is worn in mourning, distress, or death.
- Pale is associated with something horrible or frightful. When one experiences something fearful, his facial expression becomes pale. Pale indicates a lifeless body's appearance when all the blood is drained from it. Revelation 6:8 clearly points out that pale is associated with death and hell. At death, the blood no longer flows through the body, so the body becomes pale.

The Horsemen

Even though scripture bears out that the horses represent spirits or influences, one should not concern himself with the horses. The riders, not the horses, cause all the turmoil. The colors reveal a definite relationship between the spiritual influence and the rider. The horse represents a spiritual (satanic) influence; the riders of the horses represent the antichrist. Satan has no authority in heaven, and this is confirmed in Isaiah 4:12, "How art thou fallen from heaven, O Lucifer, son of the morning! how art thou cut down to the ground." He fell from his heavenly position. Satan lost his heavenly status, and his dominion is now on earth. Ephesians 2:2 bears witness that Satan is the prince of the power of the air (earth). Satan has no authority in heaven, so he will imitate God on earth through a man called the antichrist. More information about the antichrist will soon follow.

Because the horsemen cause all of the turmoil on the earth, let's take a closer look at these riders. By comparing scripture known to be referencing

Jesus (Rev. 19:11–16) with Revelation 6:2, it can be determined without a doubt whether or not the rider on the white horse in Revelation 6:2 is Jesus.

Rev. 6:2   And I saw, and behold a white horse: and he that sat on him had a bow; and a crown was given unto him: and he went forth conquering, and to conquer.

Rev. 19:11   And I saw heaven opened, and behold a white horse; and he that sat upon him was called Faithful and True, and in righteousness he doth judge and make war.

Rev. 19:12   His eyes were as a flame of fire, and on his head were many crowns; and he had a name written, that no man knew, but he himself.

Rev. 19:13   And he was clothed with a vesture dipped in blood: and his name is called The Word of God.

Rev. 19:14   And the armies which were in heaven followed him upon white horses, clothed in fine linen, white and clean.

Rev. 19:15   And out of his mouth goeth a sharp sword, that with it he should smite the nations: and he shall rule them with a rod of iron: and he treadeth the winepress of the fierceness and wrath of Almighty God.

Rev. 19:16   And he hath on his vesture and on his thigh a name written, KING OF KINGS, AND LORD OF LORDS.

It is a well-known fact that the rider on the white horse in Revelation 19 is Jesus. Taking a closer look, both riders are riding a white horse. The rider in Revelation 6:2 has a crown. The rider in Revelation 19 has many crowns. The rider in Revelation 6:2 has a bow. The rider in Revelation 19 has a sharp, two-edged sword. The title or name of the rider in Revelation 6:2 is not given or is hidden. The rider in Revelation 19 has a name (the Word of God) and a title (King of Kings and Lord of Lords).

The rider in Revelation 6:2 is definitely not Jesus, but he is an earthly leader who portrays himself as Jesus. Everybody who rides a white horse is not Jesus. This rider is a man on earth who Satan influences. He is better known as the antichrist. Satan has determined that he wants this man to carry out his evil deeds, so he deposited that desire into this man's heart or mind. Bear in mind that this individual has to be a willing participant for

Satan to use him in such a way. Satan cannot force a man to go against his will. This man imitates Christ. This man is against Christ. This man, the rider on the white horse in Revelation 6:2, is the antichrist.

Rider on the White Horse

Rev. 6:1　　And I saw when the Lamb opened one of the seals, and I heard, as it were the noise of thunder, one of the four beasts saying, Come and see.

Rev. 6:2　　And I saw, and behold a white horse: and he that sat on him had a bow; and a crown was given unto him: and he went forth conquering, and to conquer.

The rider on the white horse has a bow in his hand, and a crown was given to him. Obviously, this man has elevated himself to a lofty position because some group or organization in high positions gave him a crown. It is confirmed that this rider on the white horse was given a crown in Revelation 17:12–13, "And the ten horns which thou sawest are ten kings, which have received no kingdom as yet; but receive power as kings one hour with the beast. These have one mind, and shall give their power and strength unto the beast." Ten kings will make the antichrist the leader of their coalition by relinquishing their authority over to him and giving him a crown.

The rider on the white horse has a crown. A crown is a headdress worn by a king, queen, or some other leader. He went forth conquering on the earth. He has to be on earth because there is nothing to conquer in heaven. This rider is on a white horse. The horse represents a spiritual force or influence. The color white represents righteousness and purity. Because the rider is on a white horse, some will automatically assume that the rider is Jesus. Make no mistake about it though. This is not Jesus. It is the antichrist imitating Jesus.

Rider on the Red Horse

Rev. 6:3　　And when he had opened the second seal, I heard the second beast say, Come and see.

Rev. 6:4　　And there went out another horse that was red: and power was given to him that sat thereon to take peace from the earth, and that they should kill one another: and there was given unto him a great sword.

The rider on the red horse was given a great sword. This sword is not a double-edged sword. It's only a great sword symbolizing great authority. The horse represents a spiritual influence. The red color of the horse represents struggle or a stumbling block, so the red horse represents an evil spirit carrying a rider to initiate evil deeds on earth. The rider has authority to take peace from the earth, and he uses men to kill one another. This rider's main objective is to bring war and take away peace and safety from the earth. This rider is a man on earth, influenced by Satan. This man is also the antichrist.

This rider is the same rider who is on the white horse in Revelation 6:2. First, the rider came on a white horse, imitating Christ. Next, the rider came on a red horse and showed his true colors when he decided to wreak havoc on earth and take away peace and safety. Both the rider on the white horse and the rider on the red horse are the same rider, the antichrist. There are two different spirits represented by two different horses. Both of them reflect Satan. There is one man or one rider on both horses, and it is the same man serving in two different roles.

Rider on the Black Horse

Rev. 6:5   And when he had opened the third seal, I heard the third beast say, Come and see. And I beheld, and lo a black horse; and he that sat on him had a pair of balances in his hand.

Rev. 6:6   And I heard a voice in the midst of the four beasts say, A measure of wheat for a penny, and three measures of barley for a penny; and see thou hurt not the oil and the wine.

The black horse symbolizes famine and distress. Again, this is not a literal horse. It is a spirit of famine and distress represented by the black color of the horse. The famine is a result of the war and unrest brought on by the previous rider on the red horse. The rider on the black horse has a pair of balances in his hand, where everything is measured, weighed, and rationed.

One can get a better understanding from the book of Joel as to why there is famine and rationing in the land.

Joe. 1:6   For a nation is come up upon my land, strong, and without number, whose teeth are the teeth of a lion, and he hath the cheek teeth of a great lion.

Joe. 1:7   He hath laid my vine waste, and barked my fig tree: he hath made it clean bare, and cast it away; the branches thereof are made white.

Joe. 1:8   Lament like a virgin girded with sackcloth for the husband of her youth.

Joe. 1:9   The meat offering and the drink offering is cut off from the house of the LORD; the priests, the LORD'S ministers, mourn.

Joe. 1:10   The field is wasted, the land mourneth; for the corn is wasted: the new wine is dried up, the oil languisheth.

Joe. 1:11   Be ye ashamed, O ye husbandmen; howl, O ye vinedressers, for the wheat and for the barley; because the harvest of the field is perished.

Joe. 1:12   The vine is dried up, and the fig tree languisheth; the pomegranate tree, the palm tree also, and the apple tree, even all the trees of the field, are withered: because joy is withered away from the sons of men.

Joe. 1:13   Gird yourselves, and lament, ye priests: howl, ye ministers of the altar: come, lie all night in sackcloth, ye ministers of my God: for the meat offering and the drink offering is withholden from the house of your God.

In Joel 1, a nation or leader invaded God's land, better known as Israel. This invader of Israel was a large multitude, signifying an army, and it destroyed the wheat, barley vine, and so forth. The food supply was limited because the harvest had been sacrificed by the war and lack of peace and safety, brought on by the rider on the red horse. Because there was a shortage of food, the rider on the black horse saw this as a perfect opportunity to capitalize on this situation. There would be much black market activity. The rider on the black horse understood hunger is a powerful weapon.

The rider on the black horse is also the antichrist and riding yet another different color horse. He will establish rationing because of the famine in the land. Rationing will gain him more political and economical clout. If one can control the food supply, he can control mankind.

Rider on the Pale Horse

Rev. 6:7   And when he had opened the fourth seal, I heard the voice of the fourth beast say, Come and see.

Rev. 6:8   And I looked, and behold a pale horse: and his name that sat on him was Death, and Hell followed with him. And power was given unto them over the fourth part of the earth, to kill with sword, and with hunger, and with death, and with the beasts of the earth.

The rider on the pale horse has a symbolic name. His name is death, but that's not his given name. This name represents his agenda, to kill mankind by any possible method. The pale horse symbolizes a lifeless body with all the blood drained from it. The name of this rider is appropriate because he brings death, as his name indicates. The rider also has a shadow. Death has a close friend, and his friend's name is hell. This rider was given authority, and his mission was to kill as many as possible, using any means at his disposal. He used weapons, starvation, and even beasts to kill people. This is a vicious man, influenced by Satan, and he is also the antichrist.

Summary of the riders on the four different colored horses

The riders on these four horses are one: one rider, one man, the same person. Each time he appears on a different colored horse, he's executing another part of his strategy. The same rider (antichrist) rides all four of these spiritual influences (horses). The color of the horse he's riding determines the mission of the antichrist. All of the antichrist's actions are being manifested here on earth. There is nothing to conquer and nothing to kill in heaven, so these actions have to be earthly events. Although these evil actions originated from a spiritual nature (Satan), they manifested themselves in physical form here on earth. The color of the horses reveals the nature of these evil spirits, and their nature will be administered on earth by the antichrist. All of the events by the horsemen or riders of these four horses are literal. They are not spiritual, but they are spiritually motivated.

CHAPTER 5

144,000

Rev. 7:1   And after these things I saw four angels standing on the four corners of the earth, holding the four winds of the earth, that the wind should not blow on the earth, nor on the sea, nor on any tree.

Rev. 7:2   And I saw another angel ascending from the east, having the seal of the living God: and he cried with a loud voice to the four angels, to whom it was given to hurt the earth and the sea,

Rev. 7:3   Saying, Hurt not the earth, neither the sea, nor the trees, till we have sealed the servants of our God in their foreheads.

FOUR angels stand on the four corners of the earth. The four corners of the earth refer to the four compass directions: north, south, east, and west. One angel stands at the north direction, one is at the south, one is at the east, and one is at the west. These angels hold back the winds from blowing on the four compass directions of the earth. The word *wind* means a "breeze," but it can also be translated as "spirit."[7] A blowing wind or breeze is nothing other than air that is moving. This verse could be paraphrased. The four angels stand on the four corners of the earth, restraining the winds (spirits) from blowing (moving) on the earth, sea, and any tree. There has to be more to this verse than just the wind blowing on the earth before the servants are sealed because wind blowing on earth is a common occurrence. This verse refers to spirits moving on earth. It isn't speaking of spooky

---

[7] The New Strong's Complete Dictionary of Bible Words (Thomas Nelson Publishers, 1996), 280.

things, but a spirit in the sense of a type of consciousness or supernatural influence that is organized and controlling.

Another angel appears from the east, which has the seal of the living God. The seal of the living God is some type of a stamp, mark, or inscription. This seal or mark implies that the ones wearing this seal belong to God. When something or someone is sealed, it denotes it has a protected status. The angel ascending from the east shouts instructions to the four angels stationed at the four corners of the earth, telling them they should not hurt the earth, sea, or any trees until the servants of God were sealed on their foreheads. It appears the angels at the four corners of the earth are preparing to hurt the earth, sea, and trees, but that's not the case. They are holding back or preventing the winds or spirits from blowing (moving) on the earth until the servants of God were sealed or protected. These four angels are not angels of destruction. They are in a preventative mode. They are stationed at the four corners of the earth to prevent anything from happening on earth before the proper time. These fours angels are protectors, not destroyers, of the earth, and they are stationed at the four corners or four compass directions of the earth. Their mission is not to allow anything to hurt the earth, sea, and trees until after the sealing of the servants of God. This is a very significant point and will be addressed later.

Rev. 7:4   And I heard the number of them which were sealed: and there were sealed an hundred and forty and four thousand of all the tribes of the children of Israel.

Rev. 7:5   Of the tribe of Juda were sealed twelve thousand. Of the tribe of Reuben were sealed twelve thousand. Of the tribe of Gad were sealed twelve thousand.

Rev. 7:6   Of the tribe of Aser were sealed twelve thousand. Of the tribe of Nepthalim were sealed twelve thousand. Of the tribe of Manasses were sealed twelve thousand.

Rev. 7:7   Of the tribe of Simeon were sealed twelve thousand. Of the tribe of Levi were sealed twelve thousand. Of the tribe of Issachar were sealed twelve thousand.

Rev. 7:8   Of the tribe of Zabulon were sealed twelve thousand. Of the tribe of Joseph were sealed twelve thousand. Of the tribe of Benjamin were sealed twelve thousand.

The angels have a specific number of servants to seal, 144,000, which is not just a random group of servants. All of the servants who will be sealed at that particular time will be Jewish. There is a specific amount to be sealed from each of the twelve tribes of Israel.

John named how many would be sealed from each tribe:

1	Tribe of Judah	12,000
2	Tribe of Reuben	12,000
3	Tribe of Gad	12,000
4	Tribe of Asher	12,000
5	Tribe of Naphtalim	12,000
6	Tribe of Manasses	12,000
7	Tribe of Simeon	12,000
8	Tribe of Levi	12,000
9	Tribe of Issachar	12,000
10	Tribe of Zabulon	12,000
11	Tribe of Joseph	12,000
12	Tribe of Benjamin	12,000

The total number of people sealed from all the tribes of the children of Israel is 144,000, with twelve thousand from each tribe. This particular event of sealing the servants of God is only for Israel. No Gentiles are mentioned in the sealing of the servants of God in Revelation 7:4–8. The sealing mentioned here of the servants of God is limited to the Jewish people only.

Something else should be examined more carefully. One tribe of the original twelve tribes, Dan, isn't mentioned. This scripture does not indicate why his name is omitted, but it was probably for some type of transgression.[8] The Old Testament gives more insight pertaining to the consequences for transgressing God's law.

Deu. 29:18 Lest there should be among you man, or woman, or family, or tribe, whose heart turneth away this day from

---

[8] Torah Light Ministries, Stanley Chester, taped message.

the LORD our God, to go and serve the gods of these nations; lest there should be among you a root that beareth gall and wormwood;

Deu. 29:19 And it come to pass, when he heareth the words of this curse, that he bless himself in his heart, saying, I shall have peace, though I walk in the imagination of mine heart, to add drunkenness to thirst:

Deu. 29:20 The LORD will not spare him, but then the anger of the LORD and his jealousy shall smoke against that man, and all the curses that are written in this book shall lie upon him, and the LORD shall blot out his name from under heaven.

Deu. 29:21 And the LORD shall separate him unto evil out of all the tribes of Israel, according to all the curses of the covenant that are written in this book of the law:

Moses told the children of Israel that, if any man, woman, family, or tribe served other gods, their name would be blotted out from under heaven. Because the tribe of Dan is omitted from the list in Revelation 7:4–8, one must investigate or search the scriptures to determine if the tribe of Dan did actually serve other gods. More information about the tribe of Dan can be found in the book of 1 Kings.

1 Kin. 12:25   Then Jeroboam built Shechem in mount Ephraim, and dwelt therein; and went out from thence, and built Penuel.

1 Kin. 12:26   And Jeroboam said in his heart, Now shall the kingdom return to the house of David:

1 Kin. 12:27   If this people go up to do sacrifice in the house of the LORD at Jerusalem, then shall the heart of this people turn again unto their lord, even unto Rehoboam king of Judah, and they shall kill me, and go again to Rehoboam king of Judah.

1 Kin. 12:28   Whereupon the king took counsel, and made two calves of gold, and said unto them, It is too much for you to go up to Jerusalem: behold thy gods, O

	Israel, which brought thee up out of the land of Egypt.
1 Kin. 12:29	And he set the one in Bethel, and the other put he in Dan.
1 Kin. 12:30	And this thing became a sin: for the people went to worship before the one, even unto Dan.
1 Kin. 12:31	And he made an house of high places, and made priests of the lowest of the people, which were not of the sons of Levi.
1 Kin. 12:32	And Jeroboam ordained a feast in the eighth month, on the fifteenth day of the month, like unto the feast that is in Judah, and he offered upon the altar. So did he in Bethel, sacrificing unto the calves that he had made: and he placed in Bethel the priests of the high places which he had made.
1 Kin. 12:33	So he offered upon the altar which he had made in Bethel the fifteenth day of the eighth month, even in the month which he had devised of his own heart; and ordained a feast unto the children of Israel: and he offered upon the altar, and burnt incense.

The scriptures point out that a calf of gold was set up and worshipped in Dan. God specifically said in Exodus 20:3, "Thou shalt have no other gods before me." Perhaps this is why the tribe of Dan is omitted or blotted out from the list in Revelation 7:4–8 because they worshipped gods made with the hands of men instead of worshipping the God that created the heavens, earth, and the seas. The tribe of Dan was worshipping the golden calves as if the calves were the God that brought them out of Egypt. The golden calves were not the God that created everything, but they were the gods that the hands of men made.

The tribe of Dan was omitted, but twelve tribes are still listed in Revelation 7:4–8, so there must be a substitution for the tribe of Dan. When comparing Revelation 7:4–8 to the list of twelve tribes, one discovers that Manasses was not one of the original twelve tribes, but his name is included in the list. The book of Genesis gives more information as to the identity of Manasses.

Gen. 46:19 The sons of Rachel Jacob's wife; Joseph, and Benjamin.

Gen. 46:20 And unto Joseph in the land of Egypt were born
Manasseh and Ephraim, which Asenath the daughter of
Potipherah priest of On bare unto him.

Genesis 46:19–20 points out that Joseph, one of the original twelve tribes, had two sons, Manasses and Ephraim. Manasses was the firstborn of Joseph, but, just like Jacob, received the blessing over his older brother, Esau. Ephraim also received the blessing over his older brother Manasses (Gen. 48:9–20). Ephraim received the blessing, but his name was not listed with the twelve tribes in Revelation 7:4–8. Ephraim's name was omitted or blotted for the same reason that Dan's name was omitted. In 1 Kings 12:29, two golden calves were made. One was set up and worshipped in Dan; the other was set up and worshipped in Bethel. Bethel is a place in Ephraim, so Ephraim's name was omitted. When Ephraim's name was omitted, this created a vacancy, providing for the addition of Manasses, his brother's name.

Because the tribe of Joseph is listed as one of the twelve tribes and Manasses, Joseph's son, is listed as one of the twelve tribes in Revelation 7:5–8, Joseph will have a double inheritance. This is exactly what was prophesied by the prophet Ezekiel. Ezekiel 47:13 states, "Whereby ye shall inherit the land according to the twelve tribes of Israel: Joseph shall have two portions."

Rev. 14:1 And I looked, and, lo, a Lamb stood on the mount Sion, and with him an hundred forty and four thousand, having his Father's name written in their foreheads.

Rev. 14:2 And I heard a voice from heaven, as the voice of many waters, and as the voice of a great thunder: and I heard the voice of harpers harping with their harps:

Rev. 14:3 And they sung as it were a new song before the throne, and before the four beasts, and the elders: and no man could learn that song but the hundred and forty and four thousand, which were redeemed from the earth.

Rev. 14:4 These are they which were not defiled with women; for they are virgins. These are they which follow the Lamb whithersoever he goeth. These were redeemed from among men, being the firstfruits unto God and to the Lamb.

Rev. 14:5   And in their mouth was found no guile: for they are without fault before the throne of God.

John looked and saw a lamb standing on Mount Sion. Accompanying the lamb is 144,000, the same number sealed in Revelation 7:4–8. John explained the significance of the seal. It was the name of the lamb's father. Revelation 3:12 states, "And I will write upon him the name of my God." The seal was written in the foreheads of the 144,000. They received this seal because they were faultless in the eyes of God. This does not mean that they never sinned. It means they were born again and God had blotted out all of their previous sins. Hebrews 8:12 states, "I will be merciful to their unrighteousness, and their sins and their iniquities will I remember no more." The 144,000 were the first fruits unto God and the lamb. First fruits are exactly what the name implies, the first yield of a product at harvest. All things, whether good or evil, comes to the Jew first. Romans 2:8–10 states:

Unto them that are contentious, and do not obey the truth … tribulation and anguish, upon every soul of man that doeth evil, of the Jew first, and also of the Gentile … glory, honour, and peace, to every man that worketh good, to the Jew first, and also to the Gentile.

The 144,000 are the first fruits or first to be positioned in a protected status. Some will say that the 144,000 are in heaven with God, but that's not the case. Mount Sion is the same as Mount Zion. It is called Mount Sion in the New Testament and Mount Zion in the Old Testament, and it is a physical place in Israel. It is not in heaven, so the 144,000 are still here on earth. If they are in heaven, there is no need to be sealed. They were sealed to be protected from the turmoil that was fast approaching the earth. Revelation 7:3 states, "Hurt not the earth, neither the sea, nor the trees, till we have sealed the servants of our God." None of the seals could be broken, and none of the trumpets could be sounded until the 144,000 were sealed.

As John beheld the lamb and 144,000, he also heard voices and the sound of musical instruments coming from heaven. John also heard the 144,000 singing a new song. The singing was a new song that was sung before the throne on Mount Zion, which is on earth. Only the 144,000 sang this song because no other man could learn that song except them.

Because Revelation 14:4 states these are redeemed from among men, some take this to mean that the 144,000 are in heaven. The word *redeem* means "to be saved, bought, and paid in full." Galatians 3:13 states, "Christ hath redeemed us from the curse of the law." All born-again people are redeemed (saved), but they are still here on the earth. Because a person is redeemed, it does not mean that individual is in heaven.

Again, because the 144,000 follow the lamb wherever he goes, some think they are in heaven. Matthew 16:24 states, "Then said Jesus unto his disciples, if any man will come after me, let him deny himself, and take up his cross, and follow me." All born-again people are followers of Jesus, but they are still on earth in a physical body. The 144,000 are still here on earth. They are not in heaven.

The 144,000 are a group of born-again Jews. They are here on earth, and they have received protection from God. The seal they received on their foreheads denotes they have demonstrated they are worthy to be called sons of God. This seal they received is worn in honor. They have earned the right to be accepted by God and partake in all the fringe benefits this honor bestows. The seal worn by the 144,000 is not a brand to show ownership. It sets them apart and shows they are distinguished, a member of the house of God. This is not a physical seal, and it is not visible to other individuals. It is a spiritual seal that God has placed upon his first fruits, the 144,000.

CHAPTER 6

THE SEALS AND THE TRUMPETS

BY now, it is obvious that the book of Revelation is a book of sevens. Actually, there are several different sevens. See the chart of sevens in the back of the book for a complete list. Some of these sevens have been discussed in the previous chapters, but this chapter will focus on the seven seals and the seven trumpets.

Seals are impressions placed on an object to denote its authority or authenticity. Seals are also used to place a document into a protected status. Some documents are not official unless they have a seal, either inscribed or stamped upon them. Some examples of these documents are birth certificates and passports. Other documents are protected from unauthorized access, like court orders and classified documents.

Trumpets are musical instruments that have the appearance of a tube with keys in it to allow the passage of air. The keys open and close to produce a sound when air is blown into one end of it. The moving air vibrates and causes a reverberation. The book of Revelation refers to seven angels sounding seven trumpets. The scripture does not confirm whether or not the sounding of these trumpets are seven different sounds or one distinct sound being echoed seven different times. It really doesn't matter whether or not the sounds are different because something unique will happen each time the trumpet sounds.

The seven seals were first mentioned in Revelation 5. It was the book with seven seals that no man could open. The lamb was the only one found worthy to open the seals to reveal what the seals were concealing. The lamb was on the threshold of opening the seven seals to reveal the things of the future to John.

Seven Seals and Seven Trumpets

Rev. 8:1   And when he had opened the seventh seal, there was
            silence in heaven about the space of half an hour.
Rev. 8:2   And I saw the seven angels which stood before God; and
            to them were given seven trumpets.

Revelation 8 begins with the seventh seal being broken. After this seal
was broken, there was silence in heaven for about a half hour. From the
above scriptures, it appears that all of the seals were broken before the angels
were given the seven trumpets. Remember, the book of Revelation is not
written in chronological order. Actually, the seven seals and the seven trumpets are tied together. This will become obvious as this study progresses. In
reality, the seven trumpets are given to the seven angels just prior to the first
seal being broken. The book with the seven seals is in the throne room in
heaven, so the seals are broken in heaven. When the seals are broken, it indicates that the fullness of time or time when heavenly beings will no longer
prohibit destruction and calamity to be dispensed upon the earth.

One of the duties of the angels in heaven is to prevent certain things
from happening until the proper time. Revelation 7:3 states, "Hurt not the
earth, neither the sea, nor the trees, till we have sealed the servants of our
God." The breaking of the seals is a timer indicating that something spiritual
will happen in heaven by heavenly beings. When the trumpets are blown,
it indicates that something physical will happen on earth by human beings.
Revelation 8:7 states, "First angel sounded, and there followed hail and fire
mingled with blood, and they were cast upon the earth: and the third part
of trees was burnt up, and all green grass was burnt up." The seals represent
timers in heaven; the trumpets represent actions manifested on the earth. I
know it seems confusing now, but it's like a puzzle. When the puzzle pieces
are poured out of the box, it is confusing and frustrating because there are so
many pieces with no starting point. As one proceeds with the task of assem-
bling the puzzle and begins to find pieces that match, the puzzle begins to
take shape by becoming more revealing. The end result is a perfect picture
of what the artist intended to reveal from the beginning. Let's begin to put
this puzzle together.

The First Seal

Rev. 6:1   And I saw when the Lamb opened one of the seals, and
             I heard, as it were the noise of thunder, one of the four
             beasts saying, Come and see.

Rev. 6:2   And I saw, and behold a white horse: and he that sat on
             him had a bow; and a crown was given unto him: and
             he went forth conquering, and to conquer.

The breaking of the seals happens in heaven because John saw the book with the seven seals in the throne room in heaven. When a seal is broken, Jesus, the Lamb in heaven, breaks it. It means it is time for heavenly beings to initiate God's plan for earth and mankind. When the first seal is broken, the rider on the white horse appears. He has a crown and a bow. His mission is to go forth conquering and to conquer. This could not happen until it is the proper time, according to God's timetable. The breaking of the seals is a timer, signaling a particular event is now allowed to take place.

When the first seal is broken, this signals it is time for the spiritual influence represented by the white horse to move on the earth. Do you remember the four angels holding back the wind (spirit) so it could not blow (move) on the earth until the 144,000 were sealed (Rev. 7:1)? The four angels are actually preventing the white horse (spirit) from moving on the earth. When the first seal is broken, the spirit (white horse) is released. Once the spirit (white horse) is released, there is still no manifestation of it on the earth. The white horse (spirit) roams the earth, seeking someone (mankind) to influence or possess. The individual the white horse (spirit) deems suitable to carry out his agenda is the antichrist, the rider on the white horse. Although the white horse (spirit) has a candidate for the position of antichrist, this union cannot take place until it is the proper time according to God's calendar, signaled by the sounding of the corresponding trumpet.

Some might think that the white horse (spirit) is one of the good spirits because white represents righteousness. Although white represents righteousness, there are those who specialize in deception. Do you remember the four angels that are holding back the winds (spirits) to prevent them from hurting the earth (Rev. 7:1–3)? These angels are actually holding back evil spirits, symbolized by the four different colored horses and the roles they play (Rev. 6:1–8). All four horses are evil, including the white horse. This is clever strategy because a white horse is usually associated with righteousness, but the rider's name, antichrist, makes it crystal clear that the white horse is an evil spirit with evil intentions.

The First Trumpet

Rev. 8:6   And the seven angels which had the seven trumpets prepared themselves to sound.

Rev. 8:7   The first angel sounded, and there followed hail and fire mingled with blood, and they were cast upon the earth: and the third part of trees was burnt up, and all green grass was burnt up.

The sounding of the trumpet marks the beginning of physical things being manifested on earth and witnessed by mankind. Immediately after the release of the white horse, the first trumpet sounds, signaling it is time for the antichrist to start his reign of terror on earth. When the first trumpet sounds, hail and fire will mingle with blood and be cast into the earth. The hail and fire mingled with blood isn't hail and fire from heaven or some supernatural event. It is exploding bombs, raining down dirt, blood, and flesh. After all, the antichrist goes forth to conquer.

John described what he saw with the knowledge of that day. Not only will men be killed, but one-third of all the trees in the antichrist's war zone will be burned. All the green grass will be burned.

Remember in Revelation 7:3 when the angel from the east told the angels at the four corners of the earth not to hurt the earth, sea, or any trees until the sealing of the 144,000? Because the sounding of the first trumpet is the beginning of hurting the earth and burning of the trees, the 144,000 must be sealed before the first trumpet is sounded.

When the first trumpet sounds, this marks the beginning of the destruction on earth through war. Revelation 6:2 states, "And he went forth conquering, and to conquer." When this war begins, all the green grass and one-third of the trees in the war zone will be burned up. The destruction of the trees, grass, and other forms of vegetation indicates that a majority of all the plants used for food will be compromised. If one can sabotage the food supply, then he has succeeded in conquering the people in the affected areas.

The Second Seal

Rev. 6:3   And when he had opened the second seal, I heard the second beast say, Come and see.

Rev. 6:4   And there went out another horse that was red: and power was given to him that sat thereon to take peace from the earth, and that they should kill one another: and there was given unto him a great sword.

The second seal has just broken in heaven. This means it is time for another but different spirit to emerge. This spirit represented by the red horse is the spirit of struggle. The rider on the red horse is the antichrist, and he's carrying a great sword. The mission of the antichrist is to take peace from the earth. A great struggle will cause the elimination of the peace in the land.

The Second Trumpet

Rev. 8:8   And the second angel sounded, and as it were a great mountain burning with fire was cast into the sea: and the third part of the sea became blood;

Rev. 8:9   And the third part of the creatures which were in the sea, and had life, died; and the third part of the ships were destroyed.

When the second seal is broken, the spirit of struggle, represented by the red horse, will be released. Immediately, the second trumpet is blown. The spirit of struggle (red horse) empowers the antichrist to take peace from the earth. John saw a great mountain burning with fire as it fell into the sea. This great mountain is some type of military weapon that the antichrist (the rider on the red horse) uses. This weapon could be some type of missile or dirty bomb. Some people think this mountain is some type of meteor. Meteors are supernatural events, but the events described here, taking peace from the earth, are man-made events. The antichrist is a human being and has no control over meteors. As this study progresses, one will begin to see that all of the things done after the sounding of the trumpets are physical things on earth that man controls. When this burning mountain (bomb) falls into the seas controlled by the antichrist, one-third of the sea becomes blood, one-third of the fish and other sea life die, and one-third of the ships in the sea are destroyed. The antichrist, which the spirit of struggle (red horse) manipulates, has a mission, to take peace from the earth by first destroying vegetation and then by attacking and destroying the seas. By attacking the seas, this isolates one country from another, and this isolation creates fear. Fear and panic is the weapon of choice that the antichrist uses. His agenda is to take away peace from the earth. Now that the second trumpet is sounded, the seas are under attack. By attacking the seas, this interrupts shipping and destroys a big part of the seafood that the seas provide. This interferes with international commerce. Countries are afraid to use the sea, for fear of being attacked and knowing the sea is contaminated with blood and dead fish. The rider on the red horse has successfully taken away peace from the earth.

The Third Seal

Rev. 6:5   And when he had opened the third seal, I heard the third beast say, Come and see. And I beheld, and lo a black horse; and he that sat on him had a pair of balances in his hand.

Rev. 6:6   And I heard a voice in the midst of the four beasts say, A measure of wheat for a penny, and three measures of barley for a penny; and see thou hurt not the oil and the wine.

The third seal is broken in heaven, and the rider on the black horse appears. He has a pair of balances in his hand. The black horse represents a spirit of famine and distress. The rider is the antichrist. Everything is weighed and measured. This indicates some type of rationing. Because the whole food supply has been compromised, the supply of food is minimal, so the antichrist has initiated famine in the land. Joel 1:10 states, "The new wine is dried up, the oil languisheth." The vines used to produce the grapes for the wine has been destroyed with all of the military activity from the first two trumpets. The military needs oil for all of its military weaponry, so this sets the stage for rationing. The rider on the black horse has a pair of balances in his hand. Food, oil, and wine are in short supply. These shortages set the stage for the initiation of rationing.

The Third Trumpet

Rev. 8:10   And the third angel sounded, and there fell a great star from heaven, burning as it were a lamp, and it fell upon the third part of the rivers, and upon the fountains of waters;

Rev. 8:11   And the name of the star is called Wormwood: and the third part of the waters became wormwood; and many men died of the waters, because they were made bitter.

When the third trumpet sounds, a star will fall from heaven, burning as it is a lamp. This star will not fall on all of the world, but upon one-third of the rivers and waters of the earth. This star has a name, Wormwood. Wormwood means "bitterness" or "calamity."[9] Many men will die because the rivers will be made bitter. This will cause much misfortune and tragedy. Let's interpret what is really being said here. In Revelation 1:20, stars are interpreted as angels, so we have an angel falling from heaven. This star (angel) is burning as though it is a lamp. Revelation 4:5 tells us that lamps are spirits. Other than God, at least three types of spiritual beings are in heaven. It is considered general knowledge that there are angels in heaven. Ezekiel 10:10–22 points out that there are cherubim in heaven. Isaiah 6:2–6, points out that there are seraphim in heaven. The book of Ezekiel reveals more information concerning one spirit being in particular.

Eze. 28:13   Thou hast been in Eden the garden of God; every precious stone was thy covering, the sardius, topaz, and the diamond, the beryl, the onyx, and the jasper, the sapphire, the emerald, and the carbuncle, and gold: the workmanship of thy tabrets and of thy pipes was prepared in thee in the day that thou wast created.

---

[9] The New Strong's Complete Dictionary of Bible Words (Thomas Nelson Publisher, 1996), 592.

Eze. 28:14   Thou art the anointed cherub that covereth; and I have
             set thee so: thou wast upon the holy mountain of God;
             thou hast walked up and down in the midst of the stones
             of fire.

Eze. 28:15   Thou wast perfect in thy ways from the day that thou
             wast created, till iniquity was found in thee.

Ezekiel 28:13–15 shows a cherub (cherubim) was in the garden of Eden. The cherub was covered with all types of precious stones. He was on the holy mountain of God. This being was the anointed cherub, a position of high authority. This being was perfect until iniquity was found in him. This heavenly being or anointed cherub is none other than Satan himself.

Rev. 12:7   And there was war in heaven: Michael and his angels
            fought against the dragon; and the dragon fought and
            his angels,

Rev. 12:8   And prevailed not; neither was their place found any
            more in heaven.

Rev. 12:9   And the great dragon was cast out, that old serpent,
            called the Devil, and Satan, which deceiveth the whole
            world: he was cast out into the earth, and his angels were
            cast out with him.

Revelation 12:7–9 shows that Satan will be kicked out of heaven and onto the earth. Satan will no longer have access to heaven. At that point, his place of habitation will be on the earth. Some will say that Satan was expelled from heaven when iniquity was found in him in the book of Ezekiel, but that's not the case. Satan was in a position of high authority in heaven. Ezekiel 28:14 states, "Thou art the anointed cherub that covereth; and I have set thee so," but Satan's heart was lifted up. Ezekiel 28:15 states, "Iniquity was found in thee." Then he lost his heavenly position of authority. Ezekiel 28:16 states, "Therefore I will cast thee as profane out of the mountain of God: and I will destroy thee, O covering cherub." Satan only lost his position of authority. He still has access to heaven. Like a judge who has been impeached, he can still enter a courtroom, but he no longer has any authority in that courtroom.

The book of Job shows that Satan is having a conversation with God in heaven. Job 1:7 states, "And the LORD said unto Satan, whence comest thou? Then Satan answered the LORD, and said, from going to and fro in the earth, and from walking up and down in it." Satan has access to heaven and earth, but he has no authority in heaven. Another example that Satan still has access to heaven is in Revelation 12:9–10, "That old serpent, called the Devil, and Satan, which deceiveth the whole world: he was cast out into the earth ... for the accuser of our brethren is cast down, which accused them before our God day and night." Before Satan was cast out of heaven in Revelation 12, he had access to God. Satan is the accuser. Every time a born-again believer stumbles or miscues, there stands Satan in the presence of God, pointing out every little mistake made by born-again believers. It's all summed up in Revelation 12:12: "Woe to the inhabiters of the earth and of the sea! for the devil is come down unto you, having great wrath, because he knoweth that he hath but a short time." Satan knows it's almost time for him to be put in the bottomless pit, so he wants as much company as possible.

This star falling from heaven is an angelic being (Satan). He is being kicked out of heaven. Revelation 12:9 states, "The great dragon was cast out, that old serpent, called the Devil, and Satan ... he was cast out into the earth." His name is Wormwood, a title that signifies his disposition is bitterness. The third trumpet affects the rivers and waters. When the third trumpet sounds, this star falling from heaven is Satan being kicked out of heaven and onto the earth. As he is descending onto the earth, he is burning or giving off light as if he were the light of the world. As 2 Corinthians 11:14 states, "For Satan himself is transformed into an angel of light." Just like Satan, he's being true to his nature, a deceiver. Nothing is as it appears. In his infinite knowledge, Jesus looked in the future and saw Satan falling from heaven. Luke10:18 states, "I beheld Satan as lightning fall from heaven." When Satan is kicked out of heaven, he will destroy much of the drinking water. Many men will die when they drink this water. All of this destruction and contamination manifests the famine and rationing, represented by the pair of balances in the hand of the rider on the black horse, which was revealed when the third seal was broken.

Things are getting progressively worse with the breaking of each seal and the sounding of each trumpet. All of these events are orchestrated that way so that each one compounds the other, making it easier to control mankind. There is famine in the land because of the destruction of the food and water supply. This is a perfect situation for the rider (antichrist) on the black horse (spirit of struggle), which represent famine and distress, to introduce rationing. Revelation 6:5 states, "And he that sat on him had a pair of balances in his hand."

The Fourth Seal

Rev. 6:7   And when he had opened the fourth seal, I heard the voice of the fourth beast say, Come and see.

Rev. 6:8   And I looked, and behold a pale horse: and his name that sat on him was Death, and Hell followed with him. And power was given unto them over the fourth part of the earth, to kill with sword, and with hunger, and with death, and with the beasts of the earth.

When the fourth seal is broken in heaven, the rider on the pale horse, whose name is Death, will begin his ride. The rider on the pale horse is true to his name. He represents death, and he causes a lot of death and destruction. This rider is given power over part of the earth's population. His mission is to kill with weapons, famine, pestilence, and even animals. Revelation 12:12 points out that when Satan is kicked out of heaven onto earth, he comes with great wrath because he knows he only has a short time. He wants to deceive and destroy as many people as he possibly can.

Death, the rider on the pale horse, has someone right behind him, his friend named Hell. Death and Hell represent two kinds of death. Death himself represents physical death, death of the flesh or body. Hell represents spiritual death, the destruction of the soul. Although the rider's name is Death, this is no other than the antichrist himself. The names Death and Hell are the symbolic names for their mission, which is quite clear. They are not only seeking to kill the physical body of mankind, but their mission is also to ensure the destruction of man's soul.

The Fourth Trumpet

Rev. 8:12   And the fourth angel sounded, and the third part of the sun was smitten, and the third part of the moon, and the third part of the stars; so as the third part of them was darkened, and the day shone not for a third part of it, and the night likewise.

Rev. 8:13 And I beheld, and heard an angel flying through the midst of heaven, saying with a loud voice, Woe, woe, woe, to the inhabiters of the earth by reason of the other voices of the trumpet of the three angels, which are yet to sound!

When the fourth trumpet sounds, the sun, stars, and moon will be darkened. One-third of their light will fade. Revelation 12:9 states, "The great dragon was cast out, that old serpent, called the Devil, and Satan, which deceiveth the whole world: he was cast out into the earth." Now read the last part of Revelation 12:9, "And his angels were cast out with him." We know that stars represent angels. Revelation 1:20 states, "Seven stars are the angels." Now that we know the stars are angels and they will be expelled from heaven along with Satan, we can determine approximately how many angels will be exiled. Revelation 12:4 states, "His tail drew the third part of the stars of heaven, and did cast them to the earth." When Satan is expelled from heaven, he will bring one-third of the angels (fallen) with him. This exodus of angels (stars) from heaven will be so great that it will interfere with the natural light sources (sun, moon, and physical stars) in the heavens. It will cause the day and night to be darker than normal. The sounding of the trumpets represents manifestation of spiritual things being revealed physically on the earth. This is shown by the abnormal darkness upon the face of the earth. Joel 2:30–31 refers to wonders being shown in the heavens and the earth.

Joe. 2:30 And I will shew wonders in the heavens and in the earth, blood, and fire, and pillars of smoke.

Joe. 2:31 The sun shall be turned into darkness, and the moon into blood, before the great and the terrible day of the LORD come.

The blood, fire, and pillars of smoke are a result of the wars and commotions on earth. All the events are signs seen on earth, but there are also signs in the heavens. The sun, stars, and moon are being darkened because of the mass exodus of angels (stars) from heaven. So many angels are being expelled from heaven that their exodus obstructs the shining of the sun, moon, and physical stars.

John also saw an angel fly through heaven. This angel issued a warning. He assured John that, if one thinks things are bad because of the first four trumpets, then wait until the last three trumpets are sounded. The first four trumpets are responsible for the horrible conditions on earth, but the angel said it was going to get even worse with the sounding of each of the last three trumpets, worse than they have ever been before. Matthew 24:21 states, "For then shall be great tribulation, such as was not since the beginning of the world to this time, no, nor ever shall be." Tribulation was manifested on earth from the first four trumpets, but there will be great tribulation on earth at the sounding of the last three trumpets.

The Fifth Seal

Rev. 6:9   And when he had opened the fifth seal, I saw under the altar the souls of them that were slain for the word of God, and for the testimony which they held:

Rev. 6:10   And they cried with a loud voice, saying, How long, O Lord, holy and true, dost thou not judge and avenge our blood on them that dwell on the earth?

Rev. 6:11   And white robes were given unto every one of them; and it was said unto them, that they should rest yet for a little season, until their fellowservants also and their brethren, that should be killed as they were, should be fulfilled.

When the fifth seal was broken in heaven, John saw souls under the altar. These souls questioned God as to how much longer he was going to continue to allow all of the turmoil on the earth. These souls are the souls of people who have already died in Christ. Immediately after they died, their souls went to paradise (heaven) to be with God. An example of this is when the thief on the cross with Jesus repented. Luke 23:43 states, "Jesus said unto him, verily I say unto thee, to day shalt thou be with me in paradise." The discussion of souls being in heaven has already been addressed in chapter 3. These souls are aware of all the turmoil on the earth, and they want God to go ahead and put an end to all of the violence on earth.

> Rev. 19:8   And to her was granted that she should be arrayed in fine linen, clean and white: for the fine linen is the righteousness of saints.

The souls under the altar are given white robes. They are told that the turmoil on earth will go on a little longer. It is not quite time for it all to end. Some more born-again believers will have to first die in the flesh before the fullness of the Gentiles would be complete. Revelation 19:8 testifies that the white robes given to the souls under the altar represent the righteousness of the saints.

The Fifth Trumpet

> Rev. 9:1   And the fifth angel sounded, and I saw a star fall from heaven unto the earth: and to him was given the key of the bottomless pit.
>
> Rev. 9:2   And he opened the bottomless pit; and there arose a smoke out of the pit, as the smoke of a great furnace; and the sun and the air were darkened by reason of the smoke of the pit.
>
> Rev. 9:3   And there came out of the smoke locusts upon the earth: and unto them was given power, as the scorpions of the earth have power.
>
> Rev. 9:4   And it was commanded them that they should not hurt the grass of the earth, neither any green thing, neither any tree; but only those men which have not the seal of God in their foreheads.
>
> Rev. 9:5   And to them it was given that they should not kill them, but that they should be tormented five months: and their torment was as the torment of a scorpion, when he striketh a man.
>
> Rev. 9:6   And in those days shall men seek death, and shall not

find it; and shall desire to die, and death shall flee from them.

Rev. 9:7   And the shapes of the locusts were like unto horses prepared unto battle; and on their heads were as it were crowns like gold, and their faces were as the faces of men.

Rev. 9:8   And they had hair as the hair of women, and their teeth were as the teeth of lions.

Rev. 9:9   And they had breastplates, as it were breastplates of iron; and the sound of their wings was as the sound of chariots of many horses running to battle.

Rev. 9:10   And they had tails like unto scorpions, and there were stings in their tails: and their power was to hurt men five months.

Rev. 9:11   And they had a king over them, which is the angel of the bottomless pit, whose name in the Hebrew tongue is Abaddon, but in the Greek tongue hath his name Apollyon.

Rev. 9:12   One woe is past; and, behold, there come two woes more hereafter.

When the fifth trumpet sounded, John saw a star fall from heaven. This star is an angel. Revelation 1:20 states, "The seven stars are the angels." He is another one of Satan's followers, and he has the key to the bottomless pit. The bottomless pit is like a prison. It is the place where Satan will be held for one thousand years. Revelation 20:2–3 states, "He laid hold on the dragon, that old serpent, which is the Devil, and Satan, and bound him a thousand years, and cast him into the bottomless pit, and shut him up." When the bottomless pit opens, it releases an enormous amount of smoke into the atmosphere. So much smoke gushes into the air that the sunlight is partially blocked and the day is very dark. There was a similar situation like that during the Gulf War of 1991, when several hundred oil fires were deliberately set and the burning oil filled the sky with smoke.

When the door of the bottomless pit opens, not only did smoke come out of it, but locusts as well. These locusts are not grasshoppers, as known to mankind. They are some type of military regiment or division. The book of Joel confirms the locust is a great army.

> Joe. 2:25   And I will restore to you the years that the locust hath eaten, the cankerworm, and the caterpiller, and the palmerworm, my great army which I sent among you.

The locusts (great army) are like soldiers who are given orders from their commander. The locust are ordered not to hurt the grass, neither any green thing nor any tree, but only to hurt the men who do not have the seal of God on their foreheads. The instinct of locusts is to eat green plants and trees. If these locusts are grasshoppers, then they are requested to act abnormal. These locusts are to perform like scorpions (sting mankind), which is out of character. Scorpions have a long tail, and they sting people, inflicting excruciating pain. These locusts are not to kill people when they sting them, but they are ordered only to torment mankind for five months.

> Rev. 7:2   And I saw another angel ascending from the east, having the seal of the living God: and he cried with a loud voice to the four angels, to whom it was given to hurt the earth and the sea,
>
> Rev. 7:3   Saying, Hurt not the earth, neither the sea, nor the trees, till we have sealed the servants of our God in their foreheads.
>
> Rev. 7:4   And I heard the number of them which were sealed: and there were sealed an hundred and forty and four thousand of all the tribes of the children of Israel.

The locust are very selective in who they will be allowed to sting. They will be commanded to sting only those men who do not have the seal of God on their foreheads. The locusts are ordered not to hurt any green thing and any tree because they need to replenish the food supply.

When these locusts sting men, the men will want to die. They will be in such horrible pain and agony that they will just want to die in order to get relief from their pain. The men stung by the locust will probably be so weak that they could not commit suicide. Every time they try to commit suicide, death will flee from them.

John described these locusts. They will have shapes like horses prepared for battle. Just imagine a grasshopper looking like a horse. They will have heads that look like a crown of gold. They will have faces like the face of men, and they will have hair like the hair of women. They will have teeth like the teeth of lions and breastplates of iron. The locusts will have wings, which sound like chariots of many horses running to battle. They will have tails like scorpions. The stings of the locust will be in their tails.

The locusts will also have a king over them. The king's name in Hebrew is Abaddon, which means "destroying angel."[10] The king's name in Greek is Apollyon, which means "destroyer."[11] Either way, this king or leader's agenda is to wreak havoc upon mankind in an attempt to destroy mankind, but not his physical body because he is not to kill him. He is to destroy his very soul. If a man is agonized long enough, in an attempt to get some relief, he will eventually say and do things contrary to what he believes to be true.

The description John gave of the locusts ascending out of the bottomless pit has no resemblance at all to locusts in today's society. Remember John used knowledge of that day to describe modern-day things, perhaps even things yet in the future. When examining the description of the locusts, a picture of modern-day weapons of war emerges. The description of the locusts resembles more of a military weapon than locusts. A company of Apache helicopters spraying some type of nerve gas from the rear (sting is in the tail) resembles John's description of the locust. They are spraying a gas that does not kill, but only paralyzes or immobilizes. This nerve gas does not harm the much-needed vegetation, but it only tortures mankind.

There is something else to remember. One of the previous angels said there would be three more woes to come. Revelation 8:13 states, "Saying with a loud voice, woe, woe, woe, to the inhabiters of the earth by reason of the other voices of the trumpet of the three angels, which are yet to sound." This is the first woe, and there are two other woes to follow. Revelation 9:12 states, "One woe is past; and, behold, there come two woes more hereafter." There are two more seals to be broken and two more trumpets yet to sound. The conditions on earth are getting progressively worse.

---

[10] Strong's Complete Dictionary of Bible Words (Thomas Nelson Publishers, 1996), 1.

[11] Strong's Complete Dictionary of Bible Words (Thomas Nelson Publishers, 1996), 13.

The Sixth Seal

> Rev. 6:12   And I beheld when he had opened the sixth seal, and, lo,
> there was a great earthquake; and the sun became black
> as sackcloth of hair, and the moon became as blood;

To best understand the events of the breaking of the sixth seal, one needs to examine the breaking of the sixth seal, along with the sounding of the sixth trumpet. Remember that the breaking of the sixth seal is in heaven. This is a signal that it is time for something to happen according to God's timetable. The breaking of the sixth seal also indicates that it is time for the sixth trumpet to sound. The sounding of the sixth trumpet marks the beginning of physical things to happen on earth.

The Sixth rumpet

> Rev. 9:13   And the sixth angel sounded, and I heard a voice from
> the four horns of the golden altar which is before God,
> Rev. 9:14   Saying to the sixth angel which had the trumpet, Loose
> the four angels which are bound in the great river
> Euphrates.
> Rev. 9:15   And the four angels were loosed, which were prepared
> for an hour, and a day, and a month, and a year, for to
> slay the third part of men.

When the sixth trumpet sounds, the four angels bound or stationed at the Euphrates River are loosed. Actually, the angels will be loosed at the breaking of the sixth seal in heaven, but the manifestation of it on earth will not be seen until the sounding of the sixth trumpet. It's also important to notice that, sometimes in the book of Revelation, the Bible refers to both angels and stars. Usually, when it uses the word "angels," it is referring to messengers of God, carrying out God's work. When it uses the word "stars," most of the time, it is referring to fallen angels.

It appears that these angels are going to kill an enormous amount of the earth's population. The angels are not going to kill people. Their mission is just the opposite. Their mission is to restrain the slaying of a huge amount of people until the proper time. The angels are manning their posts so nothing unwanted will take place outside of God's timetable. They are prepared for an hour, a day, a month, and a year. This does not mean they are there for thirteen months, one day, and one hour. This means a specific year, a specific month, a specific day, and a specific hour. Nothing can happen until it coincides with the plan of God. This specific date and time will be when the sixth trumpet is sounded. This is not referring to the time that Jesus will return, but only references the releasing of the four messengers (angels) stationed at the Euphrates River.

Rev. 9:16   And the number of the army of the horsemen were two hundred thousand thousand: and I heard the number of them.

Rev. 9:17   And thus I saw the horses in the vision, and them that sat on them, having breastplates of fire, and of jacinth, and brimstone: and the heads of the horses were as the heads of lions; and out of their mouths issued fire and smoke and brimstone.

Rev. 9:18   By these three was the third part of men killed, by the fire, and by the smoke, and by the brimstone, which issued out of their mouths.

Rev. 9:19   For their power is in their mouth, and in their tails: for their tails were like unto serpents, and had heads, and with them they do hurt.

Rev. 9:20   And the rest of the men which were not killed by these plagues yet repented not of the works of their hands, that they should not worship devils, and idols of gold, and silver, and brass, and stone, and of wood: which neither can see, nor hear, nor walk:

Rev. 9:21   Neither repented they of their murders, nor of their sorceries, nor of their fornication, nor of their thefts.

A great army is at the Euphrates River, and they are on a mission to kill one-third of mankind in that region. This does not mean one-third of the earth's population, but one-third of mankind in the region where they patrol. The army is stationed at one location near the Euphrates River, not all over the world. Although this is a 200 million-man army, they do not cover all seven of the continents. They are at a particular place at a particular time, and they are to kill one-third of the people within that target area.

It appears that this army is riding on horseback. Remember when John was recording what he saw. He was unfamiliar with modern-day weapons. He described this army in terms prevalent to his day. Look at the description of the soldiers or horsemen. They have breastplates and tails. They issue fire, smoke, and brimstone (sulfur) out of their mouths and tails. Even their tails had heads (warheads). The horsemen are soldiers, and the horses are some kind of a machine that the military uses. I have noticed numerous military aircraft that have a gun mounted on the front often have a mouth, complete with teeth painted around the weapon. These military aircraft with the mouths painted on them simulates John's description of the horses issuing fire from their mouths.

The men not killed by this army do not repent for their evil deeds. They continue to worship their idols, idols made of gold, silver, brass, stone, and wood. These idols could not see, walk, or speak because human hands made them. This is ironic. Here we have human hands creating gods or idols. Gods are supposed to be creators of mankind, not the other way around. The survivors of all of this bloodshed continue with their murders, theft, fornications, and so forth.

Now let's put the sixth seal and the sixth trumpet into perspective. The sixth seal is broken. The sixth trumpet sounds. The 200 million-man army starts marching on their path of death and destruction. Most of the people not killed by this army continue to worship their man-made idols.

Summary of Sixth Seal and Sixth Trumpet

Rev. 6:12   And I beheld when he had opened the sixth seal, and, lo, there was a great earthquake; and the sun became black as sackcloth of hair, and the moon became as blood;

Rev. 6:13   And the stars of heaven fell unto the earth, even as a fig tree casteth her untimely figs, when she is shaken of a mighty wind.

Rev. 6:14   And the heaven departed as a scroll when it is rolled together; and every mountain and island were moved out of their places.

The scripture does not indicate how much time is between the sixth and the seventh seal. The first thing that will happen when the sixth seal is broken is that the angels stationed at the Euphrates River will be loosed so the 200 million-man army could start their march of destruction. Just prior to the seventh seal being broken, some other things will take place. God has finally had enough, and he sets in motion the beginning of the end of unrighteousness. There is a great earthquake. The heavens roll up like a scroll when the wind is blowing the clouds in the sky. It appears that the clouds are rolling up in one place. The most important thing that one has to see here is the stars falling from heaven to earth. We know from Revelation 1:20 that the stars represent angels. These stars (angels) falling from heaven are more fallen or wicked angels that are being kicked out because they have been found to have iniquity. They are not totally committed to God. These are lukewarm angels, so they are expelled from heaven to the earth. Revelation 3:16 states, "So then because thou art lukewarm, and neither cold nor hot, I will spue thee out of my mouth." This is God cleaning house, that is, getting rid of all heavenly beings that do not serve him and only him forever.

Rev. 6:15   And the kings of the earth, and the great men, and the rich men, and the chief captains, and the mighty men, and every bondman, and every free man, hid themselves in the dens and in the rocks of the mountains;

Rev. 6:16   And said to the mountains and rocks, Fall on us, and hide us from the face of him that sitteth on the throne, and from the wrath of the Lamb:

Rev. 6:17   For the great day of his wrath is come; and who shall be able to stand?

Men and women from every walk of life will witness all of these physical events taking place in the sky and on the earth. Mountains and islands will relocate due to the great earthquake. Not only will they witness physical events, but they will witness heavenly events as well. The sun is darkened, and the moon turns red like blood. To make matters worse, they see him coming, and they finally realize that these are indeed the acts of God. All of the physical and heavenly events induce fear into the hearts of mankind.

They are so frightened that some of them will run into dens, requesting the mountains to fall on them. They would rather be crushed to death by the mountains than face the wrath to come from the one who sits on the throne. They realize it is time for judgment because they see him sitting on the throne, coming to administer judgment. Men and women from all walks of life recognize the fact that the great day of his wrath, judgment day, has come. This setting is just prior to the breaking of the seventh seal and the sounding of the seventh trumpet.

> Mat. 24:29 Immediately after the tribulation of those days shall the sun be darkened, and the moon shall not give her light, and the stars shall fall from heaven, and the powers of the heavens shall be shaken:
> Mat. 24:30 And then shall appear the sign of the Son of man in heaven: and then shall all the tribes of the earth mourn, and they shall see the Son of man coming in the clouds of heaven with power and great glory.

All of the tribes of the earth will actually see Christ coming, and they are frightened. Matthew 24:29–30 actually parallels with Revelation 6:15–17. They realize it is time for the judgment, so they will begin to weep and mourn. They want the mountains and rocks to fall on them. Some of them will think that, if the rocks and mountains fall on them and crush them, they would escape the wrath to come. Not even death will protect them from the great day of the Lord. The only people who will be able to stand in that day will be the righteous.

> Rev. 1:7 Behold, he cometh with clouds; and every eye shall see him, and they also which pierced him: and all kindreds of the earth shall wail because of him. Even so, Amen.

Everybody will see Christ coming in the clouds. Those who are not ready will wail and plead for mercy. Bear in mind that the seventh seal has not been broken and the seventh trumpet has not yet sounded. Man knows in his heart that God is fed up with the way things have been done here on earth, and it is now time for his judgment, the wrath of God. Note, the inhabitants will see Christ coming in the clouds, but they will not be changed until the seventh and final trumpet sounds. As 1 Corinthians 15:51–51 states, "We shall not all sleep, but we shall all be changed … in a moment, in the twinkling of an eye, at the last trump: for the trumpet shall sound, and the dead shall be raised incorruptible, and we shall be changed." Only those people who are righteous according to God's definition of righteousness will be changed instantaneously at the sounding of the seventh trumpet.

> Rev. 11:13   And the same hour was there a great earthquake, and the tenth part of the city fell, and in the earthquake were slain of men seven thousand: and the remnant were affrighted, and gave glory to the God of heaven.
>
> Rev. 11:14   The second woe is past; and, behold, the third woe cometh quickly.

A great earthquake has just taken place. This is the same earthquake as the one that took place in Revelation 6:12–14, when the sun was darkened, and in Revelation 11:13, when seven thousand of the inhabitants in Jerusalem died. This is the second woe that was mentioned in Revelation 8:13. These events parallel with the events in Revelation 6:12–17 and Matthew 24:29–30, where there was a great earthquake and men were frightened and mourned and feared the wrath to come. These events are just prior to the breaking of the seventh seal and sounding of the seventh trumpet. The third and final woe will come quickly.

> Rev. 10:1   And I saw another mighty angel come down from heaven, clothed with a cloud: and a rainbow was upon his head, and his face was as it were the sun, and his feet as pillars of fire:
>
> Rev. 10:2   And he had in his hand a little book open: and he set his right foot upon the sea, and his left foot on the earth,
>
> Rev. 10:3   And cried with a loud voice, as when a lion roareth: and when he had cried, seven thunders uttered their voices.
>
> Rev. 10:4   And when the seven thunders had uttered their voices, I was about to write: and I heard a voice from heaven

saying unto me, Seal up those things which the seven thunders uttered, and write them not.

Rev. 10:5   And the angel which I saw stand upon the sea and upon the earth lifted up his hand to heaven,

Rev. 10:6   And sware by him that liveth for ever and ever, who created heaven, and the things that therein are, and the earth, and the things that therein are, and the sea, and the things which are therein, that there should be time no longer:

Rev. 10:7   But in the days of the voice of the seventh angel, when he shall begin to sound, the mystery of God should be finished, as he hath declared to his servants the prophets.

Rev. 10:8   And the voice which I heard from heaven spake unto me again, and said, Go and take the little book which is open in the hand of the angel which standeth upon the sea and upon the earth.

Rev. 10:9   And I went unto the angel, and said unto him, Give me the little book. And he said unto me, Take it, and eat it up; and it shall make thy belly bitter, but it shall be in thy mouth sweet as honey.

Rev. 10:10 And I took the little book out of the angel's hand, and ate it up; and it was in my mouth sweet as honey: and as soon as I had eaten it, my belly was bitter.

Rev. 10:11 And he said unto me, Thou must prophesy again before many peoples, and nations, and tongues, and kings.

John saw an angel that was clothed with a cloud. He had a rainbow upon his head. His face was like it was the sun, and his feet were pillars of fire. This angel closely resembled the Angel of Jesus. This angel had an open book in his hand, possibly the book with the seven seals, whereas six of the seals had already been broken. He placed his right foot on the sea and his left foot on the earth, and he gave a loud cry or shout. When he shouted, seven thunders uttered their voices. These voices of the seven thunders were sounds as claps of thunder or heavenly voices echoing from heaven. John was about to write down what the seven thunders said, but a voice from heaven told John to seal up the things that the seven thunders uttered. He was instructed not to write it down, so we do not know what the seven thunders said. One can only speculate that the seven thunders read something from the open book that the mighty angel was holding in his hand, or it was something pertaining to the sounding of the seventh trumpet. The mighty angel lifted his hand to heaven and swore by God that, at the sounding of the seventh trumpet, there would be time no longer. The sounding of the seventh trumpet would bring this present era of the earth to completion. Revelation 10:7 states, "When he shall begin to sound, the mystery of God should be finished."

Another voice came from heaven, instructing John to take the little opened book from the mighty angel and eat it up. He was informed that it would be sweet in his mouth, but it would be bitter once it reached his stomach. John took the book and ate it. It was sweet in his mouth and bitter in his stomach. Everything that tastes good is not necessarily good for you. An example would be desserts that taste good as one consumes them, but are not kind to the waistline. John was told that he had to continue to prophesy to more people from all walks of life.

Rev. 11:14 The second woe is past; and, behold, the third woe cometh quickly.

The setting of this scene is after the breaking of the sixth seal and sounding of the sixth trumpet, but prior to the breaking of the seventh seal and sounding of the seventh trumpet. Immediately after the second woe in Revelation 11:14, the third woe comes quickly. The events following the breaking of the seventh seal and sounding of the seventh trumpet will be the third and final woe. This is the moment when God's plan for this present world as we know it will be complete. Revelation 10:7 states, "The mystery of God should be finished, as he hath declared." The sounding of the seventh trumpet is the end of the period of time called grace. It is the beginning of one thousand years of peace on earth, and it is often referred to as the millennium.

The Seventh Seal

Rev. 8:1 And when he had opened the seventh seal, there was silence in heaven about the space of half an hour.

Rev. 8:2 And I saw the seven angels which stood before God; and to them were given seven trumpets.

Rev. 8:3 And another angel came and stood at the altar, having a golden censer; and there was given unto him much incense, that he should offer it with the prayers of all saints upon the golden altar which was before the throne.

Rev. 8:4 And the smoke of the incense, which came with the prayers of the saints, ascended up before God out of the angel's hand.

Rev. 8:5 And the angel took the censer, and filled it with fire of the altar, and cast it into the earth: and there were voices, and thunderings, and lightnings, and an earthquake.

The seventh seal has just been broken in heaven, and there is silence in heaven for about a half hour. After the silence in heaven has passed, an angel stands before the altar in heaven with a golden censer. The angel was given a lot of incense so he could offer it with the prayers of the saints on the golden altar, which was before the throne. When he offers the incense and the prayers of the saints, the smoke ascends to God. This is like a sacrifice, where the odor of a sweet smell ascends up to God. After the angel offers the incense with the prayers of the saints, he fills the censer with fire from the altar, and he throws it into the earth. There are voices, thundering, lightning, and an earthquake.

The Seventh Trumpet

Rev. 11:15 And the seventh angel sounded; and there were great voices in heaven, saying, The kingdoms of this world are become the kingdoms of our Lord, and of his Christ; and he shall reign for ever and ever.

Rev. 11:16 And the four and twenty elders, which sat before God

on their seats, fell upon their faces, and worshipped
God,

Rev. 11:17 Saying, We give thee thanks, O Lord God Almighty,
which art, and wast, and art to come; because thou hast
taken to thee thy great power, and hast reigned.

Rev. 11:18 And the nations were angry, and thy wrath is come,
and the time of the dead, that they should be judged,
and that thou shouldest give reward unto thy servants
the prophets, and to the saints, and them that fear thy
name, small and great; and shouldest destroy them
which destroy the earth.

Rev. 11:19 And the temple of God was opened in heaven, and
there was seen in his temple the ark of his testament:
and there were lightnings, and voices, and thunderings,
and an earthquake, and great hail.

The sounding of the seventh trumpet also brings voices, thundering,
lightning, and an earthquake. This parallels with the breaking of the seventh
seal in Revelation 8:5. The seventh trumpet also brings great hail with it.
When the seventh and final trumpet sounds, it marks the ending of this
world as it is known today, the beginning of eternity for some, and a second
chance for others. God takes over this world and rules forever. All of the
heavenly beings fall down and worship God. The unsaved people are angry
because they know it is time for the wrath of God. The sounding of the
seventh trumpet brings with it a time for all the righteous in Christ, dead
and alive, to be judged and receive their rewards. The ark of the testament
will be seen in heaven. This marks the beginning of the wrath of the lamb.
Revelation 6:17 states, "The great day of his wrath is come; and who shall be
able to stand." The sounding of the seventh trumpet also marks the beginning of eternity for those found worthy to stand. Revelation 21:4 states,
"God shall wipe away all tears from their eyes; and there shall be no more
death, neither sorrow, nor crying, neither shall there be any more pain."
Those worthy will enter into the presence of God, and they will want for
nothing for an eternity.

CHAPTER 7

THE BEAST

Rev. 13:1   And I stood upon the sand of the sea, and saw a beast rise up out of the sea, having seven heads and ten horns, and upon his horns ten crowns, and upon his heads the name of blasphemy.

Rev. 13:2   And the beast which I saw was like unto a leopard, and his feet were as the feet of a bear, and his mouth as the mouth of a lion: and the dragon gave him his power, and his seat, and great authority.

JOHN was still in the spirit, and he stood upon the seashore. He saw a beast come up out of the sea. This beast had seven heads and ten horns, and it had ten crowns, a crown for each horn. John described this beast. It looked like a leopard with feet like a bear, and his mouth was like a lion. This beast got its power from the dragon, which also gave him his seat and great authority.

This beast made up of three animals, with multiple heads and horns, sounds like a scary creature. To fully understand what is happening here, one must turn to the Old Testament. Daniel 2:1–40,[12] gives more clarity about this beast. This is a long process, but, upon completion of probing the scriptures, one will have a better understanding of this beast rising up out of the sea.

King Nebuchadnezzar's Dilemma

Dan. 2:1   And in the second year of the reign of Nebuchadnezzar

---

[12] Torah Light Ministries, Stanley Chester, taped message.

Nebuchadnezzar dreamed dreams, wherewith his spirit was troubled, and his sleep brake from him.

Dan. 2:2   Then the king commanded to call the magicians, and the astrologers, and the sorcerers, and the Chaldeans, for to shew the king his dreams. So they came and stood before the king.

Dan. 2:3   And the king said unto them, I have dreamed a dream, and my spirit was troubled to know the dream.

Dan. 2:4   Then spake the Chaldeans to the king in Syriack, O king, live for ever: tell thy servants the dream, and we will shew the interpretation.

Dan. 2:5   The king answered and said to the Chaldeans, The thing is gone from me: if ye will not make known unto me the dream, with the interpretation thereof, ye shall be cut in pieces, and your houses shall be made a dunghill.

Dan. 2:6   But if ye shew the dream, and the interpretation thereof, ye shall receive of me gifts and rewards and great honour: therefore shew me the dream, and the interpretation thereof.

Dan. 2:7   They answered again and said, Let the king tell his servants the dream, and we will shew the interpretation of it.

Dan. 2:8   The king answered and said, I know of certainty that ye would gain the time, because ye see the thing is gone from me.

Dan. 2:9   But if ye will not make known unto me the dream, there is but one decree for you: for ye have prepared lying and corrupt words to speak before me, till the time be changed: therefore tell me the dream, and I shall know that ye can shew me the interpretation thereof.

Dan. 2:10   The Chaldeans answered before the king, and said, There is not a man upon the earth that can shew the king's matter: therefore there is no king, lord, nor ruler, that asked such things at any magician, or astrologer, or Chaldean.

Dan. 2:11   And it is a rare thing that the king requireth, and there is none other that can shew it before the king, except the gods, whose dwelling is not with flesh.

Dan. 2:12 For this cause the king was angry and very furious, and commanded to destroy all the wise men of Babylon.

Dan. 2:13 And the decree went forth that the wise men should be slain; and they sought Daniel and his fellows to be slain.

Dan. 2:14 Then Daniel answered with counsel and wisdom to Arioch the captain of the king's guard, which was gone forth to slay the wise men of Babylon:

Dan. 2:15 He answered and said to Arioch the king's captain, Why is the decree so hasty from the king? Then Arioch made the thing known to Daniel.

Dan. 2:16 Then Daniel went in, and desired of the king that he would give him time, and that he would shew the king the interpretation.

Dan. 2:17 Then Daniel went to his house, and made the thing known to Hananiah, Mishael, and Azariah, his companions:

Dan. 2:18 That they would desire mercies of the God of heaven concerning this secret; that Daniel and his fellows should not perish with the rest of the wise men of Babylon.

Dan. 2:19 Then was the secret revealed unto Daniel in a night vision. Then Daniel blessed the God of heaven.

Dan. 2:20 Daniel answered and said, Blessed be the name of God for ever and ever: for wisdom and might are his:

Dan. 2:21 And he changeth the times and the seasons: he removeth kings, and setteth up kings: he giveth wisdom unto the wise, and knowledge to them that know understanding:

Dan. 2:22 He revealeth the deep and secret things: he knoweth what is in the darkness, and the light dwelleth with him.

Dan. 2:23 I thank thee, and praise thee, O thou God of my fathers, who hast given me wisdom and might, and hast made known unto me now what we desired of thee: for thou hast now made known unto us the king's matter.

Dan. 2:24 Therefore Daniel went in unto Arioch, whom the king had ordained to destroy the wise men of Babylon: he went and said thus unto him; Destroy not the wise men of Babylon: bring me in before the king, and I will shew unto the king the interpretation.

Dan. 2:25 Then Arioch brought in Daniel before the king in haste, and said thus unto him, I have found a man of the captives of Judah, that will make known unto the king the interpretation.

Dan. 2:26 The king answered and said to Daniel, whose name was Belteshazzar, Art thou able to make known unto me the dream which I have seen, and the interpretation thereof?

Dan. 2:27 Daniel answered in the presence of the king, and said, The secret which the king hath demanded cannot the wise men, the astrologers, the magicians, the sooth-sayers, shew unto the king;

Dan. 2:28 But there is a God in heaven that revealeth secrets, and maketh known to the king Nebuchadnezzar what shall be in the latter days. Thy dream, and the visions of thy head upon thy bed, are these;

Dan. 2:29 As for thee, O king, thy thoughts came into thy mind upon thy bed, what should come to pass hereafter: and he that revealeth secrets maketh known to thee what shall come to pass.

Dan. 2:30 But as for me, this secret is not revealed to me for any wisdom that I have more than any living, but for their sakes that shall make known the interpretation to the king, and that thou mightest know the thoughts of thy heart.

Dan. 2:31 Thou, O king, sawest, and behold a great image. This great image, whose brightness was excellent, stood before thee; and the form thereof was terrible.

Dan. 2:32 This image's head was of fine gold, his breast and his arms of silver, his belly and his thighs of brass,

Dan. 2:33 His legs of iron, his feet part of iron and part of clay.

Dan. 2:34 Thou sawest till that a stone was cut out without hands, which smote the image upon his feet that were of iron and clay, and brake them to pieces.

Dan. 2:35   Then was the iron, the clay, the brass, the silver, and
            the gold, broken to pieces together, and became like
            the chaff of the summer threshingfloors; and the wind
            carried them away, that no place was found for them:
            and the stone that smote the image became a great
            mountain, and filled the whole earth.

Dan. 2:36   This is the dream; and we will tell the interpretation
            thereof before the king.

Dan. 2:37   Thou, O king, art a king of kings: for the God of heaven
            hath given thee a kingdom, power, and strength, and
            glory.

Dan. 2:38   And wheresoever the children of men dwell, the beasts
            of the field and the fowls of the heaven hath he given
            into thine hand, and hath made thee ruler over them all.
            Thou art this head of gold.

Dan. 2:39   And after thee shall arise another kingdom inferior to
            thee, and another third kingdom of brass, which shall
            bear rule over all the earth.

Dan. 2:40   And the fourth kingdom shall be strong as iron: foras-
            much as iron breaketh in pieces and subdueth all things:
            and as iron that breaketh all these, shall it break in pieces
            and bruise.

Daniel 2 tells us that King Nebuchadnezzar of Babylon had a dream in the second year of Daniel's captivity. He wanted to know the interpretation of the dream, but he forgot what he had dreamed. Nevertheless, he summoned his astrologers, sorcerers, and magicians, better known as wise men, expecting them to give him the interpretation of his dream. He explained to them about the dream, but he forgot the contents of the dream. The wise men told the king they could not give an interpretation of a dream without first being given the dream's contents. The king was furious, and he wanted to kill the wise men for being incompetent. Not only did he want to kill his wise men, he wanted to kill Daniel and his friends. Daniel and his friends were captives from Israel, brought to Babylon after the Babylonians captured Jerusalem. They were brought to Babylon because they were the fairest, wisest, and most educated, and they believed in a different god. It was told to the king that no one could interpret the dream without first being given the contents of the dream, except the gods whose dwelling was not with flesh.

When Daniel heard of the decree to slay them, he requested time to pray to his god because his god would not only give the contents of the dream, but the interpretation as well. It was agreed upon, and Daniel and his friends prayed to their god. Just like Daniel said, his god gave him the dream and the interpretation.

The Contents of the Dream

Daniel went before the king to give him the dream and the interpretation. The king dreamed of a great image with a head of gold. The image had breasts and arms of silver. It had a belly and thighs of brass. It had legs of iron and feet made of iron and clay. There was a stone made without hands that hit the image on the feet. The great image was broken into pieces. There was no place found for the image anymore. The stone that broke the image became a great mountain and filled the whole earth.

The Interpretation of the Dream

Now Daniel gave the king the interpretation. He said the dream was what shall pass hereafter. King Nebuchadnezzar was the king of Babylon, which the head of gold represented. After the fall of the Babylonian kingdom, there would be another kingdom, represented by silver. The second kingdom would be inferior to Babylon. This second kingdom would fall, and there would be a third kingdom represented by brass. After the fall of the third kingdom, there would be a fourth kingdom, represented by iron and clay. The fourth kingdom would be divided. The legs, feet, and toes would make up the fourth kingdom. In the days that the toes of the beast came into power and rule, the God of heaven shall set up a kingdom that shall never be destroyed. Daniel told the king that the dream was certain and the interpretation was sure.

This great image of which King Nebuchadnezzar dreamed is just an introduction to understanding the beast. Even Daniel did not fully understand the magnitude of the king's dream. I guess some are wondering, "What is the connection between the image in the king's dream and the beast that

John saw rising up out of the sea?" The association will begin to develop as the mystery of the image unfolds. Up to this point, it is seen that the image is associated with kingdoms, but let's move on to Daniel 7:1–7 to get more information concerning the image and the beast rising out of the sea.

Daniel's Vision

Dan. 7:1   In the first year of Belshazzar king of Babylon Daniel had a dream and visions of his head upon his bed: then he wrote the dream, and told the sum of the matters.

Dan. 7:2   Daniel spake and said, I saw in my vision by night, and, behold, the four winds of the heaven strove upon the great sea.

Dan. 7:3   And four great beasts came up from the sea, diverse one from another.

Dan. 7:4   The first was like a lion, and had eagle's wings: I beheld till the wings thereof were plucked, and it was lifted up from the earth, and made stand upon the feet as a man, and a man's heart was given to it.

Dan. 7:5   And behold another beast, a second, like to a bear, and it raised up itself on one side, and it had three ribs in the mouth of it between the teeth of it: and they said thus unto it, Arise, devour much flesh.

Dan. 7:6   After this I beheld, and lo another, like a leopard, which had upon the back of it four wings of a fowl; the beast had also four heads; and dominion was given to it.

Dan. 7:7   After this I saw in the night visions, and behold a fourth beast, dreadful and terrible, and strong exceedingly; and it had great iron teeth: it devoured and brake in pieces, and stamped the residue with the feet of it: and it was diverse from all the beasts that were before it; and it had ten horns.

Some time after interpreting King Nebuchadnezzar's dream, Daniel himself had a dream or vision. In Daniel's dream, he saw four beasts come up out of the sea. All of these beasts were different from the other. He described the beasts. The first beast was like a lion. The second beast was like a bear. The third beast was like a leopard. The fourth beast was dreadful and terrible. He was diverse from the other three beasts that were before him. This beast's appearance was not normal. It had ten horns.

The four different beasts of which Daniel dreamed has a similar description to the one beast that John saw come up out of the sea in Revelation 13:1–2; "And saw a beast rise up out of the sea, having seven heads and ten horns … and the beast which I saw was like unto a leopard, and his feet were as the feet of a bear, and his mouth as the mouth of a lion." John's one beast looked like a lion, a bear, and a leopard, and it had ten horns. All four of Daniel's beasts came up out of the sea, and the beast that John saw came up out of the sea. Although Daniel's dream was about four beasts and John's vision was about one beast, there are a lot of similarities between the two.

Daniel's dream troubled him because he did not understand what it all meant. Here was a man who went to his god to get the contents and interpretation of King Nebuchadnezzar's dream and was now puzzled about his own dream. It only seemed proper that Daniel's god would also give him the interpretation of his own dream. Continuing in Daniel 7, more information is revealed pertaining to the beasts in Daniel's dream.

Dan. 7:15   I Daniel was grieved in my spirit in the midst of my body, and the visions of my head troubled me.

Dan. 7:16   I came near unto one of them that stood by, and asked him the truth of all this. So he told me, and made me know the interpretation of the things.

Dan. 7:17   These great beasts, which are four, are four kings, which shall arise out of the earth.

Dan. 7:18   But the saints of the most High shall take the kingdom, and possess the kingdom for ever, even for ever and ever.

Dan. 7:19   Then I would know the truth of the fourth beast, which was diverse from all the others, exceeding dreadful, whose teeth were of iron, and his nails of brass; which devoured, brake in pieces, and stamped the residue with his feet;

Dan. 7:20   And of the ten horns that were in his head, and of the other which came up, and before whom three fell; even of that horn that had eyes, and a mouth that spake very great things, whose look was more stout than his fellows.

Dan. 7:21 I beheld, and the same horn made war with the saints, and prevailed against them;

Dan. 7:22 Until the Ancient of days came, and judgment was given to the saints of the most High; and the time came that the saints possessed the kingdom.

Dan. 7:23 Thus he said, The fourth beast shall be the fourth kingdom upon earth, which shall be diverse from all kingdoms, and shall devour the whole earth, and shall tread it down, and break it in pieces.

Dan. 7:24 And the ten horns out of this kingdom are ten kings that shall arise: and another shall rise after them; and he shall be diverse from the first, and he shall subdue three kings.

Daniel was still actively involved in his dream. He was confused and did not fully understand what he was dreaming. He wanted the interpretation of what he was dreaming, so, while still in the dream, he asked someone who was near him, probably an angel, what his dream meant.

The angel proceeded to tell Daniel the interpretation. The four beasts were four kings that rose up out of the earth. Daniel 7:17 states, "These great beasts, which are four, are four kings, which shall arise out of the earth." Kings ruled over kingdoms, so the four beasts that were four kings were four different kingdoms. The fourth beast was the fourth kingdom. Daniel 7:23 states, "The fourth beast shall be the fourth kingdom upon earth." The fourth kingdom had ten horns. The ten horns were ten kings. Daniel 7:24 states, "And the ten horns out of this kingdom are ten kings that shall arise." The fourth kingdom was made up of ten kings, so the fourth kingdom was made up of ten horns (kings). Another horn (king) came up and overthrew three of the ten horns (kings) in the fourth kingdom, and he was now the king of the entire fourth kingdom. The king of the fourth kingdom was exceedingly dreadful, and he made war with the saints. The saints did not prevail against him. The fourth kingdom was successful until God conquered the kingdom and let the saints possess the kingdom. Daniel 7:22 states, "The time came that the saints possessed the kingdom." This kingdom now belonged to the saints forever. Daniel 7:18 states, "But the saints of the most High shall take the kingdom, and possess the kingdom for ever, even for ever and ever."

After the angel gave Daniel the interpretation of his dream, he understood it more, but he was still confused. He continued to keep the dream in his mind. Approximately two years later, Daniel had a second dream, which also pertained to his first dream.

Daniel's Second Dream

Dan. 8:1   In the third year of the reign of king Belshazzar a vision appeared unto me, even unto me Daniel, after that which appeared unto me at the first.

Dan. 8:2   And I saw in a vision; and it came to pass, when I saw, that I was at Shushan in the palace, which is in the province of Elam; and I saw in a vision, and I was by the river of Ulai.

Dan. 8:3   Then I lifted up mine eyes, and saw, and, behold, there stood before the river a ram which had two horns: and the two horns were high; but one was higher than the other, and the higher came up last.

Dan. 8:4   I saw the ram pushing westward, and northward, and southward; so that no beasts might stand before him, neither was there any that could deliver out of his hand; but he did according to his will, and became great.

Dan. 8:5   And as I was considering, behold, an he goat came from the west on the face of the whole earth, and touched not the ground: and the goat had a notable horn between his eyes.

Dan. 8:6   And he came to the ram that had two horns, which I had seen standing before the river, and ran unto him in the fury of his power.

Dan. 8:7   And I saw him come close unto the ram, and he was moved with choler against him, and smote the ram, and brake his two horns: and there was no power in the ram to stand before him, but he cast him down to the

	ground, and stamped upon him: and there was none that could deliver the ram out of his hand.
Dan. 8:8	Therefore the he goat waxed very great: and when he was strong, the great horn was broken; and for it came up four notable ones toward the four winds of heaven.
Dan. 8:9	And out of one of them came forth a little horn, which waxed exceeding great, toward the south, and toward the east, and toward the pleasant land.
Dan. 8:10	And it waxed great, even to the host of heaven; and it cast down some of the host and of the stars to the ground, and stamped upon them.

In Daniel's second vision or dream, he saw a ram. This ram had two horns, but one horn was higher than the other was. The higher horn came up last. This ram was so powerful that he could not be stopped. Next, Daniel saw a goat coming from the west, and this goat had one horn between his eyes. This goat ran directly into the ram and broke both of the ram's horns. The ram fell to the ground, and the goat stomped all over him. When the goat was very strong, his one horn was finally broken. After the goat's horn was broken, there came up four little horns in its place. Another little horn came out of the four horns, and he was very great. He turned against the south, east, and the pleasant land.

The ram that Daniel saw had two horns. Scripture points out that horns represent kings (kingdoms). Daniel 7:24 states, "The ten horns out of this kingdom are ten kings." This ram had two horns. Horns represent kings or kingdoms, depending on the context. The goat that came from the west had one horn (king). The goat (king) defeated the ram with two horns (two kings). Later, the goat's horn (king) was broken. After the goat's horn (king) was broken, there came up four more horns (four more kings) in place of the one broken horn (king). Out of the midst of the four horns (four kings) came up another little horn (king). This horn (king) was very great, and he turned against the south, east, and Israel.

Again, Daniel did not fully understand the vision. As usual, God gave Daniel more information about his visions. This time, God sent Gabriel to explain the visions to Daniel. The explanation continues in Daniel 8:16–24.

Gabriel's Explanation

Dan. 8:16   And I heard a man's voice between the banks of Ulai, which called, and said, Gabriel, make this man to understand the vision.

Dan. 8:17   So he came near where I stood: and when he came, I was afraid, and fell upon my face: but he said unto me, Understand, O son of man: for at the time of the end shall be the vision.

Dan. 8:18   Now as he was speaking with me, I was in a deep sleep on my face toward the ground: but he touched me, and set me upright.

Dan. 8:19   And he said, Behold, I will make thee know what shall be in the last end of the indignation: for at the time appointed the end shall be.

Dan. 8:20   The ram which thou sawest having two horns are the kings of Media and Persia.

Dan. 8:21   And the rough goat is the king of Grecia: and the great horn that is between his eyes is the first king.

Dan. 8:22   Now that being broken, whereas four stood up for it, four kingdoms shall stand up out of the nation, but not in his power.

Dan. 8:23   And in the latter time of their kingdom, when the transgressors are come to the full, a king of fierce countenance, and understanding dark sentences, shall stand up.

Dan. 8:24   And his power shall be mighty, but not by his own power: and he shall destroy wonderfully, and shall prosper, and practise, and shall destroy the mighty and the holy people.

Gabriel was sent to explain the vision to Daniel. Gabriel told Daniel that the vision was about the End-time. He explained the meaning of the ram and goat. The ram with the two horns were the kings of Media and Persia. Daniel 8:20 states, "The ram which thou sawest having two horns are the kings of Media and Persia." The goat with the one horn was the king of Greece. Daniel 8:21 states, "The rough goat is the king of Grecia: and the great horn that is between his eyes is the first king." Once the goat's one horn (Greece) was broken, there came up four more horns (kingdoms) in its place, but not as strong as the original kingdom. Daniel 8:22 states, "Now that being broken, whereas four stood up for it, four kingdoms shall stand up out of the nation, but not in his power." In the last days, out of one of these four kingdoms, another king would arise, and he would bring much destruction with him. Daniel 8:23–24 states, "In the latter time of their kingdom, a king of fierce countenance, and understanding dark sentences, shall stand up … he shall destroy wonderfully, and shall prosper, and prac- tise, and shall destroy the mighty and the holy people."

The ram with two horns represented the Medo-Persian kingdom. One horn represented Media; the other horn represented Persia. The goat coming from the west with one horn was the king of Greece. The king of Greece was Alexander the Great, and he attacked the Medo-Persian kingdom and overthrew it. When Alexander the Great was strong, he died, or his horn was broken. After his horn was broken, his kingdom was divided into four smaller kingdoms. These four horns came up when the goat's one horn was broken. The Grecian kingdom was divided into the Egyptian kingdom, Syrian kingdom, Macedonian kingdom, and Thracian kingdom. All of these kingdoms are recorded facts. This information can be read about in history books and encyclopedias. Daniel had these dreams while he lived in the Babylonian kingdom, under King Nebuchadnezzar and his son Belshazzar. This period of time was prior to the existence of the Medo-Persian and Grecian kingdoms.

Connecting the Dots of the Visions

Now let's tie all of this together. King Nebuchadnezzar's vision concerning the great image represents all major kingdoms ruling over Israel from Daniel's day until the End-time. The image is about the latter days. The Babylonian kingdom is the head of that great image, represented by gold. After the fall of the Babylonian kingdom, another kingdom would rise, but not as powerful. The second kingdom would be the Medo-Persian kingdom, represented by silver. This kingdom is the arms and breast of the great image. After the fall of the second kingdom (Medo-Persia), there would be a third kingdom

(Grecian) represented by brass. This kingdom is the belly and thighs of the great image. A fourth kingdom will arise, represented by iron and clay. This kingdom is the legs, feet, and toes of the great image. The fourth kingdom stands until the God of heaven comes and destroys it. This is confirmed in Daniel 2:34 and 2:44.

All major kingdoms ruling over Israel are represented here, from Babylon (the head) to the ten toes, which make up the last kingdom. Once the image is smote upon its feet (toes), all of the kingdoms of the world are destroyed. God then sets up a kingdom that will never be destroyed.

Let's examine the four beasts in Daniel 7:1–7 more closely. These four beasts are four kingdoms, just as King Nebuchadnezzar's image consisted of four kingdoms. The head of gold, the Babylonian kingdom, is the first beast that looks like a lion. The arms and breast of silver, the Medo-Persian kingdom, is the second beast that looks like a bear. The belly and thighs of brass, the Grecian kingdom, is the third beast that looks like a leopard. The legs and feet of iron and clay, the last kingdom, is the fourth beast. The fourth beast and his kingdom will be destroyed, just like King Nebuchadnezzar's image was destroyed. The king of the fourth and final kingdom will be defeated, and he will take his place in hell.

Daniel 2:29, shows that King Nebuchadnezzar's image is of future events, including the End-time. Daniel 8:23–25 clearly shows that the fourth beast in Daniel's dream is of the End-time. Both King Nebuchadnezzar's dream and Daniel's vision were referring to future events, beginning during their lifetime and continuing right up to the End-time.

It has been established that there are four beasts or kingdoms. Now let's tie all of this information into Revelation 13:1–2, concerning the beast with seven heads and ten horns rising out of the sea. How do we get heads out of kingdoms? Something else to remember, there are only four heads. John saw a beast with seven heads. Revelation 13:1 states, "I stood upon the sand of the sea, and saw a beast rise up out of the sea, having seven heads." John saw only one beast rise up out of the sea, but Daniel saw four different beasts rise up out of the sea. Daniel 7:3 states, "Four great beasts came up from the sea, diverse one from another." Let's reexamine what we have read.

A stone cut without hands hit the image on the feet and destroyed it. Daniel 2:34 states, "A stone was cut out without hands, which smote the image upon his feet that were of iron and clay, and brake them to pieces." The stone cut without hands is interpreted as the God of heaven and it will destroy all the kingdoms before it. When all of the kingdoms before it are destroyed, this stone becomes a great mountain.

In this case, mountain is symbolic for kingdom. We know God will set up an everlasting kingdom after the destruction of the kingdoms represented by the image. The stone will become a great mountain, which is an everlasting kingdom. Heads are symbolic for mountains. Revelation 17:9 states, "The seven heads are seven mountains." If heads are mountains and mountains are kingdoms, then kingdoms are heads. The seven heads that John saw refers to seven kingdoms.

It seems as though we still have a problem. John in Revelation 13:1 saw a beast with seven heads. According to Daniel, there were only four beasts or four kingdoms, or four heads. There seems to be a discrepancy because, Daniel saw four heads and John saw seven heads. To further explain, we have to examine Daniel's second vision. Daniel 8:5 states, "The goat had a notable horn between his eyes." Daniel 8:8 tells us that, when the goat's horn was broken, there came up four new horns. "The he goat waxed very great: and when he was strong, the great horn was broken; and for it came up four notable ones toward the four winds of heaven." The goat was the kingdom of Greece. When that kingdom was broken, there would arise four more kingdoms out of this kingdom, but they would not be as strong as the Grecian kingdom.

There we have the seven heads. Babylon was the first kingdom, represented by the lion. Medo-Persia was the second kingdom, represented by the bear. Greece was the third kingdom, represented by the leopard. When the Grecian kingdom fell, there arose four more horns (kingdoms). There we have seven beasts or kingdoms: Babylon, Medo-Persia, Grecian, plus the four that came out of the Grecian. Each one of the seven kingdoms represents one of the heads, so there are seven kingdoms or seven heads.

Now how do we associate this with the one beast that John saw in Revelation 13:1–2? Remember the image that King Nebuchadnezzar dreamed represented all of the kingdoms until Christ comes. This one image represents all seven of the kingdoms. The beasts are also known as kingdoms, mountains, or heads. One beast or image represents all seven kingdoms. The horns are the ten kings that make up the last (seventh) kingdom. Daniel

7:24 states, "And the ten horns out of this kingdom are ten kings." That is why we have a beast (kingdom) with:

- Seven heads (seven kingdoms represented by King Nebuchadnezzar's image)
- Ten horns (last kingdom made up of ten kings)
- Ten crowns (one crown for each king)

Now we are almost there. In Daniel 2, we read of this great image. This image has several kingdoms. The first kingdom is the head of gold, the Babylonian kingdom. The second kingdom is the breast and arms of silver, the Medo-Persian kingdom. The third kingdom is the belly and thighs of brass, the Grecian kingdom. The fourth and fifth kingdom is the two legs of iron, the Syrian and Egyptian kingdoms. The sixth kingdom is the feet of iron and clay, the Roman kingdom. The seventh kingdom is the ten toes, the antichrist's kingdom. History will confirm all of these facts right up to the sixth kingdom. The seventh kingdom, or antichrist's kingdom, is still future. It comes into existence in the last days. The antichrist's kingdom is against God, so God destroys it and sets up his own kingdom that will stand forever.

We will confirm the seven kingdoms again in Daniel 7:1–7. The first beast was the Babylonian kingdom. The second beast was the Medo-Persian kingdom. The third beast was the Grecian kingdom. The third beast or Grecian kingdom had four wings upon its back, the symbolism of four heads or four kingdoms. Daniel 7:6 states, "This I beheld, and lo another, like a leopard, which had upon the back of it four wings of a fowl; the beast had also four heads; and dominion was given to it." The four kingdoms grew out of the Grecian kingdom, and the four smaller kingdoms make up the fourth beast.

The fourth beast is really a combination of the four smaller kingdoms that came from the third beast. In this fourth beast, we have the fourth kingdom, the Syrian kingdom. The fifth kingdom is the Egyptian kingdom. The sixth kingdom is the Roman kingdom. The seventh kingdom is the antichrist's kingdom. The last four kingdoms came about because of the division of the Grecian kingdom into four smaller kingdoms. Again, history books will confirm six of the seven kingdoms. The seventh kingdom, or antichrist's kingdom, is still future. It comes into existence in the last days.

We will confirm the seven kingdoms once again in Daniel 8:1–10. Remember that Babylon was the head of gold or the first kingdom. The ram with the two horns was the Medo-Persian kingdom, the second kingdom. The goat with the one horn was the Grecian kingdom, the third kingdom. When the third kingdom was destroyed, there came up four more horns or kingdoms. These four horns represent the last four kingdoms. The fourth kingdom was the Syrian kingdom. The fifth kingdom was the Egyptian kingdom. The sixth kingdom was the Roman kingdom. The seventh kingdom is the antichrist's kingdom. The seventh kingdom, or antichrist kingdom, is still future. It comes into existence in the last days.

Rev. 13:1   And I stood upon the sand of the sea, and saw a beast rise up out of the sea, having seven heads and ten horns, and upon his horns ten crowns, and upon his heads the name of blasphemy.

Rev. 13:2   And the beast which I saw was like unto a leopard, and his feet were as the feet of a bear, and his mouth as the mouth of a lion: and the dragon gave him his power, and his seat, and great authority.

After all of that history, we will again turn to Revelation 13:1–2. John saw a beast rise up out of the sea. It had seven heads and ten horns. Upon his heads were ten crowns. The beast also had names of blasphemy upon its heads. This beast was the last earthly kingdom to rule over Jerusalem. This beast or kingdom was a combination of all of the kingdoms that ruled over Jerusalem from the Babylonian kingdom until just before the coming of the Lord. This beast rising out of the sea was also the great image of which King Nebuchadnezzar dreamed. The beast (kingdom) looked like a leopard, a bear, and a lion, just like the three beasts (kingdoms) that Daniel witnessed coming up out of the sea. Daniel 7:1–7 states, "First was like a lion … a second, like to a bear … I beheld, and lo another, like a leopard." The last kingdom came from a combination of the three previous kingdoms: Babylonian, Medo-Persian, and Grecian. So the seventh kingdom has the same characteristics as the first three kingdoms, represented by the lion, bear, and the leopard.

Identifying the Beast

Rev. 13:1   And I stood upon the sand of the sea, and saw a beast
rise up out of the sea, having seven heads and ten horns,
and upon his horns ten crowns, and upon his heads the
name of blasphemy.

Rev. 13:2   And the beast which I saw was like unto a leopard, and
his feet were as the feet of a bear, and his mouth as the
mouth of a lion: and the dragon gave him his power,
and his seat, and great authority.

The beast rising out of the sea with seven heads and ten horns is a
kingdom. This kingdom has seven heads because the heads are the kingdoms that ruled over Israel from the Babylonian kingdom until Christ's
return. This is the seventh and last kingdom to rule over Israel. There are ten
horns or kings because this seventh and final kingdom consists of ten kings.
Ten different countries unite their forces together to form the last kingdom
before Christ returns. There are ten crowns because each king within this
kingdom wears a crown representing his country. Like the United Nations,
all countries still bear their own identity or crown. The beast rising out of
the sea is a kingdom, and this kingdom has a name. Revelation 17:5 states,
"And upon her forehead was a name written, MYSTERY, BABYLON THE
GREAT, THE MOTHER OF HARLOTS AND ABOMINATIONS OF
THE EARTH." Babylon is the name of this seventh and final kingdom.
Revelation 17:5 parallels Revelation 13:1 because both verses show that the
kingdom has blasphemous names upon its head.

This beast (kingdom) has the names of blasphemy upon its heads. All
seven of the kingdoms that ruled over Israel were sovereign. They did not
believe in the God of Israel and were based solely on their military strength.

This kingdom is a blasphemous kingdom. Blasphemy is calling something the opposite of its true identity. If you say up is down and down is
up, you have just blasphemed. If you say black is white and white is black,
you have just blasphemed. If you say God is the devil and the devil is God,
you have just blasphemed.[13] All of these kingdoms were against God. The
seventh kingdom will be even more so against God than all the other

---

[13] Torah Light Ministries, Stanley Chester, taped message.

kingdoms. Revelation 13:1 states, "And upon his heads the name of blasphemy."

When a person refers to a kingdom, he sometimes refers to the kingdom itself. Other times, we refer to the head of the kingdom. An example would be the United States. The United States as a country is the kingdom, but we often refer to the United States by its president.[14] That is what happening in Revelation 13:2. The leader or president of this kingdom is the one who receives great power and authority. This is also shown in Daniel 7:25, "He shall speak great words against the most High, and shall wear out the saints of the most High." Daniel 8:8–11 states, "He magnified himself even to the prince of the host." And again in Daniel 11:36–37, it states, "The king shall do according to his will; and he shall exalt himself, and magnify himself above every god, and shall speak marvellous things against the God of gods." This whole kingdom is anti-God. This king or leader is a blasphemer. This king is better known as the antichrist.

The beast or antichrist, the leader of this kingdom, gets his power and authority from the dragon. Revelation 13:2 states, "The beast which I saw was like unto a leopard, and his feet were as the feet of a bear, and his mouth as the mouth of a lion: and the dragon gave him his power, and his seat, and great authority." The dragon has many names or titles. Some of his names or titles can be verified in Revelation 12:9, "The great dragon was cast out, that old serpent, called the Devil, and Satan, which deceiveth the whole world." He is called the devil, the serpent, and Satan. Satan himself influences the antichrist. We know that Satan is anti-God, so antichrist is the appropriate name for the leader of this blasphemous kingdom.

Deadly Wound

> Rev. 13:3   And I saw one of his heads as it were wounded to death; and his deadly wound was healed: and all the world wondered after the beast.

One of the beast's seven heads has a deadly wound that has been healed. We need to grasp what this text means because it seems to suggest that someone died and came back to life. To better understand this, we have to

---

[14] Torah Light Ministries, Stanley Chester, taped message.

go back to the book of Daniel. We see that the goat has a single horn and the goat's horn was broken. Daniel 8:5–8 states, "The goat had a notable horn between his eyes … and when he was strong, the great horn was broken." The horn, representing a kingdom, was broken or defeated. When the horn (king) was broken (died), the kingdom was dead. Previously, we saw the goat with the one horn was the Grecian kingdom. When that horn was broken or that king died, it was as though that kingdom died. When the Grecian kingdom fell, four more kingdoms rose up out of it. Daniel 8:8 states, "The great horn was broken; and for it came up four notable ones toward the four winds of heaven." One of these kingdoms is the seventh and final kingdom. So we see that the Grecian kingdom, when it fell, had a deadly wound, but out of that dead kingdom came the seventh kingdom, signifying the Grecian kingdom was yet alive or healed. This is what was meant by the deadly wound was healed.

There we have it. The beast that John saw rising up out of the sea with seven heads and ten horns is not some kind of deformed animal. It is a kingdom ruling on earth at the End-time. It has seven heads because this kingdom is a derivative of the previous six kingdoms. The name of this kingdom is Babylon. This is ironic because the (head of gold) first kingdom's name was Babylon and the final kingdom's name is Babylon.

Blasphemous Regime

Rev. 13:4   And they worshipped the dragon which gave power unto the beast: and they worshipped the beast, saying, Who is like unto the beast? who is able to make war with him?

Rev. 13:5   And there was given unto him a mouth speaking great things and blasphemies; and power was given unto him to continue forty and two months.

Rev. 13:6   And he opened his mouth in blasphemy against God, to blaspheme his name, and his tabernacle, and them that dwell in heaven.

Rev. 13:7   And it was given unto him to make war with the saints, and to overcome them: and power was given him over all kindreds, and tongues, and nations.

Rev. 13:8   And all that dwell upon the earth shall worship him,
             whose names are not written in the book of life of the
             Lamb slain from the foundation of the world.
Rev. 13:9   If any man have an ear, let him hear.

This whole kingdom is blasphemous. People worship not only the anti-christ, but Satan as well. Satan is giving the antichrist all of his authority, so people begin to think that Satan is to be worshipped instead of the God who created the heavens, the earth, and the seas. All of the heads of this kingdom are blasphemous, especially the seventh kingdom. Revelation 13:1 states, "And upon his heads the name of blasphemy." The president or leader of this kingdom is to have power for three-and-a-half years (forty-two months). He is so defiant that he blasphemes against God, the name of God, the house of God, and all of the heavenly beings dwelling in heaven with God. He also antagonizes the saints or followers of God. He stretches his authority upon many different nationalities and religious systems. Many men will worship the antichrist, but not all. Those who know their God and have become born-again will have their names written in the Book of Life. They will not worship the antichrist because they will recognize him to be a false god.

Rev. 13:10   He that leadeth into captivity shall go into captivity:
             he that killeth with the sword must be killed with the
             sword. Here is the patience and the faith of the saints.

Anyone who leads others into captivity shall himself go into captivity. We know the antichrist and the false prophet will go into the lake of fire as a captive. Revelation 19:20 states, "The beast was taken, and with him the false prophet … these both were cast alive into a lake of fire burning with brimstone."

Anyone who kills with the sword will be killed with the sword. We know the antichrist and the false prophet will be killed with the sharp, two-edged sword. Revelation 19:15 states, "Out of his mouth goeth a sharp sword, that with it he should smite the nations: and he shall rule them with a rod of iron: and he treadeth the winepress of the fierceness and wrath of Almighty God."

Just knowing that the antichrist and false prophet will eventually be defeated with the the sharp two-edged sword and held in captivity in the lake of fire forever is the patience of the saints. This inevitable fate of the antichrist and false prophet, along with eternal life of the saints, is what nourishes the patience and faith of the saints.

CHAPTER 8

THE GREAT WHORE

Rev. 17:1 And there came one of the seven angels which had the seven vials, and talked with me, saying unto me, Come hither; I will shew unto thee the judgment of the great whore that sitteth upon many waters:

Rev. 17:2 With whom the kings of the earth have committed fornication, and the inhabitants of the earth have been made drunk with the wine of her fornication.

ONE of the angels who had the seven vials wanted to show John the judgment of the great whore, but John did not have a clue as to what the angel was talking about. To make matters worse, the whore was fornicating with very elite clientele, kings of several different nations. The whore also caused the citizens of the nations, whose kings she was fornicating with, to become adversely affected. Something else was very peculiar to John: The woman was sitting upon waters, a supernatural act. Before John could understand the judgment of the whore, he had to first learn her identity.

The Great Whore

Rev. 17:3 So he carried me away in the spirit into the wilderness: and I saw a woman sit upon a scarlet coloured beast, full of names of blasphemy, having seven heads and ten horns.

Rev. 17:4 And the woman was arrayed in purple and scarlet colour, and decked with gold and precious stones and pearls,

               having a golden cup in her hand full of abominations
               and filthiness of her fornication:

Rev. 17:5   And upon her forehead was a name written, MYSTERY,
               BABYLON THE GREAT, THE MOTHER OF
               HARLOTS AND ABOMINATIONS OF THE
               EARTH.

Rev. 17:6   And I saw the woman drunken with the blood of the
               saints, and with the blood of the martyrs of Jesus: and
               when I saw her, I wondered with great admiration.

Immediately, John was in the spirit, and he was taken into the wilderness. Once in the wilderness under the influence of the spirit, John saw a woman sitting upon a scarlet-colored beast. Previously in chapter 7, it was determined that a beast symbolizes a kingdom. This beast (kingdom) has seven heads and ten horns. The names of blasphemy are written all over the beast (kingdom). The description of this beast (kingdom) in Revelation 17:3, "Beast, full of names of blasphemy, having seven heads and ten horns," is the same description as the beast (kingdom) in Revelation 13:1–2, "Beast … having seven heads and ten horns … upon his heads the name of blasphemy." In conclusion, the beast described in Revelation 17:3 is the same beast (kingdom) described in Revelation 13:1–2.

The woman sitting upon the beast (kingdom) was dressed in purple and scarlet clothing. The color purple is associated with royalty; scarlet is associated with adultery. She was wearing the finest gold and jewelry, indicating she was saturated with riches. She was holding a gold cup in her hand. The content of the cup is the filthiness and abominations committed or performed with the kings of the earth. The woman sitting upon the scarlet-colored beast had a name inscribed upon her forehead. Revelation 17:5 states, "And upon her forehead was a name written, MYSTERY, BABYLON THE GREAT, THE MOTHER OF HARLOTS AND ABOMINATIONS OF THE EARTH." The name itself is intriguing. It baffles one's understanding. It states the woman is the mother of harlots, who are not the most reputable people in the world. The woman gives birth to harlots and abominations. This name signifies that nothing about this woman is good or righteous. Not only is the woman unrighteous, but the beast (kingdom) upon which she is sitting is blasphemous, indicating it is in conflict or opposes the one and only God who created the heavens, the earth, and the seas.

This woman had a huge part of the earth's population under her influence because of her relationship with the kings of the earth. Kings rule over the inhabitants of their kingdoms or nations, so the woman indirectly had authority over the inhabitants under those kings. She also became drunk with the blood of the saints and blood of the martyrs of Jesus. She was drunk with the blood of saints and martyrs of Jesus in the sense that she was responsible for the shedding of the blood of a multitude of saints and martyrs, not in the sense that she drank their blood. John did not fully understand what he was witnessing because he wondered about the woman sitting on the scarlet-colored beast with great admiration.

The Angel Comforts John

Rev. 17:7　And the angel said unto me, Wherefore didst thou marvel? I will tell thee the mystery of the woman, and of the beast that carrieth her, which hath the seven heads and ten horns.

When John saw this woman sitting on the beast with seven heads and ten horns, he was not sure of its meaning because he had already seen a beast with seven heads and ten horns rise up out of the sea in Revelation 13:1–2, "And saw a beast rise up out of the sea, having seven heads and ten horns." Now John saw the same beast carrying a woman. Revelation 17:3 states, "A scarlet coloured beast, full of names of blasphemy, having seven heads and ten horns." John's facial expression was a look of great concern because he did not know the meaning of the beast with seven heads and ten horns. At this point, the interpretation had not been given to him. He wanted to know the identity of the woman and the meaning of the beast that carried her. The angel informed John that he would interpret the mystery of the woman and the beast with the seven heads and ten horns.

The Beast

Rev. 17:8　The beast that thou sawest was, and is not; and shall ascend out of the bottomless pit, and go into perdition:

and they that dwell on the earth shall wonder, whose
names were not written in the book of life from the
foundation of the world, when they behold the beast
that was, and is not, and yet is.

The angel explained the meaning of the beast to John. The beast that
John saw was, is not, and shall ascend out of the bottomless pit and go into
perdition. From this statement, John still did not know any more now than
he did at first.

Let's dissect the angel's statement concerning the beast. We know from
previous study that a beast is symbolic for a kingdom. The beast that was
means a kingdom was in existence at one point in time. The beast that is not
means the kingdom that was in existence before is not in existence now. The
beast ascending out of the bottomless pit and going into perdition is referring to Satan, and I will explain.

The beast that was and the beast that is not refers to a physical beast
(kingdom). The beast that shall ascend out of the bottomless pit and go into
perdition is a spiritual beast or the force that empowers the leader of the
kingdom. That authority comes from the dragon. Revelation 13:2 states,
"And the dragon gave him his power, and his seat, and great authority."
The dragon is none other than Satan himself. This is verified in Revelation
12:9, "The great dragon was cast out, that old serpent, called the Devil, and
Satan."

The beast that was is the Babylonian kingdom. It was the first kingdom
(head of gold) of the image of which King Nebuchadnezzar dreamed in
Daniel 2. The beast that is not is the Babylonian kingdom. It was not in
existence in John's day or the time the book of Revelation was written. The
kingdom in existence in John's day was the Roman kingdom, better known
as the Roman Empire. Now the text switches to the authority figure of this
beast (kingdom). The beast that shall ascend out of the bottomless pit and
go into perdition is Satan. Revelation 20:1–3 states:

An angel come down from heaven, having the key of the bottomless
pit and a great chain in his hand. And he laid hold on the dragon,
that old serpent, which is the Devil, and Satan, and bound him a

thousand years, and cast him into the bottomless pit, and shut him up, and set a seal upon him.

Satan will be confined to the bottomless pit. After one thousand years, he will be released. Revelation 20:7 states, "And when the thousand years are expired, Satan shall be loosed out of his prison." When Satan is released from the bottomless pit, he will return to his deceitful ways and eventually go into perdition. Revelation 20:10 states, "And the devil that deceived them was cast into the lake of fire and brimstone, where the beast and the false prophet are, and shall be tormented day and night for ever and ever." The lake of fire is perdition or place of eternal punishment, so Satan is the one who ascends out of the bottomless pit and goes into perdition. Many inhabitants of the kingdom will realize that the kingdom has a satanic influence. Some, but not all, will begin to wonder if they are truly saved.

The Seven Heads

> Rev. 17:9   And here is the mind which hath wisdom. The seven heads are seven mountains, on which the woman sitteth.

The angel continued to give John more information concerning the beast with seven heads and ten horns. The angel told John that the seven heads were seven mountains. In order to understand the symbolism of the mountains, let's go to the book of Daniel.

The setting in Daniel 2:31–35 is in the Babylonian kingdom when King Nebuchadnezzar was king. The king dreamed of a great image representing the world kingdoms. A stone cut without hands destroyed this image. Daniel 2:34 states, "A stone was cut out without hands, which smote the image upon his feet." The feet of this image is a kingdom. Daniel 2:42 states, "The toes of the feet were part of iron, and part of clay, so the kingdom shall be partly strong, and partly broken." The key word is *kingdom*. The stone destroys the kingdom, and the stone becomes a great mountain. Daniel 2:35 states, "The stone that smote the image became a great mountain, and filled the whole earth." Jesus is that stone. Matthew 21:42 states, "The stone which the builders rejected, the same is become the head of the corner." Jesus' gospel while he was here on earth was the introduction to that kingdom. Matthew

4:17 states, "Repent: for the kingdom of heaven is at hand." The book of Micah also confirms that a mountain is symbolic for a kingdom. Micah 4:1 states, "But in the last days it shall come to pass, that the mountain of the house of the LORD shall be established in the top of the mountains, and it shall be exalted above the hills; and people shall flow unto it." Daniel 2:44 states, "In the days of these kings shall the God of heaven set up a kingdom, which shall never be destroyed." The stone becomes a mountain; the mountain becomes an everlasting kingdom. The seven heads are seven mountains or seven kingdoms. This is synonymous with what was studied in chapter 7. Notice, it is only one beast. The beast has seven heads. Each head represents a kingdom. Concerning the seven kingdoms, each one of the seven kingdoms falls into one of three different categories: has already ruled over Israel, was ruling over Israel when the book of Revelation was written, will rule over Israel before the return of Christ.

The Place Where the Woman Sits

Rev. 17:1   And there came one of the seven angels which had the seven vials, and talked with me, saying unto me, Come hither; I will shew unto thee the judgment of the great whore that sitteth upon many waters:

Rev. 17:9   And here is the mind which hath wisdom. The seven heads are seven mountains, on which the woman sitteth.

Revelation 17:1 points out that the woman is sitting on many waters. Revelation 17:9 also points out that the woman is sitting on seven heads or seven mountains. This sounds as though it is a contradiction because the woman is sitting in two different places: waters and/or mountains. The book of Revelation actually tells us the symbolism for waters. Revelation 17:15 states, "The waters which thou sawest, where the whore sitteth, are peoples, and multitudes, and nations, and tongues." The seven heads are seven mountains. Mountains are symbolic for kingdoms. Kingdoms rule over people. Because waters represent people and kingdoms rule over people, the meanings of both statements are the same. The woman sitting on many waters represents a woman with authority over many people. The woman sitting on seven mountains (kingdoms) represents a woman with authority over many people. Both verses refer to the same woman, and she reigns over several different nations, tongues, and cultures.

The Mind Which Has Wisdom

Rev. 17:9   And here is the mind which hath wisdom. The seven heads are seven mountains, on which the woman sitteth.

Rev. 17:10   And there are seven kings: five are fallen, and one is, and the other is not yet come; and when he cometh, he must continue a short space.

In John's day, the time he received the book of Revelation, five of the kingdoms (kings) had already fallen. The five fallen kingdoms (kings) were Babylonian, Medo-Persian, Grecian, Syrian, and Egyptian. The one kingdom (king) that was in existence in John's day was the Roman kingdom, or Roman Empire. The kingdom that is yet to come is the seventh and final worldly kingdom, and it was future to John's day. When this final kingdom (king) is brought into existence or revealed, it will only last for a short time. When it arrives, it will be the antichrist's kingdom.

The Ten Horns

Rev. 17:12   And the ten horns which thou sawest are ten kings, which have received no kingdom as yet; but receive power as kings one hour with the beast.

The beast consists of seven heads (kingdoms). Five of those kingdoms have already fallen, one of those kingdoms was in authority in John's day, and there will be one more future kingdom to conquer Israel. The one kingdom that is yet to be brought into existence is the seventh and final worldly kingdom, better known as the antichrist's kingdom. The antichrist's kingdom has ten horns. Revelation 17:12 states, "The ten horns which thou sawest are ten kings." Horns are symbolic for kings, so the ten horns are ten kings or ten nations, a king for each nation. These ten kings or ten nations will unite to form one kingdom, which will be the seventh and final worldly kingdom. It is the kingdom not yet established in reference to the writing of the book of Revelation. The angel told John that the ten kings (horns) had no kingdom at that particular time, but will receive power as kings in the future. The book of Daniel confirms that the ten horns are symbolic for ten kings. Daniel 7:24 states, "The ten horns out of this kingdom are ten kings that shall arise."

The ten horns or kings that make up the seventh and final worldly kingdom did not exist in John's day. It was future to the writing of the book of Revelation. The ten kings willingly give their power and strength to the antichrist. Their rule with the antichrist will be short-lived because they only reign with antichrist for one hour. The antichrist will betray them and take dominion over the entire kingdom soon after the signing of their agreement or treaty. Revelation 17:12 states, "And the ten horns which thou sawest are ten kings, which have received no kingdom as yet; but receive power as kings one hour with the beast."

The Eighth Beast

> Rev. 17:11 And the beast that was, and is not, even he is the eighth,
> and is of the seven, and goeth into perdition.

When scripture refers to a beast, it sometimes refers to the physical kingdom. Other times, it pertains to the leader of the kingdom. The beast that was and the beast that is not refers to the physical kingdom. The beast that is the eighth refers to the leader of the final worldly kingdom, better known as the antichrist.

The seventh worldly kingdom is actually ten nations that have unified themselves in order to become one powerful coalition or kingdom. There are seven different kingdoms: Babylonian, Medo-Persian, Grecian, Syrian, Egyptian, Roman, and antichrist (unified ten nation kingdom). After the seventh kingdom (unified ten nations) is established, the antichrist will over-throw three of the seven nations, leaving only seven kings. He then assumes leadership of the seventh kingdom. Once he controls the entire kingdom, he becomes the eighth beast (king). The antichrist will be delivered into perdition. Revelation 19:20 states, "The beast was taken, and with him the false prophet ... these both were cast alive into a lake of fire burning with brimstone." The lake of fire and brimstone is the final judgment or perdi-tion. Revelation 20:14 states, "Death and hell were cast into the lake of fire.

This is the second death." The leader (antichrist) assumes leadership over the seventh and final worldly kingdom (beast), the eighth beast (king) that goes into perdition.

The Seventh Kingdom's Agenda

Rev. 17:13   These have one mind, and shall give their power and strength unto the beast.

Rev. 17:14   These shall make war with the Lamb, and the Lamb shall overcome them: for he is Lord of lords, and King of kings: and they that are with him are called, and chosen, and faithful.

Rev. 17:15   And he saith unto me, The waters which thou sawest, where the whore sitteth, are peoples, and multitudes, and nations, and tongues.

Rev. 17:16   And the ten horns which thou sawest upon the beast, these shall hate the whore, and shall make her desolate and naked, and shall eat her flesh, and burn her with fire.

Rev. 17:17   For God hath put in their hearts to fulfil his will, and to agree, and give their kingdom unto the beast, until the words of God shall be fulfilled.

These ten nations (horns or kings) all have something in common. They want to destroy the followers of Jesus. God has hardened their hearts, so they unite their nations together to form the seventh and final worldly kingdom to combat the saints. The antichrist will assume control over the ten-nation kingdom, and he then becomes the leader of the entire coalition or kingdom. This coalition will eventually make war against the lamb. The lamb and his army will destroy the antichrist and his coalition. The army that accompanies Jesus is the saints. Revelation 17:14 states, "And they that are with him are called, and chosen, and faithful."

The ten kings will hate the whore (woman on scarlet-colored beast). She caused them to commit fornication. When the ten kings hand over their nations to the antichrist, they literally give the whore authority over them. It only takes them one hour to realize they have just committed fornication with the whore. The antichrist soon betrays them after their agreement. Revelation 17:12 states, "But receive power as kings one hour with the beast." We do not know the method the antichrist uses to betray the ten kings unless he deceives them, but the antichrist somehow assumes control over the entire kingdom. For this reason, the ten kings will hate the whore and destroy her. They will hate the whore so much that they will strip her naked, eat her flesh, and burn her with fire. This will become much clearer once the identity of the whore is established.

The Whore's Identity

> Rev. 17:18 And the woman which thou sawest is that great city,
> which reigneth over the kings of the earth.

The woman sitting on the scarlet-colored beast (kingdom) is that great city. This city reigns over the nations of the kings with whom she committed fornication. The kings over whom the woman reigns is the ten kings who will join forces to form one large kingdom, a seventh and final worldly kingdom. The antichrist overthrows three kings and convinces the other seven kings to give him authority over the kingdom. The kingdom under the antichrist's control will be ruled from this city. The woman (whore) is this city.

This city becomes the capital of the antichrist's kingdom, from which the leader rules his or her kingdom, from which all of the laws and doctrines are legislated for the entire kingdom. Remember when the Angel of Jesus revealed the state of the churches to John. He stated that the church of Pergamos lived in the same place where Satan's seat is located. Revelation 2:13 states, "I know thy works, and where thou dwellest, even where Satan's seat is … my faithful martyr, who was slain among you, where Satan dwelleth." It appears that the capital of the antichrist's kingdom will be the same city as the church of Pergamos because Satan, also known as the dragon, gives the antichrist his seat and great authority. Revelation 13:2 states, "And the dragon gave him his power, and his seat, and great authority."

> Rev. 18:10 Standing afar off for the fear of her torment, saying,
> Alas, alas, that great city Babylon, that mighty city! for
> in one hour is thy judgment come.

John gave us a name for this capital city, Babylon. Revelation 18:10 states, "That great city Babylon." This is also confirmed in Revelation 17:5, "Upon her forehead was a name written, MYSTERY, BABYLON THE GREAT." Babylon is also the same name as the first kingdom with the head of gold that we read about in Daniel 2. Ironically, the first kingdom that ruled over Israel and the last worldly kingdom that will rule over Israel will have the same name. Do not confuse this great city with the great city in Revelation 21:10. There are two great cities in the book of Revelation: Babylon and Holy Jerusalem. Revelation 17 only focuses on Babylon.

Rev. 17:4   And the woman was arrayed in purple and scarlet colour, and decked with gold and precious stones and pearls, having a golden cup in her hand full of abominations and filthiness of her fornication:

Rev. 18:16   And saying, Alas, alas, that great city, that was clothed in fine linen, and purple, and scarlet, and decked with gold, and precious stones, and pearls!

A woman is described in Revelation 17:4, a woman dressed in purple and scarlet and wearing fine gold, stones, and pearls. A great city is described in Revelation 18:16, a city that is adorned in purple and scarlet and wearing fine gold, stones, and pearls. One of these verses refers to a woman while the other refers to a city, but the symbolism is the same. This woman symbolizes a great city, the capital city that reigns over the kings of the earth or seventh kingdom, also known as the antichrist's kingdom. Revelation 17:18 states, "And the woman which thou sawest is that great city, which reigneth over the kings of the earth." The beast is the kingdom of antichrist. The woman sitting on the beast (kingdom) is a great capital city that reigns over the kingdom of ten kings, better known as the antichrist's kingdom or Babylon.

Rev. 17:1   And there came one of the seven angels which had the seven vials, and talked with me, saying unto me, Come hither; I will shew unto thee the judgment of the great whore that sitteth upon many waters:

Rev. 17:2   With whom the kings of the earth have committed

fornication, and the inhabitants of the earth have been
made drunk with the wine of her fornication.

Rev. 18:2   And he cried mightily with a strong voice, saying,
Babylon the great is fallen, is fallen, and is become the
habitation of devils, and the hold of every foul spirit,
and a cage of every unclean and hateful bird.

Rev. 18:3   For all nations have drunk of the wine of the wrath of her
fornication, and the kings of the earth have committed
fornication with her, and the merchants of the earth are
waxed rich through the abundance of her delicacies.

Here we see that the whore referenced in Revelation 17:1–2 and
Babylon referenced in Revelation 18:2–3 is indeed the same city. Both
verses describe the woman and the capital city of Babylon as having made
the kings of the earth to drink the wine of the wrath of her fornication.
This is an evil city. Its name implies unrighteousness. Revelation 17:5 states,
"MYSTERY, BABYLON THE GREAT, THE MOTHER OF HARLOTS
AND ABOMINATIONS OF THE EARTH." The city's name is Babylon
the Great. The word *Babylon* actually means "confusion."[15] Babylon is the
mother of harlots and abominations. She's the birthplace of all abominable
things. It is true that there is sin and unrighteousness in the world today, but
these sins are so abominable that it initiates the return of Christ. Revelation
18:5 states, "For her sins have reached unto heaven, and God hath remembered her iniquities."

The name Babylon leaves no doubt that the business affairs of the
antichrist's capital is unrighteousness. This city requires its inhabitants to
participate in its unrighteousness. The main enemies of this city are the saints
and martyrs of Jesus. Revelation 17:6 states, "I saw the woman drunken
with the blood of the saints, and with the blood of the martyrs of Jesus."
This indicates that Babylon does not tolerate the teachings of Jesus, but
enforces the government's own religious doctrines. Because Babylon literally
means confusion and the kingdom's enemies are the saints, this kingdom
confuses or tricks many of the saints into idolatry. A multitude of saints will
be deceived into idol worship, and this constitutes a great falling away from

---

[15] The New Strong's Complete Dictionary of Bible Words (Thomas Nelson Publishers, 1996),
20.

what they originally believed. As 2 Thessalonians 2:3 states, "Let no man deceive you by any means: for that day shall not come, except there come a falling away first, and that man of sin be revealed, the son of perdition."

> Rev. 18:4   And I heard another voice from heaven, saying, Come out of her, my people, that ye be not partakers of her sins, and that ye receive not of her plagues.

John heard a voice from heaven telling the inhabitants of Babylon to leave the city. They were being warned beforehand that the city of Babylon would be destroyed and they should leave the city and not get caught up in any of her abominations and blasphemies. The sins of this city were so horrible and detestable that they had reached into heaven itself. Revelation 18:5 states, "For her sins have reached unto heaven, and God hath remembered her iniquities." This is an idolatrous city, and it would ultimately be destroyed.

The Whore's Judgment

> Rev. 18:8   Therefore shall her plagues come in one day, death, and mourning, and famine; and she shall be utterly burned with fire: for strong is the Lord God who judgeth her.
>
> Rev. 18:2   And he cried mightily with a strong voice, saying, Babylon the great is fallen, is fallen, and is become the habitation of devils, and the hold of every foul spirit, and a cage of every unclean and hateful bird.
>
> Rev. 14:8   And there followed another angel, saying, Babylon is fallen, is fallen, that great city, because she made all nations drink of the wine of the wrath of her fornication.

All of these scriptures point to the fall of Babylon. This was a great city in the eyes of the antichrist's followers. The wickedness of this city was so great that these abominations reached into heaven. Revelation 18:5 states, "For her sins have reached unto heaven, and God hath remembered her iniquities." God had to bring about the judgment of the whore because the agony the saints faced while being forced into idol worship was too great for them to endure. This city was responsible for the greatest tribulation the earth had ever witnessed. Matthew 24:21 states, "For then shall be great tribulation, such as was not since the beginning of the world to this time, no, nor ever shall be." There was a lot of confusion during this time of great tribulation. Mankind could not make rational decisions, so God judged the whore. Matthew 24:22 states, "Except those days should be shortened, there should no flesh be saved: but for the elect's sake those days shall be shortened." If God did not shorten or lessen the impact of the great tribulation, no human beings would be able to survive. Satan knew he only had a little time left, so he influenced the antichrist to turn up the heat full throttle. His strategy was to deceive people by making life extremely difficult and then causing them to question why their god did not save them. He spoke against the God of heaven, causing people to doubt. Revelation 13:6–8 states:

> There was given unto him a mouth speaking great things … he opened his mouth in blasphemy against God, to blaspheme his name, and his tabernacle, and them that dwell in heaven … it was given unto him to make war with the saints, and to overcome them.

God had to bring about judgment because the agony the saints faced while being forced into idol worship was too great for them to endure.

Summarizing the Mystery of the Woman

The woman sitting on a scarlet-colored beast referred to herself as a harlot, a woman who compromises her body for gain. The word *harlot* can also mean an "idolater."[16] This woman was playing the harlot or was engaged in an arrangement with several kings in order to gain influence over the inhabitants of their nations. Once this woman (capital city) was in place, she was in a position to make laws for the rest of the kingdom, both political and religious laws. Her religious interest was idolatry, forcing the saints to forsake their god and worship the antichrist as their god.

It is commonly accepted that fornication is having intercourse with

---

[16] The New Strong's Complete Dictionary of Bible Words (Thomas Nelson Publishers, 1996), 121.

anyone other than a spouse, but fornication has another meaning, idolatry.[17] The fornication the whore (woman) was committing with the kings of the earth was idolatry. The city of Babylon was guilty of idolatry and established an atmosphere of zero tolerance for the teachings of Jesus. She was against the saints of Jesus. Revelation 17:2 states, "The inhabitants of the earth have been made drunk with the wine of her fornication." She caused the inhabitants of the kingdom to be so confused that some of them began worshipping idols, believing they were worshipping the one and only God, the God who created the heavens, the earth, and the seas.

One of the political doctrines of the city of Babylon was to create a haven for gaining riches. The symbolism is the woman dressed in fine apparel. Revelation 17:4 states, "The woman was arrayed in purple and scarlet colour, and decked with gold and precious stones and pearls." This exact symbolism is shown again when referring to the great city. Revelation 18:16 states, "That great city, that was clothed in fine linen, and purple, and scarlet, and decked with gold, and precious stones, and pearls!" The woman and the city, both being well dressed, symbolize wealth and riches. The city of Babylon permitted many of its constituents to become very wealthy. Revelation 18:3 states, "And the merchants of the earth are waxed rich through the abundance of her delicacies." Not only was the city of Babylon a government that promoted idol worship, but it also produced an atmosphere of enormous wealth and caused many to turn from God. Matthew 24:12 states, "Because iniquity shall abound, the love of many shall wax cold." Man has a tendency to trust in his riches more than he trusts in God. Revelation 3:17 states, "Because thou sayest, I am rich, and increased with goods, and have need of nothing." Many will seek wealth more than God. As 1 Timothy 6:10 states, "For the love of money is the root of all evil: which while some coveted after, they have erred from the faith, and pierced themselves through with many sorrows."

This woman was drunk with the blood of the saints. Revelation 17:6 states, "I saw the woman drunken with the blood of the saints." Drunken usually means to consume much alcohol. What the woman consumed was not alcohol. She had consumed a lot of blood from the saints and martyrs. She did not drink their blood. She merely shed their blood because they

---

[17] The New Strong's Complete Dictionary of Bible Words (Thomas Nelson Publishers, 1996), 685, 4203.

were followers of Jesus and would not participate in the antichrist's idolatrous doctrine. The cup the woman holds in her hand symbolizes all of the
abominable and idolatrous rituals carried out in the city of Babylon. The
symbolism of the cup is shown in Revelation 18:6, "Reward her even as
she rewarded you, and double unto her double according to her works: in
the cup which she hath filled fill to her double." This kingdom is primarily
a religious regime that teaches blasphemy and idolatry to its inhabitants.
Revelation 17:3 states, "Full of names of blasphemy." This kingdom rewards
its loyal supporters with enormous wealth. Revelation 18:19 states, "Alas,
alas, that great city, wherein were made rich."

The woman rides on the back of a beast, so she is in control of the beast.
This relationship is similar to a woman riding a horse. The woman is in
control of the horse, not the horse in control of the woman. The woman
(capital city) is riding on the back of the beast (kingdom), so the woman
(capital city) is in control of the beast (kingdom) or directing the path of the
kingdom's political and religious views. The woman (capital city) legislates
all of the laws for the beast (kingdom). Thinking in terms of government,
the kingdom whose capital city is Babylon has a leader or king who is in
charge of everything in his kingdom. The king of this particular kingdom is
the antichrist, and his title explains his agenda. He is the antichrist or against
Jesus Christ. That explains why the saints will undergo much distress during
his reign.

CHAPTER 9

THE SUN-CLOTHED WOMAN: A WONDER IN HEAVEN

Rev. 12:1   And there appeared a great wonder in heaven; a woman clothed with the sun, and the moon under her feet, and upon her head a crown of twelve stars:

Rev. 12:2   And she being with child cried, travailing in birth, and pained to be delivered.

JOHN was still in heaven, under the influence of the spirit and receiving the things that must be hereafter from the Angel of Jesus. The angel showed John a pregnant woman who was clothed with the sun. She had the moon under her feet. This woman also had a crown upon her head, and the crown had twelve stars. This woman was about to give birth, but she was struggling to deliver her child. To get more insight as to the identity of this woman, let's turn to the book of Genesis.

Joseph's First Dream

Gen. 37:3   Now Israel loved Joseph more than all his children, because he was the son of his old age: and he made him a coat of many colours.

Gen. 37:4   And when his brethren saw that their father loved him more than all his brethren, they hated him, and could not speak peaceably unto him.

Gen. 37:5   And Joseph dreamed a dream, and he told it his brethren: and they hated him yet the more.

Gen. 37:6   And he said unto them, Hear, I pray you, this dream which I have dreamed:

Gen. 37:7   For, behold, we were binding sheaves in the field, and, lo, my sheaf arose, and also stood upright; and, behold, your sheaves stood round about, and made obeisance to my sheaf.

Gen. 37:8   And his brethren said to him, Shalt thou indeed reign over us? or shalt thou indeed have dominion over us? And they hated him yet the more for his dreams, and for his words.

Joseph's father Jacob, whose name was changed to Israel, had twelve sons, but he loved Joseph more than he loved his other eleven sons. Israel's love for Joseph more than his other sons was probably because Joseph was the firstborn of Rachel, the woman for which he labored fourteen years for her to become his wife. Israel loved Joseph so much that he gave him a coat with many colors. Joseph's brothers had such a high level of hatred for him that they had nothing at all nice to say about him.

Joseph had a dream, and he told the dream to his brothers. They hated him even more. He dreamed of himself and his brothers binding sheaves or bundles. He dreamed his sheaves were greater than the sheaves of his brothers. Joseph's brothers understood the interpretation of the dream, and they questioned Joseph about it. They asked Joseph if he were insinuating that he would reign over them.

Joseph's Second Dream

Gen. 37:9   And he dreamed yet another dream, and told it his brethren, and said, Behold, I have dreamed a dream more; and, behold, the sun and the moon and the eleven stars made obeisance to me.

Gen. 37:10 And he told it to his father, and to his brethren: and his father rebuked him, and said unto him, What is this dream that thou hast dreamed? Shall I and thy mother and thy brethren indeed come to bow down ourselves to thee to the earth?

Joseph had another dream. He dreamed of the sun, moon, and eleven stars, and they all bowed down to him. This dream was very similar to the first dream, and the interpretation was exactly the same. This time, Joseph also told the dream to his father, who rebuked him because he understood the interpretation of the dream. Israel interpreted the dream to mean that Joseph would have dominion over his father, mother, and brothers.

According to Israel's interpretation of the dream, the sun represented Israel. The moon represented Joseph's mother, and the stars represented the tribes of Israel, a star for each of his brothers. Israel was the father of the twelve tribes of Israel. Rachel, Joseph's natural mother, was dead at this time, so Bilhah, Rachel's handmaid was considered Joseph's mother. The eleven brothers, plus Joseph, constituted the twelve tribes of Israel, so Joseph's dream was about the country of Israel.[18]

> Rev. 12:1   And there appeared a great wonder in heaven; a woman clothed with the sun, and the moon under her feet, and upon her head a crown of twelve stars:

John saw a woman. The symbolism for a woman is a city. Revelation 17:18 states, "The woman which thou sawest is that great city." So the woman that John saw was a city. There is also a woman or great city in Revelation 17:18. Do not confuse this city in Revelation 17:18 with the woman or city in Revelation 12:1. They are entirely two different cities. This woman (city) that John saw in Revelation 12:1 was clothed with the sun (Israel). Clothing is something that one wears to cover his body. The inhabitants of a city are considered the clothing for that city. The clothing for this city is the sun (Children of Israel), so this woman (city) is in the nation of Israel. This woman clothed with the sun has the moon (Joseph's mother) under her feet. Joseph's mother was dead and buried, so the moon (Joseph's mother) is under the woman's feet because she's buried in Israel. The woman has a crown upon her head. The crown consists of twelve stars (twelve tribes). Just like the stars on the United States flag represents states, the twelve stars in the crown represents the twelve tribes of Israel. Revelation

---

18 Clarence Larkin, The Book of Revelation (1919), 90.

1:20 states that stars represents angels, but the emphasis in this case is on the crown that contains the twelve stars, not the stars themselves. The stars are a part of the crown. This city is in Israel, and this city represents the twelve tribes of Israel. So one must conclude this woman is the city of Jerusalem.

In fact, throughout the Bible, the city of Jerusalem has been the focal point. Jerusalem is where Jesus instructed the one hundred and twenty to wait for the promise of the Father. Acts 1:4 states, "Commanded them that they should not depart from Jerusalem, but wait for the promise of the Father."

Jerusalem is the city where man first experienced the power of the Holy Ghost as a group, and people from several different nations witnessed it. Jerusalem is the Holy City, and the woman clothed with the sun in Revelation 12:1.

The Man-child

Rev. 12:2   And she being with child cried, travailing in birth, and pained to be delivered.

Rev. 12:5   And she brought forth a man-child, who was to rule all nations with a rod of iron: and her child was caught up unto God, and to his throne.

Jerusalem was struggling to give birth. She was about to give birth in a difficult time. She finally gave birth, and the child was a son or a man-child. Contrary to popular belief, this son or man-child is not Jesus. Yes, it is true that Jesus was born in Israel, but remember that the book of Revelation was written after the death of Jesus, so the man-child cannot be Jesus. The Angel of Jesus is revealing things that are future (things that must be hereafter) in reference to the time the book of Revelation was written.

Let's take a closer look and determine the exact identity of the man-child. The woman (Jerusalem) brought forth a man-child, and the man-child was to rule the nations with a rod of iron. In order to understand the man-child, we must first understand the covenant that God made with Abraham. According to the terms of the covenant, all male children had to be circumcised. Genesis 17:10 states, "This is my covenant, which ye shall keep, between me and you and thy seed after thee; every man-child among you shall be circumcised." This mark in their skin was like a seal to show they belonged to God. Man-child represents the followers of God. In Revelation 2:26–27, John tells the church of Thyatira that, if they overcome, they will receive power over the nations to rule them with a rod of iron. This man-child has the same authority as the ones who overcome and keep the words of Jesus until the end. They will rule the nations with a rod of iron. This man-child is not an individual. This man-child is a group that follows the teachings of Jesus. It is a group of born-again people from Jerusalem because Jerusalem is the woman giving birth. I know that some are saying that the man-child is Jesus because Jesus was caught up to the throne. Jesus is in heaven. He was there in heaven before the book of Revelation was written. The book of Revelation was written after the ascension of Jesus into heaven. The book of Revelation is about future things, so it must be restated that the man-child cannot be Jesus.

I know most people think of a man-child as an individual. It is stated that he who overcomes will rule the nations with a rod of iron. Revelation 2:26–27, "He that overcometh, and keepeth my works unto the end, to him will I give power over the nations ... he shall rule them with a rod of iron." The reference made concerning the phrase "he who overcomes" is not singular. It is inclusive of all of those who overcome, whosoever will. The book of Isaiah can shed more light on this subject concerning the woman (city of Jerusalem) giving birth.

Isa.66:7   Before she travailed, she brought forth; before her pain came, she was delivered of a man-child.

Isa.66:8   Who hath heard such a thing? who hath seen such things? Shall the earth be made to bring forth in one day? or shall a nation be born at once? for as soon as Zion travailed, she brought forth her children.

The woman is the city of Jerusalem or inhabitants of Jerusalem. Jerusalem is pregnant, or some of its inhabitants are ready to accept Jesus Christ as their Lord and Savior. She gave birth to a man-child before her birth pains reached their peak. Isaiah 66:8 tells us that she gave birth in one day, and a nation or group of people was born (born again) at once. As soon as Zion or Jerusalem travailed, she brought forth her children. Children is the plural form of child. The man-child is not an individual, but a group of people who have just received Jesus as their Lord and Savior.

The woman (Jerusalem) gave birth to the man-child. Then she (Jerusalem or the inhabitants) fled into the wilderness. In the wilderness, the man-child was caught up to God, but not all of the inhabitants of Jerusalem. It was only the man-child, that is, those recently born again. Revelation 12:6 states, "The woman fled into the wilderness, where she hath a place prepared of God, that they should feed her there a thousand two hundred and three-score days." God had a place prepared for the man-child, and the man-child was fed in the wilderness for a specific amount of time. The man-child was nourished in the wilderness for 1,260 days.

The man-child was the 144,000 who were sealed before any green grass or trees could be burned. Revelation 7:3-4 states:

Hurt not the earth, neither the sea, nor the trees, till we have sealed the servants of our God in their foreheads ... I heard the number of them which were sealed: and there were sealed an hundred and forty and four thousand of all the tribes of the children of Israel.

The seal was protecting them from harm. Likewise in the wilderness, they were also in a protected status. The man-child receiving the mark of circumcision in their foreskins in Genesis 17:10, parallels with the man-child (144,000) receiving the seal of the living God on their foreheads in Revelation 7:3.

When the fifth seal is broken, the locust comes out of the bottomless pit. They will have authority to torment only those men who do not have the seal of God on their foreheads. Revelation 9:4 states, "And it was commanded them that they should not hurt the grass of the earth, neither any green thing, neither any tree; but only those men which have not the seal of God in their foreheads." The 144,000 are the only ones who have this seal. They are the ones protected by God in the wilderness (not in heaven) for 1,260 days. Revelation 12:6 states, "She hath a place prepared of God, that they should feed her there a thousand two hundred and threescore days." The woman's (Jerusalem) inhabitants fled into the wilderness. Not all of the inhabitants were born-again. Only the 144,000 who were previously sealed received protection in the wilderness in a place that God had prepared. The man-child is the 144,000.

Rev. 14:1   And I looked, and, lo, a Lamb stood on the mount Sion, and with him an hundred forty and four thousand, having his Father's name written in their foreheads.

Rev. 14:2   And I heard a voice from heaven, as the voice of many waters, and as the voice of a great thunder: and I heard the voice of harpers harping with their harps:

Rev. 14:3   And they sung as it were a new song before the throne, and before the four beasts, and the elders: and no man could learn that song but the hundred and forty and four thousand, which were redeemed from the earth.

Rev. 14:4   These are they which were not defiled with women; for they are virgins. These are they which follow the Lamb whithersoever he goeth. These were redeemed from among men, being the firstfruits unto God and to the Lamb.

Rev. 14:5   And in their mouth was found no guile: for they are without fault before the throne of God.

John saw 144,000 standing on Mount Sion with their father's name written on their foreheads. This name is the seal of God. Revelation 7:3 states, "Till we have sealed the servants of our God in their foreheads." This 144,000 is not in heaven, as most men visualize heaven, but they are in the presence of the Holy Spirit because they are protected. Revelation 12:6 says, "Hath a place prepared of God." If they are in heaven, there would be no need for the locust to be instructed not to hurt the men with the seal of God on their foreheads. Revelation 9:4 states, "It was commanded them that they should not hurt … but only those men which have not the seal of God in their foreheads." They are virgins on earth, not in a sexual sense, but born again where their sins are forgotten or forgiven. Hebrews 10:17 states, "And their sins and iniquities will I remember no more." They are the first ones (first fruits or first Jews) redeemed from among men on the earth. Romans

1:16 states, "To the Jew first, and also to the Greek." The 144,000 are Jewish people, not Gentiles.

Redeemed does not automatically mean they are in heaven. The word *redeemed* means they are saved from something. The something from which they are saved is Satan and his angels. For instance, Jesus came into the world to redeem mankind. Luke 1:68 states, "Blessed be the Lord God of Israel; for he hath visited and redeemed his people." Everyone who is born-again has been redeemed, but they are still right here on earth in a physical body. The act of redeeming does not mean a transformation from the physical body to the spiritual body. Redemption indicates that one is in a protected status. The 144,000 are in a place on earth, prepared by God for a specific amount of time. Revelation 12:6 states, "A thousand two hundred and threescore days."

Some will say they are on Mount Zion. The text states they are on Mount Sion. According to the Greek, Sion #4622 is a hill of Jerusalem, or capital.[19] Sion also refers back to the Hebrew word #6726, a mountain or permanent capital.[20] The Hebrew word #6726 refers to the root words #6725 and #6723, which means desert, barren, dry place, solidarity place, or wilderness.[21] This describes the conditions of the place where the inhabitants of Jerusalem fled in the wilderness. Heaven is not a barren place. God protected the 144,000 in the wilderness for 1,260 days. Mount Sion is a temporary capital whereas they will only be there a specific amount of time. Mount Zion is the permanent capital, whereas they will be there for an eternity.

In case someone is having trouble with the phrase in Revelation 12:5, "Caught up unto God," remember that Paul was caught up into paradise, but he remained in the flesh, as stated in 2 Corinthians 12:3–4: "Whether in the body, or out of the body, I cannot tell: God knoweth ... how that he was caught up into paradise, and heard unspeakable words."

---

[19] The New Strong's Complete Dictionary of Bible Words (Thomas Nelson Publishers, 1996), 235, 698.

[20] The New Strong's Complete Dictionary of Bible Words (Thomas Nelson Publishers, 1996), 235, 499.

[21] The New Strong's Complete Dictionary of Bible Words (Thomas Nelson Publishers, 1996), 235, 499.

Another Wonder in Heaven

Rev. 12:3   And there appeared another wonder in heaven; and behold a great red dragon, having seven heads and ten horns, and seven crowns upon his heads.

Rev. 13:1   And I stood upon the sand of the sea, and saw a beast rise up out of the sea, having seven heads and ten horns, and upon his horns ten crowns, and upon his heads the name of blasphemy.

Rev. 17:3   So he carried me away in the spirit into the wilderness: and I saw a woman sit upon a scarlet coloured beast, full of names of blasphemy, having seven heads and ten horns.

John also saw another wonder in heaven, a great red dragon. This dragon is none other than Satan himself. Revelation 12:9 states, "The great dragon was cast out, that old serpent, called the Devil, and Satan." Satan is the spiritual force of the beast with seven heads and ten horns. Revelation 13:1–2 states, "And saw a beast rise up out of the sea, having seven heads and ten horns … and the dragon gave him his power, and his seat, and great authority." John saw this same beast in Revelation 13:1 and 17:3, with one slight difference. The beast in Revelation 12:3 only had seven crowns while the beast in Revelation 13:1 and 17:3 both had ten crowns. Revelation 17 does not literally say the beast has ten crowns, but it does state that the beast has ten horns. Horns are symbolic for kings. Revelation 17:12 states, "The ten horns which thou sawest are ten kings." Because there are ten kings, so there are ten crowns. The book of Daniel explains why this beast or dragon only has seven crowns. Daniel 7:24 states, "The ten horns out of this kingdom are ten kings that shall arise: and another shall rise after them; and he shall be diverse from the first, and he shall subdue three kings." The ten horns (kings) join themselves together to form this beast or kingdom. Another king or leader rises after the ten-king kingdom is formed. This leader subdues three kings, leaving only seven of the original ten kings. This can be confirmed in Revelation 17, where an eighth king was mentioned. Revelation 17:11 states, "The beast that was, and is not, even he is the eighth, and is of the seven, and goeth into perdition." This leader subdues three kings and assumes leadership. The beast in Revelation 12:3 is the same beast that is in Revelation 13:1 and Revelation 17:3, but only after three of the original ten kings have been overthrown. Because each king has a crown and three kings will be overthrown, the red dragon will only be left with seven crowns.

This beast is the seventh or final worldly kingdom, and the antichrist, the eighth king, rules it. The kingdom itself is a worldly kingdom, but a spiritual influence, the great red dragon, overshadows it. Revelation 13:1–2 states, "I stood upon the sand of the sea, and saw a beast rise up out of the sea ... and the dragon gave him his power, and his seat, and great authority." We learn the identity of the great red dragon in Revelation 12:9, "The great dragon was cast out, that old serpent, called the Devil, and Satan, which deceiveth the whole world: he was cast out into the earth." The wonder in heaven that John witnessed is Satan, and he is lending his influence over the seventh and final worldly kingdom.

War in Heaven

Rev. 12:7   And there was war in heaven: Michael and his angels fought against the dragon; and the dragon fought and his angels,

Rev. 12:8   And prevailed not; neither was their place found any more in heaven.

Rev. 12:9   And the great dragon was cast out, that old serpent, called the Devil, and Satan, which deceiveth the whole world: he was cast out into the earth, and his angels were cast out with him.

John saw a war being fought in heaven. The foes in this war are Michael, the archangel, and his angels against Satan and his angels. Satan and his angels lost the battle in heaven. They were expelled from heaven and exiled to the earth. Some will say that Satan was kicked out of heaven many years ago, but here is some scripture that supports the fact that Satan still has access to heaven.

It is a known fact that Satan was in the garden of Eden. Ezekiel 28:12–15 states, "Thou hast been in Eden the garden of God." Iniquity was found in

Satan, and he lost his position in heaven. He lost his high position in heaven, but he did not lose his access to heaven.

It is a known fact that Satan will be cast down to the bottomless pit. Revelation 20:1–3 states, "He laid hold on the dragon, that old serpent, which is the Devil, and Satan … And cast him into the bottomless pit." The act of kicking Satan down to hell or the bottomless pit has not taken place yet. If so, he would not have authority to deceive the nations. Revelation 20:3 states," Shut him up, and set a seal upon him, that he should deceive the nations no more, till the thousand years should be fulfilled." This is future. Satan has not yet been confined to the bottomless pit. When he enters the bottomless pit, there will be peace on earth for one thousand years. Revelation 20:3 states, "That he should deceive the nations no more," but there will be unrest on earth once again when he is released from the bottomless pit. Revelation 20:7–8 states, "When the thousand years are expired, Satan shall be loosed out of his prison, And shall go out to deceive the nations."

There was a time when the sons of God went in to the presence of God, and Satan was with them. Job 1:6 states, "Now there was a day when the sons of God came to present themselves before the LORD, and Satan came also among them." Here we have Satan in the presence of God or in heaven. Satan was also in heaven, engaged in conversation with God. Job 2:6–7 states, "And the LORD said unto Satan, behold, he is in thine hand; but save his life … so went Satan forth from the presence of the LORD, and smote Job." Satan is there in heaven right now, pointing his finger at Christians every time they make the slightest mistake. He stands before God day and night, accusing Christians. Revelation 12:10 states, "Now is come salvation, and strength, and the kingdom of our God, and the power of his Christ: for the accuser of our brethren is cast down, which accused them before our God day and night." Satan has not been kicked out of heaven yet. He will not be kicked out until the End-time. When Satan is kicked out of heaven, the heavens will rejoice, but the earth will be devastated because Satan will bring great wrath upon the earth. Revelation 12:12 states, "Therefore rejoice, ye heavens, and ye that dwell in them. Woe to the inhabiters of the earth and of the sea! for the devil is come down unto you, having great wrath, because he knoweth that he hath but a short time." This short time is actually the End-time. This same period of time is described in the book of Matthew as the great tribulation. Matthew 24:15–21 states, "When ye therefore shall see the abomination of desolation … stand in the holy place … for then shall be great tribulation, such as was not since the beginning of the world to this time, no, nor ever shall be." When Satan is forced to leave heaven forever, it will be a time of great tribulation here on earth.

> Rev. 12:4   And his tail drew the third part of the stars of heaven, and did cast them to the earth: and the dragon stood before the woman which was ready to be delivered, for to devour her child as soon as it was born.
>
> Rev. 12:9   And the great dragon was cast out, that old serpent, called the Devil, and Satan, which deceiveth the whole world: he was cast out into the earth, and his angels were cast out with him.

Satan is the great red dragon, the spiritual influence over the antichrist's kingdom. Satan and his angels will lose the war in heaven and will be exiled to the earth, so their access to heaven will be terminated. The tail of Satan will draw one-third of the stars in heaven with him when he is cast into the earth. The stars represent angels. Revelation 1:20 states, "The seven stars are the angels." Satan corrupted one-third of the angels, and he will take them with him when he is cast into the earth. Because Satan and his angels will assume residency in the earth, he decides he will make war with the woman (Jerusalem), who recently gave birth to the man-child (144,000), in order to devour the child soon after it is born. Throughout the Bible, this has been Satan's pattern, to devour any child who he deems to be a threat to him. The man-child is no different. The man-child is the 144,000 Jews from Jerusalem who recently became born again.

Post War in Heaven

> Rev. 12:9   And the great dragon was cast out, that old serpent, called the Devil, and Satan, which deceiveth the whole world: he was cast out into the earth, and his angels were cast out with him.
>
> Rev. 12:10 And I heard a loud voice saying in heaven, Now is

come salvation, and strength, and the kingdom of our God, and the power of his Christ: for the accuser of our brethren is cast down, which accused them before our God day and night.

Rev. 12:11 And they overcame him by the blood of the Lamb, and by the word of their testimony; and they loved not their lives unto the death.

Rev. 12:12 Therefore rejoice, ye heavens, and ye that dwell in them. Woe to the inhabiters of the earth and of the sea! for the devil is come down unto you, having great wrath, because he knoweth that he hath but a short time.

Satan and his angels have just been expelled from heaven onto the earth. There will be rejoicing in heaven because Satan will no longer have access to heaven, but there will be misery and turmoil on earth because Satan will relocate here. When Satan realizes he is on the earth, he will be very angry because he knows he will not have much time before his judgment. Because his days are numbered, he will turn to the woman (Jerusalem) to persecute her.

Woman's Persecution

Rev. 12:13 And when the dragon saw that he was cast unto the earth, he persecuted the woman which brought forth the man-child.

Satan and his angels will find themselves thrown down to the earth, and their access to heaven has been terminated. Satan realizes his time is short, so he will begin a campaign of terror. The woman (Jerusalem) has just given birth to the 144,000 (man-child), so Satan will target the woman (Jerusalem) to begin his path of destruction.

Rev. 12:6 And the woman fled into the wilderness, where she hath a place prepared of God, that they should feed her there a thousand two hundred and threescore days.

The woman (inhabitants of Jerusalem) will see the antichrist's army surrounding the city of Jerusalem. They will immediately become aware that it is time to flee from the city. Luke 21:20–22 states:

When ye shall see Jerusalem compassed with armies, then know that the desolation thereof is nigh. Then let them which are in Judaea flee to the mountains ... for these be the days of vengeance, that all things which are written may be fulfilled.

Not all of the inhabitants of Jerusalem will be sealed, only the man-child or 144,000. When the inhabitants of Jerusalem flee into the wilderness, some will be killed while others will be protected. Only the ones who are sealed (man-child) will be protected.

Rev. 12:14   And to the woman were given two wings of a great eagle, that she might fly into the wilderness, into her place, where she is nourished for a time, and times, and half a time, from the face of the serpent.

Rev. 12:15   And the serpent cast out of his mouth water as a flood after the woman, that he might cause her to be carried away of the flood.

Rev. 12:16   And the earth helped the woman, and the earth opened her mouth, and swallowed up the flood which the dragon cast out of his mouth.

Rev. 12:17   And the dragon was wroth with the woman, and went to make war with the remnant of her seed, which keep the commandments of God, and have the testimony of Jesus Christ.

The woman (Jerusalem) will see an army surrounding Jerusalem (the city), thus triggering the inhabitants of Jerusalem to flee into the wilderness. Satan will be angry with the inhabitants because they will be fleeing from the city, so he will use the antichrist to send water as a flood to capture the woman (inhabitants fleeing Jerusalem). The waters represent people. Revelation 17:15 states, "The waters which thou sawest, where the whore sitteth, are peoples, and multitudes, and nations, and tongues." The waters that Satan (antichrist) will send after the woman (Jerusalem) is an actual army. The water is a flood of people. The woman (Jerusalem) will be given help from the earth. The earth will open up and swallow the army. The ones who will escape the army will be the man-child (144,000) who will be nourished in the wilderness for a time, times, and one-half time. A time is one year. Times is two years. One-half a time is one half year. When you add it together, it totals to three-and-a-half years. This is equivalent to 1,260 days. Revelation 12:6 states, "A thousand two hundred and threescore days." After the antichrist's army is swallowed up, Satan will be very angry, so he will turn and go to make war with the rest of Israel, specifically those who keep the commandments of God.

The woman clothed with the sun and the moon under her feet is Jerusalem. The twelve stars in the crown are the twelve tribes of Israel. The man-child birthed by the woman is the 144,000 Jewish people who will be the first fruits, sealed on their foreheads. The war in heaven is when Satan and his angels will be permanently exiled from heaven to earth. Once Satan realizes he is deported to earth, he will persecute the woman (Jerusalem). Satan (antichrist) will send an army after the woman, but an earthquake will swallow it up. This parallels with the Red Sea opening, allowing the children of Israel to pass through and then swallowing the Egyptian army as they pursued them. Satan (antichrist) now turns to make war with those who are left in Israel, especially the practicing Jews. The ones saved in the wilderness and nourished by God for 1,260 days is the 144,000 (man-child). These are the first fruits or first Jewish people actually protected by God from the antichrist while still here on earth. The 144,000 are at a temporary capital in the wilderness, and they will be there for 1,260 days.

CHAPTER 10

THE TWO WITNESSES

Rev. 11:1   And there was given me a reed like unto a rod: and the angel stood, saying, Rise, and measure the temple of God, and the altar, and them that worship therein.

Rev. 11:2   But the court which is without the temple leave out, and measure it not; for it is given unto the Gentiles: and the holy city shall they tread under foot forty and two months.

JOHN was still in the presence of the Angel of Jesus. The angel gave John a measuring reed, an instrument for measuring, such as a tape measure or yardstick. The angel instructed John to measure the temple of God in Jerusalem and the altar and count the people who worship in the temple. He was instructed not to measure the court outside of the temple because it will be given to the Gentiles. The period of time when the outer court of the temple and the city of Jerusalem will be trodden underfoot by the Gentiles is considered part of the times of the Gentiles. Luke 21:24 states, "And Jerusalem shall be trodden down of the Gentiles, until the times of the Gentiles be fulfilled." The Gentiles will occupy the Holy City, Jerusalem, for forty-two months. The timing of this occupation coincides with the same time period that the woman is protected in the wilderness. Revelation 12:6 states, "The woman fled into the wilderness, where she hath a place prepared of God, that they should feed her there a thousand two hundred and three-score days." Immediately after the antichrist fails to capture the fleeing woman, he then turns back to occupy Jerusalem. Revelation 12:16–17 states, "The earth helped the woman, and the earth opened her mouth, and swallowed up the flood which the dragon cast out of his mouth … the dragon was wroth with the woman, and went to make war with the remnant of her seed."

The angel told John to measure the temple and altar and count the people who worship in the temple, but not measure the outer court because it was given to the Gentiles. This indicates that the Gentiles will not have access to the inside of the temple and altar area. They will only be allowed to assemble in the outer court. John was instructed to measure the temple in Jerusalem, so the temple will have to be constructed before or at the End-time.

Two Witnesses

> Rev. 11:3   And I will give power unto my two witnesses, and they shall prophesy a thousand two hundred and threescore days, clothed in sackcloth.
>
> Rev. 11:4   These are the two olive trees, and the two candlesticks standing before the God of the earth.

The Angel of Jesus told John that power would be given to the two witnesses, and they shall prophesy for 1,260 days, which is equivalent to forty-two months, the same amount of time the Gentiles will tread the city of Jerusalem and the outer court underfoot.

Because the Gentiles will tread underfoot the outer court of the temple for forty-two months and the two witnesses' ministry will also last for forty-two months, it is reasonable to conclude that these two periods of time coincide. It is obvious that the two witnesses are in Jerusalem, the Holy City, and they are there to proclaim the word of God.

During their prophecy, the two witnesses will be wearing sackcloth or very hard, rough clothing, usually associated with mourning. The angel probably sensed that John was puzzled about the two witnesses because John was immediately given more information concerning them. The angel told John that the two witnesses were two olive trees and two candlesticks standing before the God of the whole earth. The two olive trees and two candlesticks are the two witnesses. They are not separate. One olive tree and one candlestick represent each witness. In order to better understand the symbolization of the olives trees, let's go to the book of Zechariah.[22]

Zec. 4:12   And I answered again, and said unto him, What be these two olive branches which through the two golden pipes empty the golden oil out of themselves?

Zec. 4:13   And he answered me and said, Knowest thou not what these be? And I said, No, my lord.

Zec. 4:14   Then said he, These are the two anointed ones, that stand by the Lord of the whole earth.

This text shows Zechariah talking with an angel. The angel told Zechariah that the two olive branches are two anointed ones who stand by the God of the whole earth. The two witnesses are two anointed ones, who are special and have been consecrated. In an earthly sense, olive trees produce oil. Oil is also associated with anointing. If someone is under the anointing, he is said to be controlled or led by the spirit of God.

The fact these two anointed ones are referred to as witnesses indicates these two olives trees or witnesses have been in very close proximity with God. They will come to Jerusalem in the End-time to give account of what they experienced. In this case, the two witnesses are to give account of the sacredness and righteousness of God. Their mission is to reveal God to the inhabitants of Jerusalem and keep the altar from being trodden underfoot by the Gentiles. The text does not indicate if it is all Gentiles or just the unsaved Gentiles who trod down Jerusalem, but the mere fact that Jerusalem is being overrun and the place of worship is measured by the two witnesses suggests it is only the unsaved Gentiles running rampant through Jerusalem.

The olive trees represent the anointed ones (Zec. 4:14). Now let's take a closer look at the candlesticks. The candlesticks represent churches according to Revelation 1:20, "And the seven candlesticks which thou sawest are the seven churches." Because candlesticks represent churches and there are two candlesticks or witnesses, then this represents two churches. There are two witnesses represented by two candlesticks (two churches). The olives trees that produce oil represent the anointing power of God. God always

---

[22] Torah Light Ministries, Stanley Chester, taped message.

uses man to carry out his work here on earth, so the two witnesses are two men (prophets). Revelation 11:10 states, "These two prophets" have the anointing power of God. They are the head of two churches, who are in Jerusalem proclaiming the word of God.

The scripture tells us that the two witnesses are two candlesticks or two churches. A church is not necessarily the building where religious services are rendered. The church can be that building, but it also means a calling out, congregation, Jewish synagogue, community of members, and assembly.[23] The first group of people that God called out under the Old Testament was Israel, with the covenant he made with Abraham. Later when Christ came, another group of people was called out, those who were born again under the New Testament. This invitation was even extended to the Gentiles. The two witnesses are two men who have the anointing of God, and they are proclaiming the word of God in Jerusalem. In other words, these two men are prophets of God. Revelation 11:10 states, "Because these two prophets."

Witnesses' Authority

Rev. 11:5   And if any man will hurt them, fire proceedeth out of their mouth, and devoureth their enemies: and if any man will hurt them, he must in this manner be killed.

The temple and altar is being set apart only for people who are saved or worship in the temple. Unsaved people are denied access. The two witnesses measured this area in an effort to set up boundaries or limitations for the unsaved. This area is holy ground. The two witnesses are there to protect it and keep it holy. They are in the midst of Jerusalem, prophesying to the unsaved, and their enemies do not receive them well. Revelation 11:10 states, "Because these two prophets tormented them." Although the two witnesses are righteous men, they still have the authority to protect themselves because their ministry is for a specific amount of time. Revelation 11:3 states, "And they shall prophesy a thousand two hundred and threescore days." If anyone hurts them, fire proceeds out of their mouths and destroys their enemies.

---

[23] The New Strong's Complete Dictionary of Bible Words (Thomas Nelson Publishers, 1996), 611.

This fire that proceeds out of their mouths is not some physical or literal fire. This can better be explained in the books of Jeremiah and Isaiah.

Jer. 5:14   Wherefore thus saith the LORD God of hosts, Because ye speak this word, behold, I will make my words in thy mouth fire, and this people wood, and it shall devour them.

Isa. 30:27   Behold, the name of the LORD cometh from far, burning with his anger, and the burden thereof is heavy: his lips are full of indignation, and his tongue as a devouring fire:

Other scriptures show a devouring fire does not have to be a literal fire, but the power of God. The two witnesses use the word of God to defend themselves from their enemies. They merely use words and speak them with the authority of Almighty God. Mark 11:24 states, "Therefore I say unto you, what things soever ye desire, when ye pray, believe that ye receive them, and ye shall have them." An example of words spoken with authority is in Genesis 1:3, "And God said, let there be light: and there was light." Another example of words spoken with authority is in Mark 4:39, "He arose, and rebuked the wind, and said unto the sea, peace, be still. and the wind ceased, and there was a great calm." The two witnesses have the anointing of God, so their words are received and acted upon immediately by the spirit of God.

Witnesses' Identity

Rev. 11:6   These have power to shut heaven, that it rain not in the days of their prophecy: and have power over waters to turn them to blood, and to smite the earth with all plagues, as often as they will.

During the ministry of the two witnesses, they will have the authority to stop it from raining, turn water into blood, and bring plagues on the earth at their will. Because the Bible is the source of all interpretation, let's see if we can find some biblical people who were instrumental in the same acts as the two witnesses.

In Exodus 7, we find that Moses was instrumental in plaguing the earth with locusts, flies, boils, and turning the river into blood. Moses demonstrated he possessed or had been used in the same capacity as the authority of the two witnesses.

In 1 Kings 17:1, we find that Elijah was used to shut the heavens from raining. Again in 1 Kings 18:41–46, we see Elijah was used again in causing an abundance of rain. In 2 Kings 1:10, Elijah was used to call fire down from heaven. We now have two men that, at one time or another, had been used by God in the same capacity as the authority of the two witnesses, so it is reasonable to conclude that Elijah and Moses are possible candidates for the two witnesses.

We should also consider something else. Jesus was transfigured on a mountain just before his crucifixion, and he communicated with two men. Mark 9:2–4 states, "And he was transfigured before them … there appeared unto them Elias with Moses: and they were talking with Jesus." The two men with whom Jesus talked was Moses and Elias (Elijah).

Some will say the two witnesses cannot be Moses and Elijah because Moses died many years ago. Still others will say the two witnesses are Elijah and Enoch. The reason for this line of thinking is that Elijah and Enoch never died. God took both of them in a whirlwind. They think Enoch and Elijah have to return to earth to die because it is appointed unto men once to die. Hebrews 9:27 states, "As it is appointed unto men once to die, but after this the judgment." Let's look at some other possibilities.

Mal. 4:5   Behold, I will send you Elijah the prophet before the coming of the great and dreadful day of the LORD:

Elijah the Prophet is supposed to return before the great and dreadful day of the Lord, but, when we look at the words of Jesus, we see Elias (Elijah) has already returned. Matthew 17:12 states, "I say unto you, that Elias is come already, and they knew him not." Jesus said John the Baptist was Elijah. Matthew 11:14 states, "If ye will receive it, this is Elias, which was for to come." Some will say that, because Elijah was raptured and never died, he will have to return to earth to die. We know John the Baptist was beheaded.

Matthew 14:10 states, "He sent, and beheaded John in the prison." If Elijah and John the Baptist is the same individual, then Elijah died as John the Baptist? This destroys the theory that Elijah has to return to earth to die because he died as John the Baptist.

There's not much recorded in the Bible about Enoch except that he walked with God and God took him. Genesis 5:24 states, "Enoch walked with God: and he was not; for God took him." There is a lot of information recorded about Elijah, so let's see what Jesus had to say about him.

> Mat. 17:10 And his disciples asked him, saying, Why then say the scribes that Elias must first come?
>
> Mat. 17:11 And Jesus answered and said unto them, Elias truly shall first come, and restore all things.
>
> Mat. 17:12 But I say unto you, That Elias is come already, and they knew him not, but have done unto him whatsoever they listed. Likewise shall also the Son of man suffer of them.
>
> Mat. 17:13 Then the disciples understood that he spake unto them of John the Baptist.

Jesus told the disciples that Elijah must come first and restore all things. Then he told them that Elijah had already come. This seems like double talk, but, in verse 13, it is clear that Jesus was speaking of John the Baptist. If Jesus was saying that Elijah had already returned to earth as John the Baptist, this is a close resemblance to reincarnation. The book of Luke sheds more light on this matter.

> Luk. 1:11 And there appeared unto him an angel of the Lord standing on the right side of the altar of incense.
>
> Luk. 1:12 And when Zacharias saw him, he was troubled, and fear fell upon him.
>
> Luk. 1:13 But the angel said unto him, Fear not, Zacharias: for thy prayer is heard; and thy wife Elisabeth shall bear thee a son, and thou shalt call his name John.
>
> Luk. 1:14 And thou shalt have joy and gladness; and many shall rejoice at his birth.
>
> Luk. 1:15 For he shall be great in the sight of the Lord, and shall

drink neither wine nor strong drink; and he shall be filled with the Holy Ghost, even from his mother's womb.

Luk. 1:16   And many of the children of Israel shall he turn to the Lord their God.

Luk. 1:17   And he shall go before him in the spirit and power of Elias, to turn the hearts of the fathers to the children, and the disobedient to the wisdom of the just; to make ready a people prepared for the Lord.

When the angel told Zacharias that his wife Elizabeth was going to have a son, he also told Zacharias what to name him, John. The angel also told Zacharias that John was to be great in the sight of the Lord and John was to come before Jesus in the spirit and power of Elijah. So we see that John the Baptist had the spirit and power of Elijah. These are entirely two different men, but they have the same ways, character, and intellect. They have the same spirit from God.

Because it is possible for men to be born in the same spirit and power as other men before them, we conclude these two witnesses are two mortal men of the last days that have the same spirit and power of Elijah and Moses.[24] These two men will come in the spirit and power of Moses and Elijah, and they will have authority over rain, fire, and plagues.

Some will disagree that the two witnesses will be two men with the same spirit as Elijah and Moses because they think the two men will have the same spirit as two other men, namely Elijah and Enoch. It really doesn't matter whose spirits the two witnesses will have. All of the candidates lived in the Old Testament. No one from the End-time will recognize either of these two men anyway. They never knew them.

Earlier, it was determined that the two witnesses (candlesticks) represented two churches or two congregations. These two groups are of people from both the New and Old Testaments. We know Moses lived in the Old Testament, so one of the witnesses is an individual who will live in the End-time with the same spirit and power of Moses. He is a representative of the Old Testament.

---

[24] Torah Light Ministries, Stanley Chester, taped message.

The second witness is a man who lives in the End-time with the same spirit and power as Elijah. I know some are saying Elijah lived in the Old Testament. Yes, that's true, but John the Baptist was a man who had the same spirit and power of Elijah. Actually, John the Baptist lived between the Old and New Testament. John the Baptist lived at the end of the law or Old Testament and the beginning of grace or New Testament. John the Baptist came before Christ to prepare the way for him. Matthew 3:3 states, "Prepare ye the way of the Lord, make his paths straight." John the Baptist was to precede Jesus to prepare the people and make them ready for the arrival of Jesus. Luke 1:17 states, "To turn the hearts of the fathers to the children, and the disobedient to the wisdom of the just; to make ready a people prepared for the Lord." Once again, one of the witnesses will be in the spirit and power of Elijah sent into the earth to prepare or warn the people before the return of Christ. Malachi 4:5–6 states, "I will send you Elijah the prophet before the coming of the great and dreadful day of the LORD … he shall turn the heart of the fathers to the children, and the heart of the children to their fathers."

Jesus did not come into the world to change the law. He came to fulfill the law. Matthew 5:17 states, "Think not that I am come to destroy the law, or the prophets: I am not come to destroy, but to fulfil." Jesus lived and fulfilled the law while he was here on earth. Once Jesus fulfilled the Law, mankind could now be moved into the period of grace. John the Baptist lived in a transitional period between the Old and New Testament. The second witness will have the same spirit and power as Elijah and John the Baptist, but he will live in the End-time of the New Testament. See the transformation: first Elijah from the Old Testament and then John the Baptist in a transitional period between the Old Testament and New Testament. Finally, there is the second witness from the New Testament. There we have both the Old and New Testament represented by these two witnesses.

Witnesses' Post Ministry

Rev. 11:7   And when they shall have finished their testimony, the beast that ascendeth out of the bottomless pit shall make war against them, and shall overcome them, and kill them.

Rev. 11:8   And their dead bodies shall lie in the street of the great city, which spiritually is called Sodom and Egypt, where also our Lord was crucified.

Rev. 11:9   And they of the people and kindreds and tongues and nations shall see their dead bodies three days and an half, and shall not suffer their dead bodies to be put in graves.

Rev. 11:10 And they that dwell upon the earth shall rejoice over them, and make merry, and shall send gifts one to another; because these two prophets tormented them that dwelt on the earth.

After the two witnesses finish their prophecy, the beast from the bottomless pit will make war with them, and he succeeds in killing them. The beast that ascends out of the bottomless pit is Satan. Revelation 20:1–3 states, "He laid hold on the dragon, that old serpent, which is the Devil, and Satan … cast him into the bottomless pit, and shut him up." Revelation 20:7 states, "When the thousand years are expired, Satan shall be loosed out of his prison." Satan is the spiritual force or influence that gives the antichrist his power and authority. Revelation 13:2 states, "And the dragon gave him his power, and his seat, and great authority." This beast is none other than the antichrist, the leader of the seventh and final kingdom, with the spirit of Satan.

At the completion of their mission, the two witnesses' anointing will be lifted, and the antichrist will kill them. The two witnesses' dead bodies will lie in the streets of Jerusalem for three-and-a-half days. The inhabitants will be so happy that the two witnesses are dead that they will not allow their bodies to be buried. The people even exchange gifts, and they have a huge celebration because they are so happy to see the two witnesses are finally dead. When the two witnesses were prophesying the word of God, the inhabitants of Jerusalem thought the two witnesses were tormenting them because of the witnesses' control of rain, plagues, and fire. After all, they had to endure their prophesying for three-and-a-half years. Now that the two witnesses are dead, the inhabitants of Jerusalem could go back to normal, free to live whatever lifestyle they chose without fear of reprisals from the two witnesses.

The two witnesses are two men (prophets) anointed by God, so their ministry was the true word of God. The inhabitants hated the two witnesses and were glad when they were finally dead, indicating their doctrines and beliefs were in conflict with the ministry of the two witnesses. Because the inhabitants' doctrine was not in line with the word of God, they had to be living a life of false worship or idolatry and abominations. This doctrine is the exact same doctrine or belief system that we read about in Revelation 17, where the woman (capital city) sat upon a beast (kingdom) and caused the inhabitants to become drunk (confused) with the wine (doctrine) of her fornication (idolatry).

Witnesses' Resurrection

> Rev. 11:11 And after three days and an half the Spirit of life from God entered into them, and they stood upon their feet; and great fear fell upon them which saw them.

The inhabitants celebrated the death of the two witnesses for three-and-a-half days. Suddenly, after three-and-a-half days, life entered into the two witnesses, and they stood upon their feet. Immediately, the celebrations stopped, and the party spirit turned into a spirit of fear.

> Rev. 11:14 The second woe is past; and, behold, the third woe cometh quickly.

After the turn of events at the sounding of the fourth trumpet, an angel said there would be three woes. Revelation 8:13 states, "I beheld, and heard an angel flying through the midst of heaven, saying with a loud voice, woe, woe, woe, to the inhabiters of the earth by reason of the other voices of the trumpet of the three angels, which are yet to sound!" The angel is indicating that, at least three times more, there would be lots of misery and affliction thrust upon the earth. The three woes would come with the sounding of the fifth, sixth, and seventh trumpets. The first woe begins at the sounding of the fifth trumpet in Revelation 9:1–12, when the angel of the bottomless pit had people tormented for five months. It ends just prior to the sounding of the sixth trumpet. Revelation 9:12–13 states, "One woe is past; and, behold, there come two woes more hereafter … and the sixth angel sounded."

The second woe begins with the sounding of the sixth trumpet in Revelation 9:13–21, when the 200-million-man army marches and kills a multitude of people. It ends when life suddenly entered into the two witnesses. Revelation 11:11–14 states, "After three days and an half the Spirit of life from God entered into them, and they stood upon their feet … the second woe is past; and, behold, the third woe cometh quickly." The third woe would occur quickly.

Each woe is progressively worse than the woe that preceded it. Each woe begins with the sounding of one of the last three trumpets and ends just before or at the precise time the next trumpet sounds. Revelation 8:13 states, "Woe, woe, woe, to the inhabiters of the earth by reason of the other voices of the trumpet of the three angels, which are yet to sound!" Therefore, the seventh and last trumpet sounds immediately after the two witnesses are raised from the dead. Revelation 11:14 states, "The second woe is past; and, behold, the third woe cometh quickly."

> Rev. 11:15 And the seventh angel sounded; and there were great voices in heaven, saying, The kingdoms of this world are become the kingdoms of our Lord, and of his Christ; and he shall reign for ever and ever.

The third woe will take place quickly. The first and second woe was completed with the sounding of the fifth and sixth trumpet, so the third and final woe will occur with the sounding of the seventh trumpet. The seventh trumpet sounds. The third and final woe now begins to take place.

> Rev. 11:12 And they heard a great voice from heaven saying unto them, Come up hither. And they ascended up to heaven in a cloud; and their enemies beheld them.
> Rev. 11:13 And the same hour was there a great earthquake, and the tenth part of the city fell, and in the earthquake were slain of men seven thousand: and the remnant were affrighted, and gave glory to the God of heaven.

They also hear a voice from heaven telling the two witnesses to "come up hither." The two witnesses ascend into heaven in a cloud while all the people who were previously celebrating their death watched them ascend to heaven in a cloud.

The ascension of the two witnesses parallels the ascension of Jesus. Acts 1:9 states, "And when he had spoken these things, while they beheld, he was taken up; and a cloud received him out of their sight."

The same time that the voice from heaven shouted for the two witnesses to ascend into the cloud, a great earthquake destroys one-tenth of the buildings in Jerusalem. Seven thousand people die. Immediately, some of the inhabitants of Jerusalem become born again. They just realize that the two witnesses were men of God after all, and the inhabitants of Jerusalem had been following a false god. This is the third and final woe. Revelation 11:15 states:

And the seventh angel sounded; and there were great voices in heaven, saying, the kingdoms of this world are become the kingdoms of our Lord, and of his Christ; and he shall reign for ever and ever.

The third and final woe comes at the exact time as this world government as we know it today comes to an abrupt and final end. This is the moment that Jesus begins to rule and reign forever in his kingdom.

CHAPTER 11

THE IMAGE

Rev. 13:1   And I stood upon the sand of the sea, and saw a beast rise up out of the sea, having seven heads and ten horns, and upon his horns ten crowns, and upon his heads the name of blasphemy.

Rev. 13:11   And I beheld another beast coming up out of the earth; and he had two horns like a lamb, and he spake as a dragon.

PREVIOUSLY, John witnessed a beast that rose up out of the sea (Rev. 13:1). Now he witnessed another beast that rose up out of the earth (Rev. 13:11). John witnessed two different beasts coming from two different places. The first beast had seven heads and ten horns and rose up from the sea (Rev. 13:1). The second beast had two horns and rose up from the earth (Rev. 13:11).

We have already discovered that, in Bible prophecy, the word *beast* represents a kingdom and horns represent kings or nations. The first beast with seven heads and ten horns was earlier determined to be the antichrist's kingdom. The second beast has two horns, so that beast is a kingdom formed by two horns (nations) joining together to create a much larger or stronger kingdom. The first beast that rose out of the sea is a kingdom or territory controlled by a government. It is a political system. The second beast that rose out of the earth is a different kind of kingdom. It is a kingdom within a kingdom. It rose up out of the earth from within the first beast (antichrist's kingdom). Its agenda is not political, but more of a religious or a belief system.

The second beast has two horns like a lamb. Usually when one mentions a lamb in biblical terms, the reference is almost always associated with Jesus. John 1:29 states, "The next day John seeth Jesus coming unto him, and saith, behold the Lamb of God, which taketh away the sin of the world." Jesus was the Lamb of God, but there is no mention of him having two horns or nations. He did represent two different groups of people: the Old Testament Jews under the law and the New Testament born-again believers under grace. It is confirmed again in the book of Romans that Jesus represents two different groups of people. Romans 1:16 states, "The gospel of Christ: for it is the power of God unto salvation to every one that believeth; to the Jew first, and also to the Greek." Again, horns represent kings or nations. Revelation 17:12 states, "The ten horns which thou sawest are ten kings." Nations represents groups of people. An example would be descendants of Jacob and Esau. Genesis 25:23 states, "And the LORD said unto her, two nations are in thy womb, and two manner of people shall be separated from thy bowels; and the one people shall be stronger than the other people." Because the second beast has two horns, this indicates he represents two different groups of people.

A beast by nature is a dangerous animal, but this beast has the appearance of a gentle lamb. So some deception is definitely taking place. The gentle beast is an oxymoron. When referencing a beast, the text is sometimes referring to the kingdom itself. Other times, it is referencing the leader of the kingdom. This beast looks like a lamb, meaning the beast looks like Jesus. Because this beast disguises himself to look like Jesus, it indicates the scripture refers to the leader of the kingdom. Jesus was a man, so the beast was a man.

This beast is disguised as a lamb. Because Jesus is the Lamb, the beast appears to be Jesus. Jesus was a man, but not just any man. Jesus was also a prophet. Matthew 21:11 states, "This is Jesus the prophet." The beast is disguised as a lamb or Jesus, therefore the beast is calling himself a prophet. But, in reality, he is not the prophet Jesus. He is a false prophet. The false prophet is referenced in Revelation 19:20, "The beast was taken, and with him the false prophet." The beast that rose up out of the earth is the false prophet. He is the leader of a kingdom comprised of two different groups of people, represented by the two horns.

When Jesus walked here on earth, his kingdom was not land or a territory. His kingdom was a religious kingdom. He was not interested in politics.

He was interested in the souls of mankind, so this kingdom is some type of religious organization that is also interested in the souls of mankind. This kingdom or religious organization is made up of two parts or two groups because the false prophet has two horns. These two different groups are possibly two different religions that come together to serve under the leadership of the false prophet. There are several choices as to who the two religious groups can be. The first choice that comes to mind because the setting is in and around Jerusalem is the Jews and Muslims. Others will say that the two religious groups are the Protestants and Catholics. It really doesn't matter who the two groups are because the important thing to remember is that they are under the control of the false prophet.

This false prophet speaks like a dragon. The dragon is also known as the serpent. Revelation 12:9 states, "The great dragon was cast out, that old serpent, called the Devil, and Satan." We know the serpent is very subtle. Genesis 3:1, "Now the serpent was more subtil than any beast of the field which the LORD God had made." He tricked Eve into eating the forbidden fruit. She also gave it to Adam, and he ate it as well. This one act caused Adam and Eve to be of a sinful nature and all of their offspring to be born into sin. Jesus has already died or been sacrificed for our sins, so the shed blood of Jesus saved mankind. Now the false prophet is trying to trick mankind once again into an unsaved state, where there is no more forgiveness for sin. Hebrews 10:26 states, "There remaineth no more sacrifice for sins."

Beast's Authority

Rev. 13:12   And he exerciseth all the power of the first beast before him, and causeth the earth and them which dwell therein to worship the first beast, whose deadly wound was healed.

Rev. 13:13   And he doeth great wonders, so that he maketh fire come down from heaven on the earth in the sight of men,

The false prophet has a close relationship with the antichrist. The false prophet exercises all the powers of the first beast (antichrist). The false prophet has the same authority as the antichrist, and scripture shows that his power comes from the dragon or Satan. Revelation 13:2 states, "And the dragon gave him his power, and his seat, and great authority." The power given to the antichrist and false prophet is signs and wonders. Matthew 24:24 states, "There shall arise false Christs, and false prophets, and shall shew great signs and wonders." The false prophet also causes the members of his religious organization to worship the antichrist. A multitude of people will believe the false prophet to be the true Lamb of God. Jesus has already prophesied to his disciples that false prophets would arise. Matthew 24:24 states, "For there shall arise false Christs, and false prophets, and shall shew great signs and wonders." These signs and wonders are so believable that they will even fool the most religious people, including preachers, ministers, evangelists, and so forth. Matthew 24:24 states, "And shall shew great signs and wonders; insomuch that, if it were possible, they shall deceive the very elect." Men will liken these signs and wonders to the miracles that Jesus performed during his ministry on earth, so they will readily accept the false prophet as Jesus Christ, the Lamb of God.

Beast's Agenda

> Rev. 13:14 And deceiveth them that dwell on the earth by the means of those miracles which he had power to do in the sight of the beast; saying to them that dwell on the earth, that they should make an image to the beast, which had the wound by a sword, and did live.
>
> Rev.13:15 And he had power to give life unto the image of the beast, that the image of the beast should both speak, and cause that as many as would not worship the image of the beast should be killed.

Here it is confirmed that the false prophet is definitely not Jesus Christ. The false prophet deceives people, and we know Jesus does not deceive anyone because of his doctrine in truth and righteousness. The false prophet, by virtue of his title, campaigns for mankind to worship a false god, the antichrist. The false prophet has his followers make an image in honor of the antichrist, the one who had a deadly wound that was healed. The deadly wound that was healed is not a wound with respect to someone dying. This wound is the fall of a previous kingdom. This was discussed in chapter seven. Once the image was erected, the false prophet uses more signs and wonders to make the image to appear lifelike. He will even cause the image to speak. When the false prophet requests someone to worship the image of the beast and that person refuses, the image of the beast issues an order to put that person to death.

Three-part Worship

The first beast is the antichrist, and he blasphemes God. Revelation 13:5–6 states:

> There was given unto him a mouth speaking great things and blasphemies … and he opened his mouth in blasphemy against God, to blaspheme his name, and his tabernacle, and them that dwell in heaven.

The antichrist also sets himself up as God. As 2 Thessalonians 2:4 states, "Who opposeth and exalteth himself above all that is called God, or that is worshipped." This doctrine is confirmed again in Daniel 11:36, "And he shall exalt himself, and magnify himself above every god, and shall speak marvellous things against the God of gods."

The second beast (false prophet) is a religious leader, so he is in charge of worship. He causes men to worship the first beast (antichrist) as God. He has authority to do signs and wonders while in the sight of the antichrist. This is another reason why he constructed the image of the antichrist. During the absence of the antichrist, he would have the image representing the antichrist so he could continue to do signs, wonders, and miracles in the presence of the image.

The image is a statue or some type of hologram. This image is given in honor of the antichrist, a representation of the antichrist during his absence. People are made to worship this image as though it is the antichrist himself. Through signs and wonders, the false prophet made the image to act lifelike. It was so lifelike that the image could speak and announce the death of whomsoever he willed.

Let's take a closer look at the facts. We have the antichrist calling himself

God. We have the false prophet appearing as a lamb or Jesus. We have the image of the antichrist as a deity. This is a picture of an unholy trinity, not the holy trinity. Trinity refers to three gods in one. The recognized trinity in religious circles is God the Father, God the Son, and God the Holy Ghost. These three gods are one the same. The unholy trinity is the antichrist as God, the false prophet as the son, and the image as the Holy Ghost. This particular trinity is deception. Revelation 13:14 states, "And deceiveth them that dwell on the earth."

The Mark

Rev. 13:16 And he causeth all, both small and great, rich and poor, free and bond, to receive a mark in their right hand, or in their foreheads:

Rev. 13:17 And that no man might buy or sell, save he that had the mark, or the name of the beast, or the number of his name.

Rev. 13:18 Here is wisdom. Let him that hath understanding count the number of the beast: for it is the number of a man; and his number is Six hundred threescore and six.

Not only has the false prophet convinced his followers to construct the image in the likeness of the antichrist, he also makes them worship the image as God. All the people worship the antichrist, except the people who had their names written in the Lamb's Book of Life. Revelation 13:8 states, "All that dwell upon the earth shall worship him, whose names are not written in the Book of Life of the Lamb." All the people worshipping this image are deceived. They are convinced the antichrist is God, the false prophet is Jesus, and the image is the Holy Ghost. They believe everyone whose religious beliefs was contrary to theirs were involved in satanic worship. This false prophet is very convincing. Jesus prophesied that the false prophet even deceives the very religious people. Matthew 24:24 states, "There shall arise false Christs, and false prophets, and shall shew great signs and wonders; insomuch that, if it were possible, they shall deceive the very elect."

This false prophet goes as far as to have all of his followers take a mark on their foreheads or right hands. This mark is a form of identification so all of his followers could be readily identified. Here is another deception by the false prophet. God sealed his servants with a seal on their foreheads. Revelation 7:3 states, "Sealed the servants of our God in their foreheads." Now, the false prophet is putting some type of a mark, seal, or inscription on his servants so he will know his own.[25] Revelation 13:16 states, "To receive a mark in their right hand, or in their foreheads."

The false prophet will have many people killed who refuse to take the mark. He will not kill everybody. He will kill any and all who pose a threat to his doctrine. He will kill all men who try to destroy his kingdom by teaching and preaching the true gospel. He will not hurt people who do not believe in any god because they are not a threat to him.

The false prophet is also giving special privileges to the people who take his mark. This world is set up around economic prosperity. He allows all of his followers to buy and sell or to become financially wealthy. People without the mark will not be allowed this privilege. They will be reduced to a people merely trying to survive.

We have to look more closely at the phrase "buying and selling." Many people interpret the phrase to mean that one will not be allowed to buy or sell anything, but that's not the case. The text is not talking about buying necessities of life like food and clothing. It is talking about buying and selling on a much larger scale. It's talking about becoming merchants, that is, buying and selling merchandise for profit.[26] Let's look at the phrase "buy and sell" in the Bible.

Jas. 4:13   Go to now, ye that say, To day or to morrow we will go into such a city, and continue there a year, and buy and sell, and get gain:

Here the phrase "buy and sell" refers to business activity, not buying and selling the necessities of life. The Greek word for "buy and sell" in Strong's dictionary is *emporeuomai*, represented by the number 1710. The meaning of this word is "to travel into a country as a peddler, to trade, to buy and sell, to make merchandise."[27] The phrase "buying and selling" is not talking

---

[25] Torah Light Ministries, Stanley Chester, taped message 4, The Mark of the Beast.

[26] Torah Light Ministries, Stanley Chester, taped message 4, The Mark of the Beast.

[27] The New Strong's Dictionary of Bible Words (Thomas Nelson, 1996), 614.

about grocery shopping. Under the antichrist's regime, it refers to buying and selling on a corporate level.

Revelation 18 talks about the fall of Babylon or the antichrist's kingdom. Only the merchants, the ones who profited in the antichrist's kingdom, are weeping and wailing, not the common man. The only people who profited in this organization are the people who took the mark of the beast. The false prophet will not allow people without the mark to become anybody important in his kingdom. Economic prosperity drives this present world. The false prophet uses this tactic of enormous economic prosperity to deceive people into joining his church or religious organization. He uses religion tied in with financial prosperity to deceive people into thinking that economic prosperity is a by-product of religious worship. Only the people who take the mark will be allowed to prosper. The false prophet will not kill all the people who did not take the mark. After all, he needs someone to do the work for his elite group who has taken his mark. Someone has to do the undesirable tasks like garbage detail, cleaning, farming, playing soldiers, and so forth.

> Rev. 13:17 And that no man might buy or sell, save he that had the mark, or the name of the beast, or the number of his name.
> Rev. 13:18 Here is wisdom. Let him that hath understanding count the number of the beast: for it is the number of a man; and his number is Six hundred threescore and six.

We have to look at something else concerning the mark. Most people recognize the mark as 666. The mark is something more than 666. It could be any of three different things: a mark, a name, or a number. We all know what is meant when we say the number of the beast, 666. The name could also be the name of the kingdom, which is something blasphemous. Revelation 13:1 states, "And upon his heads the name of blasphemy." It is confirmed again that the name is something blasphemous. Revelation 17:3 states, "A scarlet coloured beast, full of names of blasphemy." The mark could be something like an emblem or a symbol.

When you see certain emblems, you recognize them immediately, and you know what they mean. Some examples of symbols or emblems are peace sign, hazardous materials, the cross, the dove, the flag, and so forth. People should be aware of any and everything that is anti-God or requires one to denounce Jesus Christ as his Lord and Savior. Anything contrary to the death, burial, and resurrection of Jesus Christ of Nazareth and his ascension can be used to symbolize this false religious organization, whether it is a name, mark, or number.

Satan empowers the false prophet, and he is very cunning. He is ingenious enough to have everybody going to hell from the moment he is born. The only way to escape that fate is to become born-again. The false prophet is deceiving people into thinking the image is in honor of God. One must beware and focus on the word of God in order to minimize the chance of being deceived. As 2 Timothy 2:15 states, "Study to shew thyself approved unto God, a workman that needeth not to be ashamed, rightly dividing the word of truth." By studying the word of God, a person enhances his understanding and recognizes the pitfalls and obstacles that the antichrist and false prophet put in place, therefore improving their chances of not being deceived. After all, Jesus said the antichrist would fool the very elect.

Concurrent Events

Many things are happening simultaneously. We read that the Holy City will be tread underfoot and the Gentiles will be given the outer court for forty-two months. Revelation 11:2 states, "The holy city shall they tread under foot forty and two months." This translates to three-and-a-half years. We read that the two witnesses prophesied for 1,260 days. Revelation 11:3 states, "I will give power unto my two witnesses, and they shall prophesy a thousand two hundred and threescore days." This also translates to three-and-a-half years.

We read about the woman fleeing into the wilderness, where she has a place prepared for her for 1,260 days. Revelation 12:6 states, "Where she hath a place prepared of God, that they should feed her there a thousand two hundred and threescore days." This is three-and-a-half years. It is confirmed again when the woman is nourished in the wilderness for a time (one year),[28] times (two years), and a half time (one-half year). Revelation 12:14 states,

---

[28] The New Strong's Dictionary of Bible Words (Thomas Nelson Publishers, 1996), 259, 469.

"Where she is nourished for a time, and times, and half a time." This adds up to be three-and-a-half years.

The antichrist will rule for forty-two months or three-and-a-half years. Revelation 13:5 states, "And power was given unto him to continue forty and two months." The false prophet sets up an image in honor of the antichrist. The image is also being worshipped approximately three-and-a-half years. It has been shown previously that the beast or kingdom in Revelation 17 is the same beast as the one in Revelation 12–13. All the events taking place in Revelation 11, 12, 13, and 17 are all happening at approximately the same time and all the same length of time. Scripture does not give the exact context of the three-and-a-half-year ministry of the two witnesses, but it is a good possibility that their ministry warns people of their immediate damnation if they worship the antichrist, the false prophet, or his image.

The Warning

Rev. 14:9   And the third angel followed them, saying with a loud voice, If any man worship the beast and his image, and receive his mark in his forehead, or in his hand,

Rev. 14:10 The same shall drink of the wine of the wrath of God, which is poured out without mixture into the cup of his indignation; and he shall be tormented with fire and brimstone in the presence of the holy angels, and in the presence of the Lamb:

Rev. 14:11 And the smoke of their torment ascendeth up for ever and ever: and they have no rest day nor night, who worship the beast and his image, and whosoever receiveth the mark of his name.

Rev. 14:12 Here is the patience of the saints: here are they that keep the commandments of God, and the faith of Jesus.

Rev. 14:13 And I heard a voice from heaven saying unto me, Write, Blessed are the dead which die in the Lord from henceforth: Yea, saith the Spirit, that they may rest from their labours; and their works do follow them.

John saw an angel, and the angel told him that if any man worshipped the beast (antichrist) or his image or received his mark, then he shall suffer the wrath of God. The time frame here is about the same time that the image is set up. When the image is set up, the angel then issues this clear warning. If you worship the antichrist in any way, whether you receive his name, number, or mark, you will burn in hell forever. It's not just the mark or 666 that will cause you to suffer eternal damnation. It can be any form of worship or acceptance of anything that identifies you with the antichrist, false prophet, or his image. John also heard a voice from heaven telling him that anyone who dies in the Lord for refusing to receive the mark of the beast from the time the image is set up until the end of antichrist's reign will be blessed. Here is a time when death will be better than life because that person will no longer have to go through the antichrist's reign of terror. He will be blessed on the other side because he will have overcome. Revelation 2:26 states, "And he that overcometh, and keepeth my works unto the end, to him will I give power over the nations … and he shall rule them with a rod of iron." Under normal circumstances, it is better to choose life over death, but, if faced with taking the mark of the beast or death, then choosing death is far better.

Rev. 14:6   And I saw another angel fly in the midst of heaven, having the everlasting gospel to preach unto them that dwell on the earth, and to every nation, and kindred, and tongue, and people,

Rev. 14:7   Saying with a loud voice, Fear God, and give glory to him; for the hour of his judgment is come: and worship him that made heaven, and earth, and the sea, and the fountains of waters.

This angel reinforced the fact that man should fear God and worship him only. He is teaching the everlasting gospel. The angel distinguished who man should serve. He proclaimed that man should fear the God who made the heavens, the earth, the sea, and the fountains of waters. There is only one god, so do not worship or identify with any other. Your eternal destiny is dependent solely upon the god you serve.

CHAPTER 12

THE HARVEST

Rev. 8:1   And when he had opened the seventh seal, there was
             silence in heaven about the space of half an hour.
Rev. 8:2   And I saw the seven angels which stood before God; and
             to them were given seven trumpets.

THE seventh seal has just been opened. There is silence in heaven for
about a half hour. This seal is broken just prior to the seventh trumpet
being sounded. It appears the seven trumpets are being given to the seven
angels at this particular time, but that's not the case. It was determined earlier
that the breaking of the seven seals and the sounding of the seven trumpets
alternates: first seal broken, first trumpet sounds, second seal broken, second
trumpet sounds, and so forth. Remember the book of Revelation is not
written in chronological order. It is written in segments, similar to the way
a person dreams. Revelation 8:1 is the end of the segment concerning the
seals. Revelation 8:2 is the beginning of the segment concerning the trumpets, but the breaking of the seals and sounding of the trumpets intertwine.
The seven angels stood before God and received the seven trumpets at or
about the time the first seal was broken.

Altar Call

Rev. 8:3   And another angel came and stood at the altar, having
             a golden censer; and there was given unto him much
             incense, that he should offer it with the prayers of
             all saints upon the golden altar which was before the
             throne.

Rev. 8:4   And the smoke of the incense, which came with the prayers of the saints, ascended up before God out of the angel's hand.

Rev. 8:5   And the angel took the censer, and filled it with fire of the altar, and cast it into the earth: and there were voices, and thunderings, and lightnings, and an earthquake.

John was still in the spirit in heaven. The Angel of Jesus was revealing End-time events to him. John saw an angel come down and stand before the altar. He had a golden censer, and he was given a huge amount of incense. He was to offer the incense with the prayers of the saints upon the golden altar. When the angel offered the incense upon the golden altar, the smoke from the incense and the prayers of the saints ascended up before God. The angel then took the censer, filled it with coal from the altar, and threw it into the earth. John then heard thunder and saw lightning and an earthquake.

To better understand, let's look at Numbers 16:42–50. God was in the process of destroying some Israelites who came against Moses and Aaron. Moses told Aaron to take a censer and some coals from off the altar and go make atonement for the people. The plague had already begun, but Aaron took a censer and filled it with coal from the altar. Then he put incense on the coal to make the atonement for the people. The plague stopped immediately.

This was happening in heaven as the angel took fire from the golden altar. Remnants of the fire could be seen burning on the floor of the sea of glass (Rev. 15:2). Iniquity abounded on earth, but, when the golden censer filled with fire was thrown onto the earth, the iniquity ended because the angel had just made the atonement for the saints. At the same time the iniquity abounded on the earth, the great tribulation was also taking place. All of these things will come to an abrupt end when the angel makes atonement for the saints, beginning at the breaking of the seventh seal and followed by the sounding of the seventh trumpet. The atonement for the saints will take place after the breaking of the seventh seal. Immediately after the atonement is complete, the seventh trumpet will sound.

John's Briefing

Rev. 10:5 And the angel which I saw stand upon the sea and upon the earth lifted up his hand to heaven,

Rev. 10:6 And sware by him that liveth for ever and ever, who created heaven, and the things that therein are, and the earth, and the things that therein are, and the sea, and the things which are therein, that there should be time no longer:

Rev. 10:7 But in the days of the voice of the seventh angel, when he shall begin to sound, the mystery of God should be finished, as he hath declared to his servants the prophets.

John also saw an angel standing with one foot upon the earth and the other foot upon the sea. This indicates the angel has authority over the entire world. The angel swore by the Lord God Almighty that there would be time no longer when the seventh trumpet sounds. He declared the mystery of God would be finished at that time. When the seventh trumpet sounds, it will then be too late to get your house in order. God has given man a lifetime to get his heart in good standing. Once the seventh trumpet sounds, all of those who are born-again will no longer be bound by time. They will enter into eternity. Even though a person can be born again any time before death, there is only one way to get born again, and it should have already taken place. Romans 10:9–10 states, "If thou shalt confess with thy mouth the Lord Jesus, and shalt believe in thine heart that God hath raised him from the dead, thou shalt be saved … with the heart man believeth unto righteousness; and with the mouth confession is made unto salvation." Time stops for the born-again saints precisely at that moment the seventh trumpet sounds. At that moment, they will enter into eternity.

Sounding of Seventh Trumpet

Rev. 11:15 And the seventh angel sounded; and there were great voices in heaven, saying, The kingdoms of this world are become the kingdoms of our Lord, and of his Christ; and he shall reign for ever and ever.

Rev. 11:16 And the four and twenty elders, which sat before God

on their seats, fell upon their faces, and worshipped
God,

Rev. 11:17 Saying, We give thee thanks, O Lord God Almighty,
which art, and wast, and art to come; because thou hast
taken to thee thy great power, and hast reigned.

Rev. 11:18 And the nations were angry, and thy wrath is come,
and the time of the dead, that they should be judged,
and that thou shouldest give reward unto thy servants
the prophets, and to the saints, and them that fear thy
name, small and great; and shouldest destroy them
which destroy the earth.

Rev. 11:19 And the temple of God was opened in heaven, and
there was seen in his temple the ark of his testament:
and there were lightnings, and voices, and thunderings,
and an earthquake, and great hail.

John had just heard the angel proclaim that, when the seventh trumpet
sounds, it would be time no longer. When the seventh trumpet sounds,
it brings the reigning of Christ in his kingdom with it, and he will reign
forever. The sounding of the seventh trumpet is the beginning of several
things. It signals it is time for the wrath to begin, the dead to be judged, the
prophets, saints, and all who fear his name to be rewarded. It is a time for
those who destroyed the earth to be destroyed.

At the sounding of the seventh trumpet, Jesus will take his throne. The
nations will be angry, especially those nations that gave their authority to the
antichrist. Jesus spoke of the gathering of the nations during his ministry.

Mat. 25:31 When the Son of man shall come in his glory, and all the
holy angels with him, then shall he sit upon the throne
of his glory:

Mat. 25:32 And before him shall be gathered all nations: and he
shall separate them one from another, as a shepherd
divideth his sheep from the goats:

Mat. 25:33 And he shall set the sheep on his right hand, but the
goats on the left.

Mat. 25:34 Then shall the King say unto them on his right hand,

> Come, ye blessed of my Father, inherit the kingdom
> prepared for you from the foundation of the world:

The angry nations are the nations referred to as the goats that will be gathered on the left-hand side of Jesus. The inhabitants of these nations have not been living a godly life, and they will become angry. They are angry because they now realize they have not entered into the kingdom of God. On the other hand (right hand), the nations referred to as the sheep nations will inherit the kingdom of heaven. All of these actions will be set in motion at the sounding of the seventh trumpet.

The temple of God was opened in heaven, and the ark of his testament was visible. The ark of his testament is synonymous with the ark of the covenant. Moses was instructed to build the ark of the covenant so God could dwell there among the Israelites. Exodus 25:8 states, "And let them make me a sanctuary; that I may dwell among them." God also instructed Moses to build a lid or mercy seat with two cherubim setting upon it. The throne of God is on the mercy seat between the two cherubim. Exodus 25:22 states:

> And there I will meet with thee, and I will commune with thee from
> above the mercy seat, from between the two cherubims which are
> upon the ark of the testimony, of all things which I will give thee in
> commandment unto the children of Israel.

The throne of God is upon the ark of his testament. This is where God will communicate with his followers.

When the seventh trumpet sounds, the saints of God will have their eyes opened. They will be able to see the throne of God. They will see the same throne room that John witnessed. Revelation 4:1–2 states:

> A door was opened in heaven: and the first voice which I heard was
> as it were of a trumpet talking with me; which said, come up hither,
> and I will shew thee things which must be hereafter … and imme-
> diately I was in the spirit: and, behold, a throne was set in heaven,
> and one sat on the throne.

The saints will now see things in the spirit world as well as things in the physical or natural world. For the first time, they will see the throne of God. Revelation 11:19 states, "The temple of God was opened in heaven, and there was seen in his temple the ark of his testament."

An example of the natural eyes versus the spiritual eyes is when Elisha prayed that the eyes of his servant be opened so he may see. The servant's eyes were opened, and he was then capable of seeing the multitude of horses and chariots of fire all around them. As 2 Kings 6:17 states, "And the LORD opened the eyes of the young man; and he saw: and, behold, the mountain was full of horses and chariots of fire round about Elisha." A better description of this is given in 1 John 3:2: "Beloved, now are we the sons of God, and it doth not yet appear what we shall be: but we know that, when he shall appear, we shall be like him; for we shall see him as he is." When he returns, the spiritual eyes of the saints will be opened. The things that are hidden from us now will then be visible. As 1 John 3:2 states, "When he shall appear … for we shall see him as he is."

The Harvest

Rev. 14:14 And I looked, and behold a white cloud, and upon the cloud one sat like unto the Son of man, having on his head a golden crown, and in his hand a sharp sickle.

Rev. 14:15 And another angel came out of the temple, crying with a loud voice to him that sat on the cloud, Thrust in thy sickle, and reap: for the time is come for thee to reap; for the harvest of the earth is ripe.

Rev. 14:16 And he that sat on the cloud thrust in his sickle on the earth; and the earth was reaped.

The timing of this scene is immediately after the sounding of the seventh trumpet. John looked and saw a white cloud. Someone was sitting on the cloud. The figure on the cloud looked like the son of man. A golden crown was on his head, and a sharp sickle was in his hand. The figure on the white cloud is Jesus Christ, and every eye will see him as he returns. Revelation 1:7 states, "Behold, he cometh with clouds; and every eye shall see him, and they also which pierced him: and all kindreds of the earth shall wail because of him." When Jesus ascended into heaven, he was received in a cloud. Acts 1:9

states, "While they beheld, he was taken up; and a cloud received him out of their sight." Two men stood nearby who informed the people that Jesus would return to earth in the same manner as he ascended into heaven. Acts 1:11 states, "This same Jesus, which is taken up from you into heaven, shall so come in like manner as ye have seen him go into heaven." This is that moment when he returns to earth in the clouds, the same way he ascended into heaven.

The sounding of the seventh trumpet is the beginning of the harvest or reaping of the world. Matthew 13:39 states, "The harvest is the end of the world." He throws his sickle into the earth, and the earth is reaped. A sickle is an instrument like a knife or hook used for harvesting or cutting wheat. This cutting of the wheat is not a literal cutting, but is symbolic for saints being reaped, harvested, or transformed from a natural body to a spiritual body and entering into the kingdom of God. As 1 Corinthians 15:42–44 states:

So also is the resurrection of the dead. It is sown in corruption; it is raised in incorruption: It is sown in dishonour; it is raised in glory: it is sown in weakness; it is raised in power: It is sown a natural body; it is raised a spiritual body.

At death, the earthly body is buried because of an accident, sickness, or old age. At the resurrection or sounding of the seventh trumpet, that individual will be raised from the dead with a new spiritual body that will never die.

When the seventh trumpet sounds, the harvesting of the saints takes place immediately. As 1 Corinthians 15:51–52 states:

Behold, I shew you a mystery; we shall not all sleep, but we shall all be changed, in a moment, in the twinkling of an eye, at the last trump: for the trumpet shall sound, and the dead shall be raised incorruptible, and we shall be changed.

The righteous dead will be raised from their graves. The people who are alive and worthy will be changed instantaneously at the sounding of the seventh trumpet. Philippians 3:20–21 states, "From whence also we look for the Saviour, the Lord Jesus Christ: who shall change our vile body, that it may be fashioned like unto his glorious body." At that moment, the righteous dead are raised. The bodies of the saints who are still alive are changed. They will be in the presence of the Lord. As 1 Thessalonians 4:16–17 states:

> For the Lord himself shall descend from heaven with a shout, with the voice of the archangel, and with the trump of God: and the dead in Christ shall rise first: then we which are alive and remain shall be caught up together with them in the clouds, to meet the Lord in the air: and so shall we ever be with the Lord.

At the sounding of the seventh trumpet, all the righteous, dead and alive, will be given a new body that isn't capable of death. They will spend eternity with God.

> Mat. 24:30 And then shall appear the sign of the Son of man in heaven: and then shall all the tribes of the earth mourn, and they shall see the Son of man coming in the clouds of heaven with power and great glory.
> Mat. 24:31 And he shall send his angels with a great sound of a trumpet, and they shall gather together his elect from the four winds, from one end of heaven to the other.

This is the same picture as described in Revelation 14:16; "He that sat on the cloud thrust in his sickle on the earth; and the earth was reaped." Jesus will return to the earth in the clouds, and all will witness his return. Revelation 1:7 states, "He cometh with clouds; and every eye shall see him." Many will mourn when they see him returning in the clouds because they realize it is too late for them. He shall send his angels to reap the earth of all who are born again at the time of his return. Matthew 24:30–31 and Revelation 14:14–16 are synonymous because the same elements are mentioned: the clouds, trumpet, and the harvesting of the saints or the elect. All of these events will take place at the sounding of the seventh trumpet.

Sea of Glass

Rev. 4:6   And before the throne there was a sea of glass like unto crystal: and in the midst of the throne, and round about the throne, were four beasts full of eyes before and behind.

The scene is in the throne room. The Angel of Jesus requested that John ascend into heaven so he could reveal future things to him. There, before the throne, John witnessed a sea of glass like a ballroom floor. The sea of glass was empty because there is no mention of the sea of glass being occupied. Bear in mind that John had already witnessed the throne room before any of the seals were broken or any of the trumpets sounded. Now compare Revelation 15:2–4 to Revelation 4:6. Remember, Revelation 4:6 is before the sounding of any trumpet, and Revelation 15:2–4 is after the sounding of the seventh trumpet.

Rev. 15:2   And I saw as it were a sea of glass mingled with fire: and them that had gotten the victory over the beast, and over his image, and over his mark, and over the number of his name, stand on the sea of glass, having the harps of God.

Rev. 15:3   And they sing the song of Moses the servant of God, and the song of the Lamb, saying, Great and marvellous are thy works, Lord God Almighty; just and true are thy ways, thou King of saints.

Rev. 15:4   Who shall not fear thee, O Lord, and glorify thy name? for thou only art holy: for all nations shall come and worship before thee; for thy judgments are made manifest.

This sea of glass is now occupied. It is filled with those who are born-again and those who had not worshipped the antichrist. They did not take the mark of the beast, nor did they worship the image. They are standing before the throne of God on the sea of glass, singing and praising God. The timing of this scene is immediately after the sounding of the seventh trumpet. These are the ones gathered together in the harvest when Jesus threw his sickle onto the earth, and the earth was reaped. The sea of glass also has fire on it. This is the fire from the golden altar when the angel threw the golden censer into the earth. Revelation 8:5 states, "And the angel took the censer, and filled it with fire of the altar, and cast it into the earth." The fire from the golden altar is the angel making atonement for the saints.

Rev. 7:9   After this I beheld, and, lo, a great multitude, which no man could number, of all nations, and kindreds, and people, and tongues, stood before the throne, and before the Lamb, clothed with white robes, and palms in their hands;

Rev. 7:10   And cried with a loud voice, saying, Salvation to our God which sitteth upon the throne, and unto the Lamb.

Rev. 7:11   And all the angels stood round about the throne, and about the elders and the four beasts, and fell before the throne on their faces, and worshipped God,

Rev. 7:12   Saying, Amen: Blessing, and glory, and wisdom, and thanksgiving, and honour, and power, and might, be unto our God for ever and ever. Amen.

Rev. 7:13   And one of the elders answered, saying unto me, What are these which are arrayed in white robes? and whence came they?

Rev. 7:14   And I said unto him, Sir, thou knowest. And he said to me, These are they which came out of great tribulation, and have washed their robes, and made them white in the blood of the Lamb.

Rev. 7:15   Therefore are they before the throne of God, and serve him day and night in his temple: and he that sitteth on the throne shall dwell among them.

Rev. 7:16   They shall hunger no more, neither thirst any more; neither shall the sun light on them, nor any heat.

Rev. 7:17   For the Lamb which is in the midst of the throne shall feed them, and shall lead them unto living fountains of waters: and God shall wipe away all tears from their eyes.

Here we see a multitude of people standing before the throne, just as we saw in Revelation 15:2–4. These are from every nation, kindred, and tongue, and they are standing before the throne. These people came out of the great tribulation. They are dressed in white because they were born-again and they endured until the end. These saints did not take the mark of the beast or worship his image. They are in the presence of God praising him. Here we see that they are in heaven where God will wipe away all of their tears. They will no longer hunger or thirst. Neither will they get too hot from the sun. They will serve God in his temple, and God will dwell with them. The lamb will lead them to living fountains of waters. The fountains of living waters are the living waters Jesus mentioned in John 4:14, "But whosoever drinketh of the water that I shall give him shall never thirst; but the water that I shall give him shall be in him a well of water springing up into everlasting life." The living water Jesus mentioned is not literal water. It is the Holy Spirit that individuals receive when they believe in Jesus Christ and follow him. This is verified in John 7:38–39, "He that believeth on me … out of his belly shall flow rivers of living water … But this spake he of the Spirit."

The sounding of the seventh trumpet marks the beginning of eternity. This is the point when saints will receive their glorious body. Philippians 3:20–21 states, "We look for the Saviour, the Lord Jesus Christ: who shall change our vile body, that it may be fashioned like unto his glorious body." The glorified body is the new body the saints will receive immediately after the seventh trumpet sounds. As 1 Corinthians 15:51–52 states, "Behold, I shew you a mystery; we shall not all sleep, but we shall all be changed … at the last trump: for the trumpet shall sound, and the dead shall be raised incorruptible, and we shall be changed."

The new body the saints will receive at the sounding of the seventh trumpet will look like the body that Jesus had when he was raised from the dead. This new body will enable saints to literally walk through walls.

CHAPTER 13

THE VIALS

W E should note something very important. There is a lot of talk about the great tribulation and the wrath of God. These are two different and separate events. Satan initiates the great tribulation through the antichrist. The wrath of God is the outpouring of the seven vials of wrath, initiated by God. Angelic beings pour out the seven vials of wrath upon the earth, and it begins soon after the great tribulation ends. The sounding of the seventh trumpet ends the great tribulation and marks the beginning of the wrath of God. The angels will not gather together the elect or the harvest until after the great tribulation. Matthew 24:29–31 states:

> Immediately after the tribulation of those days … and then shall appear the sign of the Son of man in heaven … and they shall see the son of man coming in the clouds of heaven with power and great glory … and he shall send his angels with a great sound of a trumpet, and they shall gather together his elect from the four winds.

The gathering together of his elect or the harvest is better known as the second coming, and it takes place at the sounding of the seventh trumpet. The wrath of God follows the second coming of Christ. Revelation 11:18 states, "And the nations were angry, and thy wrath is come." This is the order of events: first the great tribulation, then the second coming, and finally the wrath of God. The wrath of God is the outpouring of the seven vials of the wrath of God mentioned in Revelation 16.

There is a lot of indifference concerning the great tribulation and wrath of God. Many people think the great tribulation and the wrath of God will be applied equally throughout the whole world. The great tribulation and wrath of God will be concentrated in the kingdom of the antichrist. There has never been one kingdom that has ruled the entire world. The only kingdom that will ever rule the entire world will be the kingdom of God. Many nations have tried to rule the entire world, but all of them have failed. Even the antichrist's kingdom will fall. The fall of the antichrist's kingdom creates a domino effect, where nations will fall one after the other, because the world's commerce is intertwined.

The Bible only records events in parts of Asia, Europe, and Africa. The rest of the world existed during the time of Adam, Noah, Abraham, David, and the death of Jesus, but the Bible never mentions these lands. The Bible concentrates only on the seven kingdoms that controlled Israel. The great tribulation and the wrath of God are not global. Their main focus is on the kingdom of the antichrist and the surrounding areas.

Seven Last Plagues

Rev. 15:1   And I saw another sign in heaven, great and marvellous, seven angels having the seven last plagues; for in them is filled up the wrath of God.

Rev. 15:5   And after that I looked, and, behold, the temple of the tabernacle of the testimony in heaven was opened:

Rev. 15:6   And the seven angels came out of the temple, having the seven plagues, clothed in pure and white linen, and having their breasts girded with golden girdles.

Rev. 15:7   And one of the four beasts gave unto the seven angels seven golden vials full of the wrath of God, who liveth for ever and ever.

Rev. 15:8   And the temple was filled with smoke from the glory of God, and from his power; and no man was able to enter into the temple, till the seven plagues of the seven angels were fulfilled.

This scene is immediately after the sounding of the seventh trumpet. After John saw this multitude of people standing on the sea of glass and worshipping God, he noticed something else in Revelation 7:9–14 and

15:2–4. He saw the seven angels who were to administer the seven last plagues. One of the four beasts (seraphim) gave each of the angels one of the seven vials full of the wrath of God. No man could enter the temple until the vials of wrath were poured out.

The Wrath

Rev. 16:1 And I heard a great voice out of the temple saying to the seven angels, Go your ways, and pour out the vials of the wrath of God upon the earth.

The seven angels are ready to pour out the vials full of the wrath of God upon the earth. The vials of wrath are poured out in succession, one at a time, one after another, until all seven are emptied upon the earth. This pouring out of the vials of wrath is not like pouring a liquid out of a container. It is the word of God recompensing the unrighteous. Hebrews 10:30 states, "Vengeance belongeth unto me, I will recompense, saith the Lord. And again, the Lord shall judge his people." This is verified in Revelation 19:15, "And out of his mouth goeth a sharp sword, that with it he should smite the nations: and he shall rule them with a rod of iron: and he treadeth the winepress of the fierceness and wrath of Almighty God."

First Vial

Rev. 16:2 And the first went, and poured out his vial upon the earth; and there fell a noisome and grievous sore upon the men which had the mark of the beast, and upon them which worshipped his image.

The first angel pours out his vial of the wrath of God upon the earth, immediately resulting in a sore only upon the people who had the mark of the beast and those who worshipped the image. We should note here that the people with the sores did not die. They just have these awful, fowl sores covering their bodies.

Second Vial

Rev. 16:3   And the second angel poured out his vial upon the sea;
             and it became as the blood of a dead man: and every
             living soul died in the sea.

The second angel pours out his vial of the wrath of God upon the sea. Immediately, the waters of the sea become stagnant as the blood of a dead man. Every living soul in the sea dies. We have to conclude that any man in the sea, died, along with and all the other sea life when the second vial was poured upon the sea. We should note that the seventh trumpet has already sounded. All of those who were born-again have already been changed into their heavenly bodies. All of those who are left were in an unsaved state at the sounding of the seventh trumpet. A remnant of the inhabitants of Jerusalem repented just in time. Revelation 11:12–13 states, "And the remnant were affrighted, and gave glory to the God of heaven." Because the seventh trumpet had not already sounded, they were eligible to take part in the first resurrection. Revelation 20:6 states, "Blessed and holy is he that hath part in the first resurrection: on such the second death hath no power, but they shall be priests of God and of Christ, and shall reign with him a thousand years." All of those whose repentance came too late to take part in the first resurrection are now considered born-again, but will have to wait to receive an immortal body until the second death, which takes place more than one thousand years later. Revelation 20:5 states, "But the rest of the dead lived not again until the thousand years were finished." Mankind does not live to be one thousand years old, so they will not be raised from the dead for at least one thousand years.

Third Vial

Rev. 16:4   And the third angel poured out his vial upon the rivers
             and fountains of waters; and they became blood.

Rev. 16:5   And I heard the angel of the waters say, Thou art righ-
             teous, O Lord, which art, and wast, and shalt be, because
             thou hast judged thus.

Rev. 16:6   For they have shed the blood of saints and prophets,

and thou hast given them blood to drink; for they are
worthy.

Rev. 16:7 And I heard another out of the altar say, Even so, Lord
God Almighty, true and righteous are thy judgments.

The third angel pours his vial of the wrath of God upon the fountains
of waters, and they become blood. This refers to rivers, streams, brooks,
and so forth. This vial turns the fresh water or drinking water into blood.
The angels comment that the judgment of turning the pure waters into
blood is just because these people on earth had shed the innocent blood of
the prophets and the saints. This judgment is not for the whole world, but
predominantly for those in the antichrist's kingdom who are guilty by association of shedding the blood of the prophets and saints. The wrath of God
is quite selective.

Fourth Vial

Rev. 16:8 And the fourth angel poured out his vial upon the sun;
and power was given unto him to scorch men with fire.

Rev. 16:9 And men were scorched with great heat, and blasphemed
the name of God, which hath power over these plagues:
and they repented not to give him glory.

The fourth angel pours out his vial of the wrath of God upon the sun.
The sun becomes very hot, and people are scorched with great heat. They
continue to blaspheme the name of God. Obviously, these people followed
the antichrist and received the mark of the beast. They continue to believe
that the antichrist was God. They think some other deity is torturing them.
With all of their pain and agony, they do not repent nor give glory to the one
true god who created the heavens, the earth, and the seas. They continue to
look to the antichrist as their god, expecting him to intervene and end the
wrath of the Almighty God. But their prayers yield no fruit. This selective
wrath should have caused one to question the antichrist. If he were their
god, why was the wrath only affecting his followers?

Fifth Vial

> Rev. 16:10 And the fifth angel poured out his vial upon the seat
>   of the beast; and his kingdom was full of darkness; and
>   they gnawed their tongues for pain,
> Rev. 16:11 And blasphemed the God of heaven because of their
>   pains and their sores, and repented not of their deeds.

The fifth angel pours out his vial of the wrath of God upon the seat of the beast. The kingdom of the beast is full of darkness, and people gnaw their tongues because of the severe pain. They still do not believe they were following the wrong God. They continue to think the antichrist is God, and they blaspheme the God of heaven because of the pain they suffered.

The seat of the beast is the antichrist's kingdom. This kingdom had his followers take the mark of the beast. His kingdom becomes dark when the fifth vial is poured out upon the seat or capital city of his kingdom. Revelation 17:18 states, "The woman which thou sawest is that great city, which reigneth over the kings of the earth." That great city is the capital of his kingdom, just like Washington DC is the capital of the United States. Every kingdom must have a capital. The seat is like the county seat, the capital of the county.

When the Angel of Jesus talked to John concerning the church at Pergamos, he told John that he knew the inhabitants of Pergamos were dwelling where Satan's seat was located. Revelation 2:12–13 states, "To the angel of the church in Pergamos write … I know thy works, and where thou dwellest, even where Satan's seat is." It appears that Satan's dwelling place or his seat is Pergamos.

The fifth angel pours out his vial of the wrath of God upon the seat of Satan, Pergamos or Babylon. Babylon is a descriptive or symbolic name. An example would be like Las Vegas being called Sin City. The people still refuse to believe they are following the wrong god because, with all of their pain and suffering, they repent not for their evil deeds. Because they believe the antichrist is the one and only god, why did they not look to him to save them from all of this pain and suffering?

Rev. 14:8   And there followed another angel, saying, Babylon is fallen, is fallen, that great city, because she made all nations drink of the wine of the wrath of her fornication.

Rev. 18:1   And after these things I saw another angel come down from heaven, having great power; and the earth was lightened with his glory.

Rev. 18:2   And he cried mightily with a strong voice, saying, Babylon the great is fallen, is fallen, and is become the habitation of devils, and the hold of every foul spirit, and a cage of every unclean and hateful bird.

Rev. 18:3   For all nations have drunk of the wine of the wrath of her fornication, and the kings of the earth have committed fornication with her, and the merchants of the earth are waxed rich through the abundance of her delicacies.

The fifth angel pours out his vial upon the seat of Satan. John then saw an angel proclaiming that Babylon had fallen. Babylon is the symbolic name of the antichrist's kingdom. Pergamos or Babylon is the literal seat or capital of Satan. This city caused man to commit fornication (idolatry). The fifth angel pours out his vial upon Babylon, the capital city. Great is the fall of the antichrist's kingdom because it was responsible for deceiving mankind and turning him away from God.

Rev. 18:5   For her sins have reached unto heaven, and God hath remembered her iniquities.

Rev. 18:6   Reward her even as she rewarded you, and double unto her double according to her works: in the cup which she hath filled fill to her double.

Rev. 18:7   How much she hath glorified herself, and lived deliciously, so much torment and sorrow give her: for she saith in her heart, I sit a queen, and am no widow, and shall see no sorrow.

Rev. 18:8   Therefore shall her plagues come in one day, death, and mourning, and famine; and she shall be utterly burned with fire: for strong is the Lord God who judgeth her.

Rev. 18:9   And the kings of the earth, who have committed

fornication and lived deliciously with her, shall bewail her, and lament for her, when they shall see the smoke of her burning,

Rev. 18:10 Standing afar off for the fear of her torment, saying, Alas, alas, that great city Babylon, that mighty city! for in one hour is thy judgment come.

Rev. 18:11 And the merchants of the earth shall weep and mourn over her; for no man buyeth their merchandise any more:

Rev. 18:12 The merchandise of gold, and silver, and precious stones, and of pearls, and fine linen, and purple, and silk, and scarlet, and all thyine wood, and all manner vessels of ivory, and all manner vessels of most precious wood, and of brass, and iron, and marble,

Rev. 18:13 And cinnamon, and odours, and ointments, and frankincense, and wine, and oil, and fine flour, and wheat, and beasts, and sheep, and horses, and chariots, and slaves, and souls of men.

Rev. 18:14 And the fruits that thy soul lusted after are departed from thee, and all things which were dainty and goodly are departed from thee, and thou shalt find them no more at all.

Rev. 18:15 The merchants of these things, which were made rich by her, shall stand afar off for the fear of her torment, weeping and wailing,

Rev. 18:16 And saying, Alas, alas, that great city, that was clothed in fine linen, and purple, and scarlet, and decked with gold, and precious stones, and pearls!

Rev. 18:17 For in one hour so great riches is come to nought. And every shipmaster, and all the company in ships, and sailors, and as many as trade by sea, stood afar off,

Rev. 18:18 And cried when they saw the smoke of her burning, saying, What city is like unto this great city!

Rev. 18:19 And they cast dust on their heads, and cried, weeping and wailing, saying, Alas, alas, that great city, wherein were made rich all that had ships in the sea by reason of her costliness! For in one hour is she made desolate.

Rev. 18:20 Rejoice over her, thou heaven, and ye holy apostles and prophets; for God hath avenged you on her.

Rev. 18:21 And a mighty angel took up a stone like a great millstone, and cast it into the sea, saying, Thus with violence shall that great city Babylon be thrown down, and shall be found no more at all.

Rev. 18:22 And the voice of harpers, and musicians, and of pipers, and trumpeters, shall be heard no more at all in thee; and no craftsman, of whatsoever craft he be, shall be found any more in thee; and the sound of a millstone shall be heard no more at all in thee;

Rev. 18:23 And the light of a candle shall shine no more at all in thee; and the voice of the bridegroom and of the bride shall be heard no more at all in thee: for thy merchants were the great men of the earth; for by thy sorceries were all nations deceived.

Rev. 18:24 And in her was found the blood of prophets, and of saints, and of all that were slain upon the earth.

Most of Revelation 18 describes the fall of Babylon. The capital city of Babylon has just been totally destroyed. She was burned with fire. This city by its name alone symbolizes unrighteousness. The kings of the earth are surprised that such a great city has fallen. The destruction of this city is devastating to the merchants of the earth because they live deliciously in this city. They stand far off and can see the smoke from the burning city. They begin to weep because their great city just went up in smoke. This is a perfect example of the phrase "buying and selling." The merchants weep because of the fall of the city. The merchants got rich from this city. The average citizen could buy food if he had the money because his goal was to survive. The merchant's goal was to make more money, and they would accept anybody's money, including the small, great, rich, poor, saved, or unsaved.

All of the products bought and sold are also listed. The items listed here are not the kind of items that a man looking to feed his family would be seeking. People who become prosperous under the antichrist's regime would be looking to acquire these items. They are not necessity items. The merchants buy slaves as well. This is another form of wealth. Men were probably volunteering to become slaves in order to feed their families. Greed and prosperity drives this economic system. Sadly, they have to sell their souls to the devil in order to become a part of it.

Remember at the breaking of the fifth seal when the souls of people who were under the altar cried out to God to avenge their blood on the people who still lived on earth. Revelation 6:6–10 states, "They cried with a loud voice, saying, how long, O Lord, holy and true, dost thou not judge and avenge our blood on them that dwell on the earth." All the righteous were changed at the sounding of the seventh trumpet and the souls under the altar were just avenged. Now is a time of celebration. Revelation 18:20 states, "Rejoice over her, thou heaven, and ye holy apostles and prophets; for God hath avenged you on her."

The great capital is destroyed. There will never be a light from a candle in this city again. There will be no craftsmen, musicians, and weddings in the capital city of Babylon, no more at all … forever. This city has become a habitation for devils and every foul spirit. It appears that the great city of Babylon has become some type of hell on earth. Revelation 18:2 states, "Saying, Babylon the great is fallen, is fallen, and is become the habitation of devils, and the hold of every foul spirit, and a cage of every unclean and hateful bird." This place will become a graveyard. No life-form of any kind will ever exist there again.

Sixth Vial

> Rev. 16:12   And the sixth angel poured out his vial upon the great river Euphrates; and the water thereof was dried up, that the way of the kings of the east might be prepared.

The sixth angel pours out his vial of the wrath of God upon the Euphrates River. When the vial is poured out upon the Euphrates River, the waters dry up. Once the waters dry up, it becomes a highway for the kings of the east. Remember when the sixth angel sounded his trumpet, the angels at the Euphrates River were loosed. Revelation 9:13–16 states, "The sixth angel sounded … the sixth angel which had the trumpet, Loose the four angels which are bound in the great river Euphrates." This large 200-million man army at the Euphrates River use the dry riverbed as a highway. They are obviously angry about the destruction of their capital city, which was destroyed when the fifth vial was poured out upon the seat or capital of the antichrist.

> Rev. 14:17 And another angel came out of the temple which is in heaven, he also having a sharp sickle.
>
> Rev. 14:18 And another angel came out from the altar, which had power over fire; and cried with a loud cry to him that had the sharp sickle, saying, Thrust in thy sharp sickle, and gather the clusters of the vine of the earth; for her grapes are fully ripe.
>
> Rev. 14:19 And the angel thrust in his sickle into the earth, and gathered the vine of the earth, and cast it into the great winepress of the wrath of God.
>
> Rev. 14:20 And the winepress was trodden without the city, and blood came out of the winepress, even unto the horse bridles, by the space of a thousand and six hundred furlongs.

The sixth vial of the wrath of God has just been poured out upon the Euphrates River. John saw an angel come out of the temple with another sharp sickle. The angel having power over fire told him to cast his sickle into the earth. When he cast it into the earth, the vine of the earth was reaped. Not only were the grapes reaped, but the vine that supports or sustains the grapes was also reaped. The grapes in this particular case are the unsaved who are in the antichrist's army warring against God. These are the ones that will be thrown into the winepress of the wrath of God. The vines are all the avenues that support the lifestyle of the unrighteous.

A winepress is commonly thought of as a machine for extracting juice from grapes. The word *winepress* in Greek means "trough."[29] A trough is a long, narrow opening that contains a liquid and sometimes allows a liquid to flow through it. An example of a trough would be a gutter or narrow stream.

---

[29] The New Strong's Complete Dictionary of Bible Words (Thomas Nelson Publishers, 1996), 652.

The trough is the path taken by the juice squeezed from the grapes, but, in this case, it is blood, not juice. It is the blood of those who rebelled against God.

When the angel thrust his sickle into the earth, he gathered the vine of the earth. The Greek meaning of *vine* is "as coiling about a support."[30] A grapevine is the life support system that coils and winds around objects in order to sustain the clusters of grapes. The vine or support system is thrown into the winepress of the wrath of God. We have to first identify this vine to get the full scope of what is happening. When the sixth seal was broken in Revelation 9, the 200-million man army was loosed at the Euphrates River. Armies are sometimes considered the life support of a nation. The Euphrates River coils and winds as it runs through the countryside. The waters of the Euphrates River are dried up during the wrath of God when the sixth vial is poured out upon this river. This dry riverbed makes a highway for the 200-million man army from the east. Revelation 16:12 states, "The sixth angel poured out his vial upon the great river Euphrates; and the water thereof was dried up, that the way of the kings of the east might be prepared." The clusters of grapes are the actual soldiers. The dry riverbed is the vine that supports the soldiers. When the soldiers enter the dry riverbed, it will become the winepress. They will eventually be killed in the dry riverbed or winepress. Their bodies and blood of the soldiers will be stretched out along the floor of the Euphrates River for a distance of sixteen hundred furlongs (two hundred miles).

When the vines and the grapes are put in the winepress of the wrath of God, a tremendous amount of blood is squeezed out. The soldiers will be marching toward Jerusalem by way of the Euphrates dry riverbed. They will be killed in the riverbed before they reach the city. Revelation 14:20 states, "The winepress was trodden without the city." There will be a continuous stream of blood up to the horses' bridles, headgear put on a horse to steer him, for a distance of sixteen hundred furlongs. That is a lot of blood to reach up to the horses' bridles. The average horse bridle is more than three feet from the ground when he is standing. It is indicated that the horses are dead because the fowls are invited to eat their flesh. Revelation 19:17–18 states:

---

[30] The New Strong's Complete Dictionary of Bible Words (Thomas Nelson Publishers, 1996), 575.

And he cried with a loud voice, saying to all the fowls that fly in the midst of heaven, Come and gather yourselves together unto the supper of the great God; that ye may eat the flesh of kings, and the flesh of captains, and the flesh of mighty men, and the flesh of horses.

Even if the horses are dead and lying on the ground, that's a lot of blood to flow for that distance. Another possibility of the blood rising to the horse bridle is the blood flow stretches for a distance of two hundred miles and collects into a valley or ravine as high as a horse's bridle. With that much blood, one has to conclude that there will be a great multitude of people, the 200-million man army, who are put into the winepress of the wrath of God because they chose to follow the antichrist.

The winepress of the wrath of God is only physical death. This death is not the second death or lake of fire spoken of in Revelation 20:14. This is not the eternal punishment where there will be the gnashing of teeth. Matthew 13:42 states, "Shall cast them into a furnace of fire: there shall be wailing and gnashing of teeth." The eternal punishment will take place at the second death when the unrighteous will be thrown into the lake of fire. Revelation 20:14–15 states, "Death and hell were cast into the lake of fire. This is the second death … whosoever was not found written in the book of life was cast into the lake of fire."

Rev. 16:13 And I saw three unclean spirits like frogs come out of the mouth of the dragon, and out of the mouth of the beast, and out of the mouth of the false prophet.

Rev. 16:14 For they are the spirits of devils, working miracles, which go forth unto the kings of the earth and of the whole world, to gather them to the battle of that great day of God Almighty.

Rev. 16:15 Behold, I come as a thief. Blessed is he that watcheth, and keepeth his garments, lest he walk naked, and they see his shame.

Rev. 16:16 And he gathered them together into a place called in the Hebrew tongue Armageddon.

John saw three unclean spirits come out of the mouth of the dragon, the beast, and the false prophet. These are the spirits of devils, and they have the likeness of frogs. They are like frogs because they leap from place to place, seeking someone to devour. They are the spirits that cause man to do his evil deeds. John was in the presence of the Holy Spirit. That was why he could see these spirits. These spirits have one mission, to wreak havoc on as many people as they can because they know they only have a short time. Devils know there is a time when they will be tormented, so they are making one last stand. Matthew 8:28–29 states:

> There met him two possessed with devils, coming out of the tombs, exceeding fierce, so that no man might pass by that way … behold, they cried out, saying, what have we to do with thee, Jesus, thou Son of God? art thou come hither to torment us before the time.

They have put together this great army, 200 million men strong, who now march down the dry riverbed of the Euphrates River to the great Battle of Armageddon. Some people believe the Battle of Armageddon will take place in Megiddo. This could very well be, but the Euphrates River does not run through Israel. In Hebrew, the word *Megiddon* means "rendezvous."[31] The Strong's reference number is #4203. *Rendezvous* means "a specific time and place of a meeting."[32] The Battle of Armageddon could not take place until a specific time, a specific place, and a specific enemy. In this case, the enemy is the army of the antichrist. According to Genesis 2:10–14, a river ran out of the garden of Eden and parted into four rivers. One of those rivers is the Euphrates. Satan first deceived man in the garden of Eden, so it might just be possible that Satan's deception of the world will all end in the garden of Eden as well.

Rev. 19:11 And I saw heaven opened, and behold a white horse; and he that sat upon him was called Faithful and True, and in righteousness he doth judge and make war.

Rev. 19:12 His eyes were as a flame of fire, and on his head were

---

[31] Torah Light Ministries, Stanley Chester, taped message.

[32] The World Book Dictionary (Doubleday & Company, Inc., 1983), 1769.

many crowns; and he had a name written, that no man knew, but he himself.

Rev. 19:13 And he was clothed with a vesture dipped in blood: and his name is called The Word of God.

Rev. 19:14 And the armies which were in heaven followed him upon white horses, clothed in fine linen, white and clean.

Rev. 19:15 And out of his mouth goeth a sharp sword, that with it he should smite the nations: and he shall rule them with a rod of iron: and he treadeth the winepress of the fierceness and wrath of Almighty God.

Rev. 19:16 And he hath on his vesture and on his thigh a name written, KING OF KINGS, AND LORD OF LORDS.

Rev. 19:17 And I saw an angel standing in the sun; and he cried with a loud voice, saying to all the fowls that fly in the midst of heaven, Come and gather yourselves together unto the supper of the great God;

John saw heaven open, and a white horse appeared. This white horse had a rider on him, and the rider had many crowns. His clothes had been dipped in blood. This rider's eyes were like flames of fire. Out of his mouth was a sharp sword. This rider had a name written on his clothes and on his thigh.

This rider has many names. He is called faithful and true, along with a name written that no one knows except himself. He is also called the Word of God, King of Kings, and Lord of Lords. This rider is none other than Jesus Christ himself. His clothes are full of blood from the tremendous lashing he endured and the agony of the nails in his hands at his crucifixion.

Jesus Christ has returned to judge the antichrist's great 200-million man army and make war against them. This battle that Jesus Christ came to fight is the Battle of Armageddon. His weapon is the sharp sword that goes out of his mouth. Ephesians 6:17 states, "The sword of the Spirit, which is the word of God." He will defeat the army with his sword. He merely speaks the defeat of the antichrist's army into existence. After the completion of the Battle of Armageddon, he will rule the nations with a rod of iron. In the Battle of Armageddon, Jesus Christ treads the winepress of the fierceness of the wrath of Almighty God. Revelation 14:19 states, "Cast it into the great winepress of the wrath of God."

Jesus has armies that were with him in heaven following him to this battle. The armies are also on white horses, and they are clothed in fine linen that is clean and white. These armies are the saints who took part in the first resurrection. Revelation 20:5 states, "This is the first resurrection." They stand on the sea of glass before the throne in Revelation 15:2 and 7:9. They are the ones of which Jude made reference. Jude 1:14–15 states:

> Behold, the Lord cometh with ten thousands of his saints ... to execute judgment upon all, and to convince all that are ungodly among them of all their ungodly deeds which they have ungodly committed, and of all their hard speeches which ungodly sinners have spoken against him.

These are the ten thousands of his saints or the multitude who were standing on the sea of glass who arrived with Jesus to execute judgment. These saints are not limited to only ten thousand. They are a multitude. Revelation 7:9 states, "A great multitude, which no man could number, of all nations, and kindreds, and people, and tongues." The saints come with Jesus Christ to execute judgment and bring the wrath of God.

John heard an angel proclaim to the fowls of the air to come to the great supper of God. The angel had just given the fowls of the air an invitation to a smorgasbord. At this party, they would enjoy the flesh of kings, captains, armies, important people, and horses. This great feast that the fowls of the earth would enjoy will be the flesh of all those slain in the Battle of Armageddon.

The pouring out of the sixth vial is just a preparation for the Battle of Armageddon. It dries up the Euphrates River to provide a highway for the armies who are marching against Jesus Christ. It brought out the three unclean spirits or devils to make one final stand. All of these events are the preparation leading up the Battle of Armageddon that will take place when the seventh and final vial will be poured out.

Seventh Vial

Rev. 16:17 And the seventh angel poured out his vial into the air; and there came a great voice out of the temple of heaven, from the throne, saying, It is done.

Rev. 16:18 And there were voices, and thunders, and lightnings; and there was a great earthquake, such as was not since men were upon the earth, so mighty an earthquake, and so great.

Rev. 16:19 And the great city was divided into three parts, and the cities of the nations fell: and great Babylon came in remembrance before God, to give unto her the cup of the wine of the fierceness of his wrath.

Rev. 16:20 And every island fled away, and the mountains were not found.

Rev. 16:21 And there fell upon men a great hail out of heaven, every stone about the weight of a talent: and men blasphemed God because of the plague of the hail; for the plague thereof was exceeding great.

The seventh angel pours out his vial of the wrath of God into the air because Satan is prince of the power of the air. Ephesians 2:2 states, "In time past ye walked according to the course of this world, according to the prince of the power of the air, the spirit that now worketh in the children of disobedience." The seventh vial destroys the powers of Satan, the antichrist, and the false prophet. This vial signals the beginning and end of the Battle of Armageddon. The Battle of Armageddon is not a long-drawn-out war. It is over in an instant. God merely speaks victory into existence. Revelation 19:21 states, "The remnant were slain with the sword of him that sat upon the horse, which sword proceeded out of his mouth." They will be destroyed with the sword out of his mouth. The sword out of his mouth is the word of God. Ephesians 6:17 states, "And the sword of the Spirit, which is the word of God." It is just like God formed the world by his word. Hebrews 11:3 states, "We understand that the worlds were framed by the word of God." He will also end the dominion of mankind by his word. Revelation 19:21

states, "The remnant were slain with the sword of him that sat upon the horse, which sword proceeded out of his mouth."

With the outpouring of the seventh vial into the air, the kingdoms of this world are finished. Man will no longer rule this world. This is the beginning of the everlasting kingdom that God established.

> Zec. 14:12 And this shall be the plague wherewith the LORD will smite all the people that have fought against Jerusalem; Their flesh shall consume away while they stand upon their feet, and their eyes shall consume away in their holes, and their tongue shall consume away in their mouth.

The Lord will come on a white horse with a multitude of his saints to fight the Battle of Armageddon. The Lord will fight the battle with the sword of his mouth, the word of God. When the Lord comes with the saints to the Battle of Armageddon, the flesh of all the people who fought against Jerusalem or the kingdom of God will melt away from their bones where they are standing. Their eyes will dissolve in their sockets, and their tongues will vaporize in their mouths. This is the end of the wrath of the Lamb.

> Rev. 19:18 That ye may eat the flesh of kings, and the flesh of captains, and the flesh of mighty men, and the flesh of horses, and of them that sit on them, and the flesh of all men, both free and bond, both small and great.
>
> Rev. 19:19 And I saw the beast, and the kings of the earth, and their armies, gathered together to make war against him that sat on the horse, and against his army.
>
> Rev. 19:20 And the beast was taken, and with him the false prophet that wrought miracles before him, with which he deceived them that had received the mark of the beast, and them that worshipped his image. These both were cast alive into a lake of fire burning with brimstone.
>
> Rev. 19:21 And the remnant were slain with the sword of him that sat upon the horse, which sword proceeded out of his mouth: and all the fowls were filled with their flesh.

At the conclusion of the Battle of Armageddon, the fowls of the air have a great feast. The beast or the antichrist and false prophet will both be taken and thrown into the lake of fire burning with brimstone or sulfur. Notice that the wrath of God is very selective. The antichrist and false prophet are not killed. They are cast alive into the lake of fire. There is something else to note. Of all the vials being poured out, no one died except on the second vial poured upon the sea and seventh vial poured into the air. People died in the sea when the waters of the sea became as the blood of a dead man. People died in the Battle of Armageddon when the seventh vial was poured into the air. Man's eyes and tongues were consumed from their bodies.

Zec. 14:1   Behold, the day of the LORD cometh, and thy spoil shall be divided in the midst of thee.

Zec. 14:2   For I will gather all nations against Jerusalem to battle; and the city shall be taken, and the houses rifled, and the women ravished; and half of the city shall go forth into captivity, and the residue of the people shall not be cut off from the city.

Zec. 14:3   Then shall the LORD go forth, and fight against those nations, as when he fought in the day of battle.

Zec. 14:4   And his feet shall stand in that day upon the mount of Olives, which is before Jerusalem on the east, and the mount of Olives shall cleave in the midst thereof toward the east and toward the west, and there shall be a very great valley; and half of the mountain shall remove toward the north, and half of it toward the south.

The book of Zechariah informs us that the Lord will gather all of his enemies for the day of the Lord. He will then go forth to destroy all of his enemies at the Battle of Armageddon. Immediately after the Battle of Armageddon, the Lord will stand in that day upon Mount Olives. This is the beginning of the everlasting kingdom. This is the beginning of the thousand-year rule of the saints, also known as the millennium. Revelation 20:4 states, "And they lived and reigned with Christ a thousand years."

The angel with the seventh vial of the wrath of God poured it into the air. A great voice came out of the temple of heaven, proclaiming it was done. Revelation 16:17 states, "And the seventh angel poured out his vial into the air; and there came a great voice out of the temple of heaven, from the throne, saying, it is done." John also heard voices and thunder. He also witnessed a great earthquake. All islands fled away, and mountains could not be found. There were great hailstones. The weight of each one of these hailstones was about fifty-seven to eighty pounds. After all of that, men still continued to blaspheme God.

Revelation 11:15 tells us that the kingdoms of this world have become the kingdoms of our Lord and of his Christ, and he shall reign forever and ever. It is done.

Rev. 19:1   And after these things I heard a great voice of much people in heaven, saying, Alleluia; Salvation, and glory, and honour, and power, unto the Lord our God:

Rev. 19:2   For true and righteous are his judgments: for he hath judged the great whore, which did corrupt the earth with her fornication, and hath avenged the blood of his servants at her hand.

Rev. 19:3   And again they said, Alleluia. And her smoke rose up for ever and ever.

Rev. 19:4   And the four and twenty elders and the four beasts fell down and worshipped God that sat on the throne, saying, Amen; Alleluia.

Rev. 19:5   And a voice came out of the throne, saying, Praise our God, all ye his servants, and ye that fear him, both small and great.

Rev. 19:6   And I heard as it were the voice of a great multitude, and as the voice of many waters, and as the voice of mighty thunderings, saying, Alleluia: for the Lord God omnipotent reigneth.

Rev. 19:7   Let us be glad and rejoice, and give honour to him: for the marriage of the Lamb is come, and his wife hath made herself ready.

Rev. 19:8   And to her was granted that she should be arrayed in fine linen, clean and white: for the fine linen is the righ-teousness of saints.

Rev. 19:9   And he saith unto me, Write, Blessed are they which are called unto the marriage supper of the Lamb. And he saith unto me, These are the true sayings of God.

Rev. 19:10   And I fell at his feet to worship him. And he said unto me, See thou do it not: I am thy fellowservant, and of thy brethren that have the testimony of Jesus: worship God: for the testimony of Jesus is the spirit of prophecy.

The setting here is after the Battle of Armageddon. We know the battle is over because the context is past tense. The great whore was judged. The blood of the servants has been avenged. The battle is over. There is more praise and worshipping in heaven. It is time for the marriage of the lamb to take place. The wife has made herself ready for the bride's groom. Whosoever is called to the marriage supper of the Lamb is blessed. Revelation 19:9 states, "Blessed are they which are called unto the marriage supper of the Lamb." The blessing is confirmed again. Revelation 20:5–6 states, "This is the first resurrection …. blessed and holy is he that hath part in the first resurrection: on such the second death hath no power, but they shall be priests of God and of Christ, and shall reign with him a thousand years."

When Jesus accomplished all things and died on the cross, he stated, "It is finished." John 19:30 states, "He said, It is finished: and he bowed his head, and gave up the ghost." This signifies that the Old Testament is finished. When the seventh vial was poured out into the air, a voice from heaven stated, "It is done." Revelation 16:17 states, "A great voice out of the temple of heaven, from the throne, saying, It is done." This signifies the end of the New Testament and now begins another segment of time for all of the participants of the first resurrection. This new segment of time is a state of being where everything is perfect, the end of the physical and beginning of the spiritual. This new segment of time is called the millennium, where there are no more tears, sorrow, pain, or death, for those that participated in the first resurrection.

Some seem to think that all unsaved people were either killed by the antichrist in the great tribulation or by God in the wrath of God. This just isn't the case. There are still people who survived both of these events. If all unsaved people were killed by the great tribulation or the wrath of God, who then would enter into the millennium? It cannot be the saved people because they were gathered together at the second coming and are now in their glorified bodies in the presence of God. Those who overcome are to rule and reign with Christ. Revelation 2:26–27 states, "He that overcometh, and keepeth my works unto the end, to him will I give power over the nations… and he shall rule them with a rod of iron." If all the unsaved people are dead, who then will the saints (overcomers) rule over with a rod of iron?

CHAPTER 14

POST ARMAGEDDON

Rev. 19:20   And the beast was taken, and with him the false prophet that wrought miracles before him, with which he deceived them that had received the mark of the beast, and them that worshipped his image. These both were cast alive into a lake of fire burning with brimstone.

Rev. 19:21   And the remnant were slain with the sword of him that sat upon the horse, which sword proceeded out of his mouth: and all the fowls were filled with their flesh.

Rev. 20:1   And I saw an angel come down from heaven, having the key of the bottomless pit and a great chain in his hand.

Rev. 20:2   And he laid hold on the dragon, that old serpent, which is the Devil, and Satan, and bound him a thousand years,

Rev. 20:3   And cast him into the bottomless pit, and shut him up, and set a seal upon him, that he should deceive the nations no more, till the thousand years should be fulfilled: and after that he must be loosed a little season.

The Imprisonment

THE timing is immediately after the Battle of Armageddon, when the seventh and final vial of wrath has been poured into the air. The scriptures show the imprisonment of the beast, false prophet, and Satan. Actually, two different imprisonments are taking place. First, the beast and false prophet are thrown into the lake of fire while still alive. Then John saw an angel come down from heaven. This angel had the key of the bottomless pit and a great chain in his hand. He grabbed hold of the dragon (Satan) and threw him into the bottomless pit. He put a seal on the pit so Satan could not escape. Satan will be bound in the bottomless pit for one thousand years.

Satan is not bound in the same place where the antichrist and the false prophet are bound. Revelation 19:20 states, "The beast was taken, and with him the false prophet ... both were cast alive into a lake of fire burning with brimstone." Satan is in the bottomless pit; the antichrist and false prophet are in the lake of fire.

The bottomless pit is a place like hell. It is the same place where the rich man went after he died in Luke 16:19–31, that is, hell. Luke 16:22–23 states, "The rich man also died, and was buried ... in hell he lift up his eyes, being in torments." He is in a place of torment, and he is conscious of all the things happening on earth, but he is powerless to change his circumstances.

The lake of fire burns continuously, and brimstone or sulfur fuels it. There is a vast difference between the lake of fire and hell. The lake of fire is greater than hell because it will eventually contain death and hell. Revelation 20:14 states, "Death and hell were cast into the lake of fire. This is the second death." The lake of fire is several degrees of intensity worse than hell.

Satan is going to be bound for one thousand years to prevent him from deceiving the nations anymore. Revelation 20:3 states, "That he should deceive the nations no more." There will finally be peace here on earth. This thousand-year period without Satan is better known as the thousand-year millennium, often referred to as the millennium. Satan will have to complete a prison sentence of one thousand years. Once the sentence is complete, he will be released from the bottomless pit.

The Priesthood

Rev. 20:4   And I saw thrones, and they sat upon them, and judgment was given unto them: and I saw the souls of them that were beheaded for the witness of Jesus, and for the word of God, and which had not worshipped the beast, neither his image, neither had received his mark upon their foreheads, or in their hands; and they lived and reigned with Christ a thousand years.

Rev. 20:5   But the rest of the dead lived not again until the thousand years were finished. This is the first resurrection.

Rev. 20:6   Blessed and holy is he that hath part in the first resurrection: on such the second death hath no power, but they shall be priests of God and of Christ, and shall reign with him a thousand years.

The setting is in the throne room after the Battle of Armageddon. Soon after John witnessed Satan being bound and confined to the bottomless pit, he also saw thrones in heaven. The thrones were occupied. John saw the souls of them that were killed for the witness of Jesus and the word of God. John also saw the ones who were alive and had not worshipped the beast or his image or received the mark of the beast. All of the souls of the people that John saw in the throne room are living and will reign with Christ for one thousand years. They took part in the first resurrection, and they will live forever. Their first term of duty is for one thousand years, and that's the same amount of time that Satan will be bound in the bottomless pit. Although they rule and reign with Christ for only a thousand years, they will spend eternity in heaven in the presence of God. Their thousand-year reign begins and ends with the imprisonment of Satan.

Something to note, only the people who were born-again at the time of their death and those who were still alive and born again at the return of Christ were at this gathering standing before the throne. All of the unsaved individuals who were dead prior to the sounding of the seventh trumpet will remain dead. Everyone who dies after the sounding of the seventh trumpet, saved or unsaved, will remain dead. They will not be judged until sometime after the thousand-year imprisonment of Satan has been completed. Revelation 20:5 states, "But the rest of the dead lived not again until the thousand years were finished." They will live again at the great white throne judgment. Revelation 20:11–12 states, "And I saw a great white throne, and him that sat on it … and I saw the dead, small and great, stand before God; and the books were opened." At the great white throne judgment, only the righteous individuals who lived in the millennium will be rewarded and spend eternity with God. All others will be sentenced to spend eternity in the lake of fire.

The sounding of the seventh trumpet initiated the first resurrection, a resurrection of people being given their new or glorified bodies, like the body that Jesus received after his resurrection. Do not confuse this resurrection with the resurrection of Lazarus. Lazarus was resurrected in the same fleshly body. He had to die again because he did not have a new body, nor did he have his new name. Revelation 2:17 states, "To him that overcometh will I give to eat of the hidden manna, and will give him a white stone, and in the stone a new name written, which no man knoweth saving he that receiveth it." The first resurrection is when born-again people will be given their new bodies. They will eat from the tree of life and be given hidden manna. They will be given a white stone and a new name that no one knows except themselves. They will rule the nations with a rod of iron. They will not experience anymore dying, pain, thirst, hunger, and so forth. The first resurrection is when an individual has endured until the end. In other words, he has earned the right to dwell with God forever.

Whosoever that takes part in the first resurrection will be blessed. Revelation 20:6 states, "Blessed and holy is he that hath part in the first resurrection." The second death will not affect them because they have already received their glorified bodies and will live forever. Those who have part in the first resurrection will become kings and priests and reign on earth for a thousand years. Revelation 5:10 states, "Hast made us unto our God kings and priests: and we shall reign on the earth." They will rule and reign with Christ for one thousand years, and they will dwell with God. Please note that their reign will be on earth.

Some might ask, "Over whom will the first resurrection saints be ruling? Who will be left here on earth after the great tribulation and the wrath of God?" The first resurrection saints will be reigning over those people who were not killed by the antichrist during the great tribulation and those people who were not killed by the vials of wrath. All of which were not born again at the sounding of the seventh trumpet. Contrary to popular belief, the antichrist did not kill everybody who did not take his mark. He only killed those who stood in the way of his agenda. After all, the antichrist needed somebody to do the work so his followers could live lavishly. The vials predominately killed those who worshipped the beast or his image, received the mark of the beast, or fought against Jesus in the Battle of Armageddon. There have to be some people left on earth after the first resurrection because the first resurrection saints have to rule over someone. The only people left here on earth will be those who were not born-again at the sounding of the seventh trumpet and survivors of both the great tribulation of the antichrist and the wrath of God. The first resurrection saints will rule over these people. The people who were not included in the first resurrection will have a good chance to become born again because Satan will be imprisoned for one thousand years. While Satan is incarcerated, the world will not be deceived. Things will be exactly as they appear because the deceiver is bound for one thousand years and he will have no influence over mankind. All of mankind's attention can now be focused on God and righteousness because Satan is no longer free to deceive or hinder him.

Post Millennium

Rev. 20:7   And when the thousand years are expired, Satan shall be loosed out of his prison,

Rev. 20:8   And shall go out to deceive the nations which are in the four quarters of the earth, Gog and Magog, to gather them together to battle: the number of whom is as the sand of the sea.

Rev. 20:9   And they went up on the breadth of the earth, and compassed the camp of the saints about, and the beloved city: and fire came down from God out of heaven, and devoured them.

It has been one thousand years of peace. Satan has reached the end of his thousand-year sentence. He will be released from the bottomless pit for a little season. Revelation 20:3 states, "Till the thousand years should be fulfilled: and after that he must be loosed a little season." We do not know how long this little season is going to be. Jesus said that no one knows the day and hour that he will return. Matthew 24:36 states, "Of that day and hour knoweth no man, no, not the angels of heaven, but my Father only." It will be the same way concerning the amount of time in the little season. No one knows how long it will be. We do know that the little season will be long enough for Satan to deceive enough people to mass a huge army as large as the sand of the sea (Rev. 20:8).

Evidently, Satan was not rehabilitated because he goes right back to his old tricks. Revelation 20:7–8 states, "When the thousand years are expired, Satan shall be loosed out of his prison ... and shall go out to deceive the nations which are in the four quarters of the earth." He goes out and deceives the people again, just like he deceived Eve in the garden of Eden. His influence saturates the entire world. Once again, he has a multitude of followers. People should know Satan's tactics by now. He is a deceiver and a counterfeiter, especially after having one thousand years where there was no satanic influence.

Gog and Magog go all over the world for one purpose and one purpose only, to deceive the world. Gog is a symbolic name for a future antichrist[33] or Satan. Magog is a symbolic name for an Anti-Christian Party,[34] or the followers of Satan. Satan and his followers gather a great multitude of people. The number is as the number of the sands of the sea. Satan and his multitude encircle New Jerusalem, the Holy City that John witnessed descending down from heaven. The Holy City is where God will dwell with his saints. Revelation 21:3 states, "The tabernacle of God is with men, and he will dwell with them, and they shall be his people, and God himself shall be with them, and be their God." Satan's intent is to destroy this city, but God sends fire down from heaven. All of them are devoured. You think Satan would have learned his lesson from the Battle of Armageddon. Over one thousand years have passed, and Satan is still attempting to destroy God's people with his strong will and determination, but to no avail.

> Rev. 20:10 And the devil that deceived them was cast into the lake of fire and brimstone, where the beast and the false prophet are, and shall be tormented day and night for ever and ever.

After the Battle of Armageddon, the antichrist and false prophet will be cast into the lake of fire. Satan will be thrown into the bottomless pit. Satan will be released after one thousand years have passed. Immediately after Satan's release, he will persuade a great multitude to turn from God,

---

[33] The New Strong's Complete Dictionary of Bible Words (Thomas Nelson Publishers, 1996), 598.

[34] The New Strong's Complete Dictionary of Bible Words (Thomas Nelson Publishers, 1996), 654.

whom they have followed for more than a thousand years, and convince them to follow him. They will encircle New Jerusalem, and God will send fire down from heaven. They will be destroyed. Satan will be imprisoned again, but he will be sent to a maximum security prison, the lake of fire where the antichrist and false prophet have been sentenced. This time, his sentence will not be one thousand years. It will be the maximum sentence allowed by law, forever.

Great White Throne Judgment

Rev. 20:11   And I saw a great white throne, and him that sat on it, from whose face the earth and the heaven fled away; and there was found no place for them.

Rev. 20:12   And I saw the dead, small and great, stand before God; and the books were opened: and another book was opened, which is the book of life: and the dead were judged out of those things which were written in the books, according to their works.

Rev. 20:13   And the sea gave up the dead which were in it; and death and hell delivered up the dead which were in them: and they were judged every man according to their works.

Rev. 20:14   And death and hell were cast into the lake of fire. This is the second death.

Rev. 20:15   And whosoever was not found written in the book of life was cast into the lake of fire.

After God destroyed Satan's massive army and Satan was thrown in the lake of fire, John saw one sitting on a great white throne, God. The heavens and earth fled from his face. John also saw a multitude of people who were formerly dead standing before God. The setting is the great white throne judgment, that is, when all the people who did not take part in the first resurrection, both alive and dead, going as far back as Adam and Eve, stand before God to be judged.

At the great white throne judgment, the books will be opened. Notice, books are plural, so there is more than one book opened. We know one book is the Book of Life. The other books are the ones that have recorded all of the deeds that man has done during his lifetime of which he never repented. Man will be judged out of these books according to the life he lived. All names written in the Book of Life will enter into the kingdom of God. All names not written in the Book of Life will be thrown into the lake of fire. The great white throne judgment is when all who have not previously been judged will receive their judgment. Hebrews 9:27 states, "It is appointed unto men once to die, but after this the judgment." This is that judgment, the second death.

At the great white throne judgment, even death and hell will be cast into the lake of fire. Satan, death, and hell will all be tormented forever. Now there is no more death because all the inhabitants in the kingdom of God are immune from death. They will live forever with God in his kingdom.

CHAPTER 15

NEW JERUSALEM

THE setting of this chapter is after the first resurrection and after the seven vials of the wrath of God is poured out upon the earth, but, just before the second death or second resurrection. This is at the beginning of the millennium. The word millennium does not appear in the Bible, but it means a period of one thousand years. The Bible refers to a thousand-year period in Revelation 20:4, "And they lived and reigned with Christ a thousand years." This is the period when Satan will be confined to the bottomless pit and the world will be free of his influence. Revelation 20:3 states, "Cast him into the bottomless pit, and shut him up, and set a seal upon him, that he should deceive the nations no more."

New Heaven New Earth

Rev. 21:1   And I saw a new heaven and a new earth: for the first heaven and the first earth were passed away; and there was no more sea.

John saw a new heaven and a new earth because the first heaven and the first earth had passed away or changed. Neither did John see any more sea. This does not mean that heaven and earth no longer existed. It had only been reconstructed. The earth will never end. Psalms 78:69 states, "Like the earth which he hath established for ever." God said the earth will be here forever. Psalms 104:5 states, "Who laid the foundations of the earth, that it should not be removed for ever." It is confirmed again that the earth is everlasting. Ecclesiastes 1:4 states, "One generation passeth away, and another generation cometh: but the earth abideth for ever." The landscape of the earth will be changed when the seventh vial is poured out into the air. There will be a great earthquake, and the islands and mountains will be moved out of their places. Revelation 16:20 states, "Every island fled away, and the mountains were not found." The earth will change in appearance, but it is still the same earth.

Rev. 16:17 And the seventh angel poured out his vial into the air; and there came a great voice out of the temple of heaven, from the throne, saying, It is done.

Rev. 16:18 And there were voices, and thunders, and lightnings; and there was a great earthquake, such as was not since men were upon the earth, so mighty an earthquake, and so great.

Rev. 16:19 And the great city was divided into three parts, and the cities of the nations fell: and great Babylon came in remembrance before God, to give unto her the cup of the wine of the fierceness of his wrath.

Rev. 16:20 And every island fled away, and the mountains were not found.

When the seventh vial of the wrath of God was poured into the air, there was the greatest earthquake ever. Every island and mountain was leveled. The face of the earth had taken on a new appearance. It is the same earth, but it has been reconstructed. It's like a room full of furniture. When you rearrange the furniture, the room has a different look and feel to it, but it is the same room and the same furniture. This is what John meant by a new heaven and a new earth, not that the present earth no longer existed.

Holy City

Rev. 21:2 And I John saw the holy city, new Jerusalem, coming down from God out of heaven, prepared as a bride adorned for her husband.

John saw the Holy City, New Jerusalem, coming down from God out of heaven, prepared as a bride adorned for her husband. A bride is the most beautiful thing when seen for the first time by the groom. A bride goes through a lot of preparation to make herself ready for her wedding. This is similar to all the preparation that born-again believers go through to ready themselves for the return of Jesus. While the born-again believers ready themselves for the return of Christ, he is away preparing a place to receive them. John 14:3 states, "And if I go and prepare a place for you, I will come again, and receive you unto myself; that where I am, there ye may be also." The Holy City or New Jerusalem is the place that Jesus went to prepare for those who love him.

Rev. 21:3   And I heard a great voice out of heaven saying, Behold, the tabernacle of God is with men, and he will dwell with them, and they shall be his people, and God himself shall be with them, and be their God.

Rev. 21:4   And God shall wipe away all tears from their eyes; and there shall be no more death, neither sorrow, nor crying, neither shall there be any more pain: for the former things are passed away.

John heard a great voice from heaven, and the voice stated the tabernacle of God was with men. The tabernacle is the Holy City or New Jerusalem, the city John saw coming down from heaven. This voice from heaven was an angel or servant of God, possibly even God himself. The voice proclaimed that God would dwell with the people in this New Jerusalem and he would be their God. The people the voice refers to are all of the saints who were involved in the first resurrection. The angel also proclaimed that God would wipe away all their tears and there would be no more death, sorrow, crying, or pain in New Jerusalem. All of the old habits, sorrows, the cares of this world, and problems had passed away. All these things were things of the former world, and all of them passed away for all who had a part in the first resurrection.

Rev. 21:5   And he that sat upon the throne said, Behold, I make all things new. And he said unto me, Write: for these words are true and faithful.

Rev. 21:6   And he said unto me, It is done. I am Alpha and Omega, the beginning and the end. I will give unto him that is athirst of the fountain of the water of life freely.

Rev. 21:7   He that overcometh shall inherit all things; and I will be his God, and he shall be my son.

Rev. 21:8   But the fearful, and unbelieving, and the abominable, and murderers, and whoremongers, and sorcerers, and idolaters, and all liars, shall have their part in the lake which burneth with fire and brimstone: which is the second death.

Someone was sitting on a throne in the New Jerusalem, talking to John. This was not the Angel of Jesus talking to John. It was God himself. God spoke to John, and he proclaimed he had made all things new. He also told John to write down these things because they were faithful and true. He informed John that it was done and he was Alpha and Omega. He would freely give to those who were thirsty from the fountain of the water of life. All of those who overcome shall inherit all things. God will be their God, and they will be the sons of God. He made a stipulation that those who were fearful, unbelieving, abominable, murderers, whoremongers, sorcerers, idolaters, and liars would have a place reserved in the lake of fire that burned with brimstone. This lake of fire will be populated at the second death or the great white throne judgment, where mankind will be judged according to the life he led. Revelation 20:11–13 states, "I saw a great white throne … I saw the dead, small and great, stand before God … and they were judged every man according to their works."

In Revelation 21:8, the people to whom God was talking are not the people who took part in the first resurrection. They are already in New Jerusalem. God is already their God, and they are dwelling with him. He was talking to the people who did not take part in the first resurrection. They are the ones who were not born-again at the sounding of the seventh trumpet. These people will live in the millennium, the thousand years when Satan is bound. They will have a second chance to make things right with God, that is, to become born-again. If they fail to become born-again during the millennium, they will be lost forever.

The Bride

Rev. 21:9   And there came unto me one of the seven angels which had the seven vials full of the seven last plagues, and talked with me, saying, Come hither, I will shew thee the bride, the Lamb's wife.

Rev. 21:10 And he carried me away in the spirit to a great and high mountain, and shewed me that great city, the holy Jerusalem, descending out of heaven from God,

Rev. 21:11 Having the glory of God: and her light was like unto a stone most precious, even like a jasper stone, clear as crystal;

One of the angels who had one of the vials of the wrath of God approached John. The angel told John that he would show him the bride, the Lamb's wife. Immediately, John was taken into a high mountain. The angel showed John a great city, descending out of heaven from God. It was the Holy City, New Jerusalem. John saw this same city in Revelation 21:2. Notice that John did not see the church. He saw New Jerusalem.

I know this is a controversial subject, but the bride of Christ is New Jerusalem. The Lamb's wife is the Holy City. Scripture references a woman as being a city. Revelation 17:18 states, "The woman which thou sawest is that great city." A bride is a woman, and a wife is a woman. In scripture, a woman is symbolic for a city, so the bride is a city, New Jerusalem. The bride of Christ or the Lamb's wife is the Holy City or New Jerusalem, not the church. The church is not the bride of Christ. The church is the body of Christ. To all of those who are disappointed, there is some consolation. Cities are made up of people. The bride is the Holy City, and the inhabitants of any city make it unique. The inhabitants of New Jerusalem are the saints who took part in the first resurrection.

The New Jerusalem is the bride of Christ. This city has the glory of God in it. The glory of God is in the Holy City because God himself will dwell in the Holy City with all the saints or participants of the first resurrection. The light in the city is like a stone most precious. The stone referred to is the jasper stone, which represents the tribe of Benjamin. See the list of twelve tribes in the back of the book. The meaning of the name of Benjamin is "son of the right hand." Jesus Christ is the son of God. Christ being on the right hand of the father is referenced in Colossians 3:1, Hebrews 10:12, and 1 Peter 3:22.

> Col. 3:1   If ye then be risen with Christ, seek those things which are above, where Christ sitteth on the right hand of God.
>
> Heb. 10:12 But this man, after he had offered one sacrifice for sins for ever, sat down on the right hand of God;
>
> 1 Pet. 3:22 Who is gone into heaven, and is on the right hand of God; angels and authorities and powers being made subject unto him.

We know Jesus to be that light. John 8:12 states, "I am the light of the world: he that followeth me shall not walk in darkness, but shall have the light of life." He was the light when he was in this world. John 9:5 states, "As long as I am in the world, I am the light of the world." In New Jerusalem, he will also be that light. Revelation 22:5 states, "There shall be no night there; and they need no candle, neither light of the sun; for the Lord God giveth them light: and they shall reign for ever and ever." Jesus Christ has provided that light to all mankind. All mankind has to do to receive that light is to repent and follow Jesus Christ, our Lord and Savior.

New Jerusalem

> Rev. 21:12 And had a wall great and high, and had twelve gates, and at the gates twelve angels, and names written thereon, which are the names of the twelve tribes of the children of Israel:
>
> Rev. 21:13 On the east three gates; on the north three gates; on the south three gates; and on the west three gates.
>
> Rev. 21:14 And the wall of the city had twelve foundations, and in them the names of the twelve apostles of the Lamb.
>
> Rev. 21:15 And he that talked with me had a golden reed to measure the city, and the gates thereof, and the wall thereof.

John was looking at New Jerusalem or the bride of Christ, soon after it descended out of heaven from God. He saw a great wall that was very high. This wall had four sides in the shape of a square. He saw twelve gates with three gates on each of the four sides. Each gate had an angel and a name written on it. The names are the names of the twelve tribes of Israel. This wall also had twelve foundations. Each foundation had a name. The names are the names of the twelve apostles of Christ.

As the angel was showing John the Holy City, he took a golden reed or measuring instrument and measured the wall of the city. Notice the reed was golden. When in the presence of God, only the best materials are used because God is holy.

> Rev. 21:17 And he measured the wall thereof, an hundred and forty and four cubits, according to the measure of a man, that is, of the angel.
>
> Rev. 21:18 And the building of the wall of it was of jasper: and the city was pure gold, like unto clear glass.
>
> Rev. 21:19 And the foundations of the wall of the city were garnished with all manner of precious stones. The first foundation was jasper; the second, sapphire; the third, a chalcedony; the fourth, an emerald;
>
> Rev. 21:20 The fifth, sardonyx; the sixth, sardius; the seventh, chrysolite; the eighth, beryl; the ninth, a topaz; the tenth, a chrysoprasus; the eleventh, a jacinth; the twelfth, an amethyst.
>
> Rev. 21:21 And the twelve gates were twelve pearls; every several gate was of one pearl: and the street of the city was pure gold, as it were transparent glass.

The measurement of the wall was one hundred and forty-four cubits. A cubit is an ancient unit of length equal to about eighteen inches. Using this calculation, the wall was two hundred and sixteen feet high. This wall was like a jasper stone, which is clear as crystal and unimaginably beautiful.

The foundations the walls sit upon are made of twelve stones. These twelve stones are the same stones that represent the twelve tribes of Israel.

The names of the stones listed in Revelation 21 are a little different from the ones listed in Exodus 28, but they are the same stones.

The wall that sits upon the twelve foundations has twelve gates. The gates are made of twelve pearls. Each gate is made of a different pearl. Three gates are on each side of the wall: three gates on the north side, three gates on the south side, three gates on the east side, and three gates on the west side.

> Rev. 21:16 And the city lieth foursquare, and the length is as large as the breadth: and he measured the city with the reed, twelve thousand furlongs. The length and the breadth and the height of it are equal.

The wall of the city is the shape of a square. The city inside the walls is in the shape of a cube. A Rubik's Cube comes to mind. The length, the width, and the height are all equal. The measurement of the city is twelve thousand furlongs. A furlong is a unit of distance equal to two hundred and twenty yards. This measurement calculates to one-eighth mile. The city is approximately fifteen hundred miles in width, length, and height. This is a huge city, and this will be the dwelling place of God and all who takes part in the first resurrection, born-again saints.

> Rev. 21:21 And the twelve gates were twelve pearls; every several gate was of one pearl: and the street of the city was pure gold, as it were transparent glass.
>
> Rev. 21:22 And I saw no temple therein: for the Lord God Almighty and the Lamb are the temple of it.
>
> Rev. 21:23 And the city had no need of the sun, neither of the moon, to shine in it: for the glory of God did lighten it, and the Lamb is the light thereof.
>
> Rev. 21:24 And the nations of them which are saved shall walk in the light of it: and the kings of the earth do bring their glory and honour into it.
>
> Rev. 21:25 And the gates of it shall not be shut at all by day: for there shall be no night there.

This city has a street made of pure gold, and it is transparent like glass.

This street is not a street as we know it. The meaning of the word *street* is "wide place or open square." This street is a large, open area, such as a park or large space like Red Square. This city does not have a temple, church, place to worship, or sanctuary in it. The Lord God Almighty and the Lamb is the temple. This city has no need of the sun and the moon because the glory of God gives it light, and the Lamb is that light. Jesus is that light. John 8:12 states, "Then spake Jesus again unto them, saying, I am the light of the world: he that followeth me shall not walk in darkness, but shall have the light of life."

The twelve gates in the wall that surrounds the city are never shut. They are not shut during the day, and there is no night in the city. The gates will not be shut because the kings of the earth will have to bring their glory into the walls of the city. These kings survived the pouring out of the vials of the wrath of God. The kings of the earth are to go to New Jerusalem every year. Zechariah 14:16 states, "And it shall come to pass, that every one that is left of all the nations which came against Jerusalem shall even go up from year to year to worship the King, the Lord of hosts, and to keep the feast of tabernacles." The feast of tabernacles is a solemn feast or ceremonial dinner. When the kings of the earth bring their glory into the walls of the city, they are actually going to give honor, praise, and worship to the Lord God Almighty.

The bride of Christ is the Holy City, New Jerusalem. It is both huge and beautiful. The city's foundations are named after the twelve apostles of the New Testament and the city's gates are named after the twelve tribes of the Old Testament. Therefore, this city is built on both the promises in the Old Testament and the promises in the New Testament. It is built on solid rocks or stones. New Jerusalem is built on the word of God.

Rev. 21:26 And they shall bring the glory and honour of the nations into it.

Rev. 21:27 And there shall in no wise enter into it any thing that defileth, neither whatsoever worketh abomination, or maketh a lie: but they which are written in the Lamb's book of life.

When these kings come up to the feast of tabernacles each year, they will not enter into the city itself. They only enter into the outer court, inside the walls, but not in the city itself. The city is like the Holy of Holies. Not just anyone can enter into it. Only those whose names are written into the Lamb's Book of Life can enter into the city. All others can only enter the court inside the walls, but must remain outside of the city itself.

Heavenly Food

Rev. 22:1   And he shewed me a pure river of water of life, clear as crystal, proceeding out of the throne of God and of the Lamb.

Rev. 22:2   In the midst of the street of it, and on either side of the river, was there the tree of life, which bare twelve manner of fruits, and yielded her fruit every month: and the leaves of the tree were for the healing of the nations.

Inside New Jerusalem, John saw a river proceeding out of the throne of God and the Lamb. This river has pure water in it. This water is as clear as crystal. This is the water of life or living water that Jesus mentioned in John 4:5–14 when he talked with the woman at the well. The water of the river flows in the middle of the street or wide-open square. On both sides of this river are the trees of life. These trees bear twelve kinds of fruit, and they bear fruit every month. The leaves of the trees are used for the healing of the nations. I guess some are wondering why it is necessary for the nations to need healing. When the first resurrection took place, only those who were born again were changed into their spiritual bodies. All of those who did not participate in the first resurrection are still in their physical bodies. They still have whatever sickness and disease they had prior to the first resurrection. The leaves from the trees of life will aid in the healing process of all those who were left behind.

Inside New Jerusalem, the saints can eat freely from the tree of life. Revelation 2:7 states, "To him that overcometh will I give to eat of the tree of life, which is in the midst of the paradise of God." Man was prohibited from eating from the tree of life after Adam ate from the tree of knowledge. God would not allow man to continue to eat from the tree of life because man would then live forever. Genesis 3:22–24 states:

The LORD God said, behold, the man is become as one of us, to know good and evil: and now, lest he put forth his hand, and take also of the tree of life, and eat, and live for ever … therefore the LORD God sent him forth from the garden of Eden … and he placed at the east of the garden of Eden Cherubims, and a flaming sword which turned every way, to keep the way of the tree of life.

Now that the first resurrection has taken place, the saints reside in New Jerusalem. Eating from the tree of life causes the saints to live forever. Because the saints can freely eat from the tree of life, that's why they will have life eternal.

All Things Become New

Rev. 22:3   And there shall be no more curse: but the throne of God and of the Lamb shall be in it; and his servants shall serve him:

Rev. 22:4   And they shall see his face; and his name shall be in their foreheads.

Rev. 22:5   And there shall be no night there; and they need no candle, neither light of the sun; for the Lord God giveth them light: and they shall reign for ever and ever.

John saw the throne of God and the Lamb in the Holy City or New Jerusalem. All of the servants will be in New Jerusalem, and they will serve him. The servants are the ones who took part in the first resurrection, the born-again saints. They will see the face of God, and they will have his name on their foreheads. Revelation 3:12 states:

Him that overcometh will I make a pillar in the temple of my God, and he shall go no more out: and I will write upon him the name of my God, and the name of the city of my God, which is new Jerusalem, which cometh down out of heaven from my God: and I will write upon him my new name.

There will not be any need for sunlight, moonlight, or lamplight in New Jerusalem because there will be no darkness there. The Lord God Almighty provides the light of New Jerusalem. The glory of the Lord God Almighty will provide the light of New Jerusalem continuously. This is appropriate because Jesus is the light of the world. From New Jerusalem, the servants will rule and reign over the whole earth forever. New Jerusalem will be the capital of the world. All things will become new or changed from this present world as we know it today. The saints will have a new name, and they will dwell with God. There will be no more curses and no more night. No more candles will be needed. The saints will become kings and priests. Revelation 5:10 states, "Hast made us unto our God kings and priests." They will reign with God, and they will live forever. Revelation 22:5 states, "And they shall reign for ever and ever."

Rev. 22:6   And he said unto me, These sayings are faithful and true: and the Lord God of the holy prophets sent his angel to shew unto his servants the things which must shortly be done.

Rev. 22:7   Behold, I come quickly: blessed is he that keepeth the sayings of the prophecy of this book.

Rev. 22:8   And I John saw these things, and heard them. And when I had heard and seen, I fell down to worship before the feet of the angel which shewed me these things.

Rev. 22:9   Then saith he unto me, See thou do it not: for I am thy fellowservant, and of thy brethren the prophets, and of them which keep the sayings of this book: worship God.

The angel had just finished showing John all of the things that must be hereafter. The things that must be hereafter are all future events from the time the book of Revelation was written. Notice the angel said he was sent to show the things that must shortly be done. By using the phrase "shortly be done," it is implied that these events are future and have not already passed when John received and wrote the book of Revelation. The revealing of the things that must come hereafter began in Revelation 4:1 and ended in Revelation 22:21. All of these events are reserved for the End-time.

Offering of the Kingdom

Rev. 22:10 And he saith unto me, Seal not the sayings of the prophecy of this book: for the time is at hand.

Rev. 22:11 He that is unjust, let him be unjust still: and he which is filthy, let him be filthy still: and he that is righteous, let him be righteous still: and he that is holy, let him be holy still.

Rev. 22:12 And, behold, I come quickly; and my reward is with me, to give every man according as his work shall be.

Rev. 22:13 I am Alpha and Omega, the beginning and the end, the first and the last.

The angel was still giving John instructions. He told him not to seal up the prophecy that he just received. He was to write this prophecy in a book and send it to the seven churches. John did not seal this prophecy. He wrote what he saw, and it became the book of Revelation.

The angel also informed John that the time of this prophecy was near. Because the book of Revelation was written around 96 AD, some will say that the time of these events was not near or close by at all. You have to remember that the timetable of man is not the timetable of God. Using the timetable of God, we see that a thousand years is as a day and a day is as a thousand years. As 2 Peter 3:8 states, "Be not ignorant of this one thing, that one day is with the Lord as a thousand years, and a thousand years as one day." Using this analogy, it has only been about two days in God's time since John received this revelation, so the time is near.

The angel implied to John that, although he revealed these things of the future to mankind, some will continue in their wicked ways. He told John that some would continue to be unjust. Some will continue to be filthy. On the flip side, there will be some who are already righteous and holy. They will continue to be righteous and holy. The good news though is that one does not have to continue to be unrighteous. He can and should repent because, when Jesus returns, he will repay every person according to his works or deeds. Matthew 16:27 states, "The Son of man shall come in the glory of his Father with his angels; and then he shall reward every man according to his works." He will come quickly. When he returns, it is too late to repent.

The time is at hand, or the time is now. Jesus is the beginning, and Jesus is the end. Revelation 1:8 states, "I am Alpha and Omega, the beginning and the ending." Jesus is our first chance to be born-again, and Jesus is our last chance to be born-again. John 14:6 states, "Jesus saith unto him, I am the way, the truth, and the life: no man cometh unto the Father, but by me." Jesus provides eternal life for all. Without being born-again, all are lost. John 11:25 states, "I am the resurrection, and the life: he that believeth in me, though he were dead, yet shall he live." Jesus Christ is the only way to enter into New Jerusalem.

> Rev. 22:14 Blessed are they that do his commandments, that they may have right to the tree of life, and may enter in through the gates into the city.
> Rev. 22:15 For without are dogs, and sorcerers, and whoremongers, and murderers, and idolaters, and whosoever loveth and maketh a lie.

The angel continued to extend an invitation for mankind to become a citizen of New Jerusalem. He proclaimed that, if you do the commandments of God, then you will inherit the right to the tree of life and can enter New Jerusalem. If you do not inherit the right to the tree of life, then you will remain outside of Holy City or New Jerusalem. All who cannot enter the city are labeled as dogs, sorcerers, sexually immoral, murderers, idolaters, and everyone who loves and practices falsehood. This label could be summed up in one word, unrighteousness.

> Rev. 22:16 I Jesus have sent mine angel to testify unto you these things in the churches. I am the root and the offspring of David, and the bright and morning star.
> Rev. 22:17 And the Spirit and the bride say, Come. And let him that heareth say, Come. And let him that is athirst come. And whosoever will, let him take the water of life freely.

The angel revealing the revelation to John is a fellow servant of Jesus. This angel went to John as a representative of Jesus to speak the words of Jesus to the churches. We know the angel is a representative of Jesus because it is stated in the text. We know these are the words of Jesus because he describes himself as the root and offspring of David and the bright and morning star, better known as Jesus. The message the angel brings is simple. The message is "Come." Come to the Lord Jesus Christ. If you come to the Lord Jesus Christ and keep his commandments, you will be counted worthy to take the water of life freely.

Rev. 22:18 For I testify unto every man that heareth the words of the prophecy of this book, If any man shall add unto these things, God shall add unto him the plagues that are written in this book:

Rev. 22:19 And if any man shall take away from the words of the book of this prophecy, God shall take away his part out of the book of life, and out of the holy city, and from the things which are written in this book.

Rev. 22:20 He which testifieth these things saith, Surely I come quickly. Amen. Even so, come, Lord Jesus.

Rev. 22:21 The grace of our Lord Jesus Christ be with you all. Amen.

Most products we buy in stores today comes with a warning label. This label usually explains the correct way to use the product and gives some safety tips. The book of Revelation is no different. It also has a warning label. If anyone adds anything to this prophecy, God shall add unto him the plagues written in the book of Revelation. If anyone shall take away from the words in this prophecy, God shall take away his part out of the Book of Life and the Holy City and take from him the things written in the book of Revelation.

The final information the Angel of Jesus gave John is that Jesus is coming. He assured John that Jesus is coming quickly. It is a known fact that Jesus is going to return soon, so mankind should be ready. We should become born again. We should come to the Lord Jesus Christ with all of our heart, all of our soul, and our entire mind. If we do these things, the grace of our Lord Jesus Christ will be with us all. Amen.

Appendices

APPENDIX A

PROMISES

THIS is an overview of the positive promises made to those churches that overcome the world and the negative promises to all those churches that do not overcome the world.

CHURCHES	OVER-COMERS	NON-OVERCOMERS
Ephesus Rev. 2:1-7	• Eat of the tree of life	• Come unto you quickly • Remove thy candlestick
Smyrna Rev. 2:8–11	• Not hurt of the second death	
Pergamos Rev. 2:12–17	• Eat of the hidden manna • Give him a white stone • Give him a new name written • New name unknown to others	• Will come to him quickly • Fight him with the sword
Thyatira Rev. 2:18–29	• Give power over the nations • He will rule with a rod of iron • Will give him the morning star	• Cast them into a bed (state of great tribulation)
Sardis Rev. 3:1–6	• Clothed in white raiment • Not blot out his name from book • Confess his name to the Father	• Will come on him as a thief • Will not know when I come

Philadelphia Rev. 3:7–13	• Make a pillar in the temple • Write God's name on him • Write the City of God on him • Write my new name upon him	
Laodicea Rev. 3:14–22	• Will sit with me in my throne	

APPENDIX B

BLESSINGS AND CURSES

THIS is an itemized list of the blessings and curses promised to individuals. They receive the blessings if they overcome the world and curses if they do not overcome the world.

Blessings	Curses
• Will feed him from the tree of life • Will give him a crown of life • Will not be hurt by the second death • Will give him hidden manna • Will give him a white stone • Will give him a new name that is unknown to others • Will give him power over the nations • Will give him the morning star • Will give him white raiment • Will not blot out his name from the Book of Life • Will confess his name before God and the angels • Will give him pillars in the temple of God • Will write the name of God upon him • Will write the city of my God upon him • Will write his new name upon him • Will grant him to sit with him in his throne	• Will come unto you quickly and remove your candlestick from its place • Will come unto you quickly and fight against you with the sword of his mouth • Will blot name out of the Book of Life • Will spew you out of his mouth (lukewarm) • Will make the unrighteous to worship at your feet • Will make the unrighteous know that God loves us

APPENDIX C

TWELVE TRIBES

THIS table lists the twelve tribes of Israel, with their respective stone and the meaning of their names.

Tribe Name	Tribe Stone	Meaning of Tribe Name	Father	Mother
Reuben	Sardis	See a son, Lord looked upon my affliction	Jacob	Leah
Simeon	Topaz	God hears Lord heard she was hated	Jacob	Leah
Levi	Carbuncle	Adherence, joined, husband joined unto her	Jacob	Leah
Judah	Emerald	Praise, praise the Lord	Jacob	Leah
Dan	Sapphire	Judge, God judged me and heard my voice	Jacob	Billah
Naphtali	Diamond	Wrestled, great wrestling with her sister	Jacob	Billah
Gad	Ligure	A troop cometh	Jacob	Zilpah
Asher	Agate	Happy, I will be called blessed	Jacob	Zilpah
Issachar	Amethyst	Hire, God has given me my hire	Jacob	Leah
Zebulon	Beryl	Dwelling, gift, wife price	Jacob	Leah
Joseph	Onyx	He will increase	Jacob	Rachel
Benjamin	Jasper	Son of sorrow (name given by Rachel) Son of right hand (name given by Jacob)	Jacob	Rachel

Billah is Rachael's handmaiden; Zilpah is Leah's handmaiden.

APPENDIX D

SEVENS

THE number seven is known as God's number of completion. This chart lists all the times seven is mentioned in the book of Revelation.

Phrase	Scripture	Excerpts
Seven	Rev. 17:11	• And is of the seven, and goeth into perdition
Seven Angels	Rev. 8:2	• Seven angels which stood before God; and to them
	Rev. 8:6	• Seven angels which had the seven trumpets prepared
	Rev. 15:1	• Seven angels having the seven last plagues; for in
	Rev. 15:6	• Seven angels came out of the temple, having the
	Rev. 15:7	• Seven angels seven golden vials full of the wrath of
	Rev. 15:8	• The seven plagues of the seven angels were fulfilled
	Rev. 16:1	• Seven angels, Go your ways, and pour out the vials
	Rev. 17:1	• Seven angels which had the seven vials, and talked
	Rev. 21:9	• Seven angels which had the seven vials full of the
Seven Candlesticks	Rev. 1:13	• Seven candlesticks *one* like unto the Son of man
	Rev. 1:20	• Seven candlesticks which thou sawest are the seven

Phrase	Scripture	Excerpts
Seven Golden Candlesticks	Rev. 1:12	• Being turned, I saw seven golden candlesticks
	Rev. 1:20	• In my right hand, and the seven golden candlesticks
	Rev. 2:1	• In the midst of the seven golden candlesticks
Seven Churches	Rev. 1:4	• Seven churches which are in Asia: Grace *be* unto
	Rev. 1:11	• Send *it* unto the seven churches which are in Asia
	Rev. 1:20	• The seven stars are the angels of the seven churches
		• Which thou sawest are the seven churches
Seven Crowns	Rev. 12:3	• And ten horns, and seven crowns upon his heads
Seven Eyes	Rev. 5:6	• And seven eyes, which are the seven Spirits of God
Seven Heads	Rev. 12:3	• Seven heads and ten horns, and seven crowns upon
	Rev. 13:1	• Having seven heads and ten horns, and upon his
	Rev. 17:3	• Names of blasphemy, having seven heads and ten
	Rev. 17:7	• Which hath the seven heads and ten horns
	Rev. 17:9	• The seven heads are seven mountains, on which the
Seven Horns	Rev. 5:6	• Having seven horns and seven eyes, which are the
Seven Kings	Rev. 17:10	• And there are seven kings: five are fallen, and one is,

Phrase	Scripture	Excerpts
Seven Lamps	Rev. 4:5	• Seven lamps of fire burning before the throne
Seven Last Plagues	Rev. 15:1	• Seven last plagues; for in them is filled up the wrath
	Rev. 21:9	• Had the seven vials full of the seven last plagues
Seven Mountains	Rev. 17:9	• Are seven mountains, on which the woman sitteth
Seven Plagues	Rev. 15:6	• The seven plagues, clothed in pure and white linen
	Rev. 15:8	• The seven plagues of the seven angels were fulfilled
Seven Seals	Rev. 5:1	• Within and on the backside, sealed with seven seals
	Rev. 5:5	• Open the book, and to loose the seven seals thereof
Seven Spirits	Rev. 1:4	• From the seven Spirits which are before his throne
	Rev. 3:1	• Things saith he that hath the seven Spirits of God
	Rev. 4:5	• Before the throne, which are the seven Spirits of God
	Rev. 5:6	• The seven Spirits of God sent forth into all the earth

Phrase	Scripture	Excerpts
Seven Stars	Rev. 1:16 Rev. 1:20 Rev. 2:1 Rev. 3:1	• And he had in his right hand seven stars • The mystery of the seven stars which thou sawest • Seven stars are the angels of the seven churches • Saith he that holdeth the seven stars in his right hand • Hath the seven Spirits of God, and the seven stars
Seven Thousand	Rev. 11:13	• In the earthquake were slain of men seven thousand
Seven Thunders	Rev. 10:3 Rev. 10:4	• He had cried, seven thunders uttered their voices • When the seven thunders had uttered their voices • Which the seven thunders uttered, and write them not
Seven Trumpets	Rev. 8:2 Rev. 8:6	• Before God; and to them were given seven trumpets • The seven trumpets prepared themselves to sound
Seven Golden Vials	Rev. 15:7	• Gave unto the seven angels seven golden vials full of
Seven Vials	Rev. 17:1 Rev. 21:9	• One of the seven angels which had the seven vials • Had the seven vials full of the seven last plagues

APPENDIX E

WORLD KINGDOMS

THIS is a diagram of the kingdoms of the world that was prophesied to affect Israel.

WORLD KINGDOMS

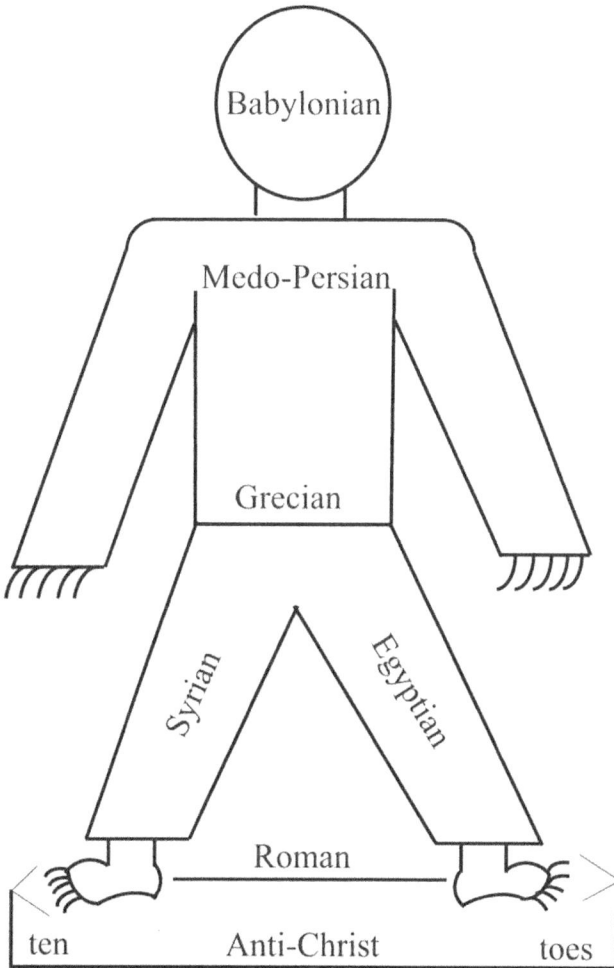

Babylonian

Medo-Persian

Grecian

Syrian

Egyptian

Roman

ten   Anti-Christ   toes

APPENDIX F

REVELATION TIMELINE

THIS is a timeline relative to events taking place throughout the end-time period.

Timers in Heaven	Chronological Order of Events	Timers on Earth
	Sealing of the 144,000	
1st seal broken	Beginning of the tribulation period	1st trumpet sounds
2nd seal broken		2nd trumpet sounds
3rd seal broken		3rd trumpet sounds
4th seal broken	Middle of the tribulation period	4th trumpet sounds
5th seal broken		5th trumpet sounds
6th seal broken		6th trumpet sounds
7th seal broken	End of the tribulation period	7th trumpet sounds
1st vial	Wrath of God	Poured out
2nd vial		Poured out
3rd vial		Poured out
4th vial		Poured out
5th vial		Poured out
6th vial		Poured out
7th vial	Armageddon	Poured out
Satan bound 1000 yrs	Millennium	Peace on earth 1000 yrs

		New Jerusalem descends
		Saints rule and reign
End of Millennium	**Little Season**	No more peace on earth
Satan loosed		Satan assembles a great army
Second death/ resurrection	**Great White Throne Judgment**	Fire destroys Satan's army
		Dead judged from the books
		Satan thrown into the lake of fire
		Death and hell thrown into lake of fire
In heaven	**Eternity**	In the lake of fire

Appendix G

Breaking of the Seals

THIS is an itemized list of the events taking place and their relationship to the breaking of the respective seal.

Seals	Events
First Seal	• White horse • Rider given a crown goes forth conquering and to conquer
Second Seal	• Red horse • Rider given power to take peace from the earth • Man should kill one another • Given a great sword
Third Seal	• Black horse • Rider has a pair of balances in his hand • A measure of wheat for a penny • Three measure of barley for a penny • See that thou hurt not the oil and the wine
Fourth Seal	• Pale horse • Rider named Death • Hell followed him • Given power over fourth part of earth to kill with sword with hunger with death and with the beasts of the earth
Fifth Seal	• Souls under the altar are slain for word of God and the testimony they held • Cry to God, "How long does thou not judge and avenge our blood on them that dwell on earth?" • Given white robes and told to wait a little season until their fellow servants and brethren also be killed as they were

Seals	Events
Sixth Seal	• Great earthquake • Sun become black as sackcloth of hair • Moon become as blood • Stars of heaven fall to earth • Heavens depart as a scroll when rolled together • Every mountain and island moved from its place • Men want rocks and mountains to fall on them to hide from the one who sits on the throne to hide them from the wrath of the Lamb because the great day of his wrath has come
Seventh Seal	• Silence in heaven for about a half hour

APPENDIX H

SOUNDING OF THE TRUMPETS

THIS is an itemized list of the events taking place and their relationship to the sounding of the respective trumpets.

Trumpets	Events
First Trumpet	• Hail and fire mingle with blood cast into the earth • One-third of the trees burn up • All of the green grass burn up
Second Trumpet	• A great mountain burning with fire is cast into the sea • One-third of the sea becomes blood • One-third of the creatures in the sea die • One-third of the ships are destroyed
Third Trumpet	• Great star falls from heaven, burning as it was a lamp • Star falls upon one-third of the rivers fountains of waters • Name of star is "Wormwood" • One-third part of the waters become wormwood • The waters were made bitter • Many men die from the waters
Fourth Trumpet	• One-third of the sun is smitten • One-third of the moon is smitten • One-third of the stars are smitten • Day and night shine only for one-third of it
Fifth Trumpet	• Star fall from heaven to earth • Bottomless pit opens • Smoke come out of the pit, darkening the sun and air • Locust comes out of the smoke and are given power as the scorpions of the earth • Commanded they should not hurt grass of the earth any green thing, or any tree • Could hurt men who do not have the seal of God on their foreheads • Could not kill them, but could torment them for five months • Men shall seek death, but death will flee from them • Shapes of locust are like horses prepared to battle

Trumpets	Events
Sixth Trumpet	• Loosed four angels that are bound at the Euphrates River • Number of the army is 200 million • Riders of the horses have breastplates of fire, jacinth, and brimstone • Heads of the horses as the heads of lions • Out of their mouths issue fire, smoke, and brimstone • By these, one-third part of men killed • Their power is in their mouths and their tails • Men not killed do not repent
Seventh Trumpet	• Great voice from heaven says, "The kingdoms of this world have become the kingdom of our Lord and of his Christ and he shall reign forever and ever." • Elders worship God

APPENDIX I

OUTPOURING OF THE VIALS

T HIS is an itemized list of the seven vials and the events that take place with the outpouring of each vial.

Vials	Events
First Vial	• Pours his vial upon the earth • A noisome and grievous sore formed: on men that had the mark of the beast and men that worshipped the image of the beast
Second Vial	• Pours his vial upon the sea • Sea become as the blood of a dead man • Every living thing in the sea dies
Third Vial	• Pours out his vial upon the rivers and fountains of waters • Waters become blood
Fourth Vial	• Pours out his vial upon the sun • Power given to him to scorch men with fire • Men scorched with great heat • Men blasphemes the name of God • Men repents not to give him glory
Fifth Vial	• Pours out his vial upon the seat of the beast • His kingdom is full of darkness • They gnaw their tongues for pain • They blaspheme the God of heaven because of pain from their sores • They repent not for their deeds
Sixth Vial	• Pours out his vial upon the great Euphrates River • Waters dry up to prepare a way for the kings of the east • Three unclean spirits like frogs come out of the mouths of the dragon, the beast, and the false prophet • These spirits are devils that gather the kings of the earth to the Battle of Armageddon

Vials	Events
Seventh Vial	• Pours his vial into the air • Voices, thundering, and lightning • Great earthquake • Babylon punished • It is done

www.ingramcontent.com/pod-product-compliance
Lightning Source LLC
LaVergne TN
LVHW051501080426
835509LV00017B/1853